THE
36 STRATEGIES
OF THE
CHINESE

ADAPTING
ANCIENT CHINESE
WISDOM TO THE
BUSINESS WORLD

BY

WEE CHOW HOU
LAN LUH LUH

 Addison-Wesley

Singapore • Reading, Massachusetts • Menlo Park, California
New York • Harlow, England • Don Mills, Ontario
Amsterdam • Bonn • Sydney • Tokyo • Madrid • San Juan
Milan • Mexico City • Seoul • Taipei

Addison Wesley Longman Singapore Pte Ltd
25, First Lok Yang Road, Singapore 629734

*Associated companies, branches and
representatives throughout the world*

First published 1998
Reprinted 1998
Second reprint with corrections 1999

ISBN 981-235-832-3

Produced by Addison Wesley Longman Singapore Pte Ltd
Printed in Singapore

Concept & design by PublishWrite Consultancy
Editorial support by PublishWrite Consultancy

ABOUT THE AUTHORS

WEE CHOW HOU, PH.D., M.B.A., B.B.A.(HONS), P.P.A.

Dr Wee is currently Professor of Business Policy, Dean of the Faculty of Business Administration and Director of the Graduate School of Business, National University of Singapore.

A former Merit, Colombo Plan and Commonwealth scholar, he was the winner of the Academy of Marketing Science (USA) 1984 Ph.D. Paper Award, and the 1985 Doctoral Dissertation Award. In 1995, he was awarded the Public Administration Medal (Silver) by the Singapore Government.

Currently, he has over 200 publications in various international, regional and local journals and proceedings. He was the editor of the Singapore Marketing Review from 1985 to 1990, and is currently on the editorial boards of Advances in International Marketing (USA), the Asia Pacific Journal of Management (Singapore), Cross Cultural Management: An International Journal (UK), and the Journal of Strategic Marketing (UK), an Associate Editor of The International Executive (USA), and a Consulting Editor on the Asia-Pacific Series of Addison-Wesley Publishing Co Inc (USA).

He has consulted for organisations throughout the world, including the United States International Trade Centre, London (Canada) Downtown Business Improvement Area, United Nations Development Program in China, Kikkoman Corporation (Japan), Pacific Rim Consulting Group, Keppel Corporation, Bon Food Pte Ltd (franchise-holder of Burger King, Singapore), and the National University of Singapore Hospital.

Dr Wee, an international conference speaker, has conducted executive training for over 120 major organisations in Australia, Brunei, China, Finland, Germany, Hong Kong, India, Indonesia, Malaysia, New Zealand, Singapore, Spain, South Africa, Thailand, the UK, and the US. Some of his major clients include Singapore Airlines, Port of Singapore Authority, Ministry of Health, Jurong Town Corporation, Housing and Development Board, Wellcome Singapore Pte Ltd, Stryker Pacific Ltd, Far East Organisation, Singapore Broadcasting Corporation, Neptune Orient Lines, Jurong Shipyard and Keppel Shipyard from Singapore; Pacific Bank, Public Bank, Sunrise Sdn Bhd, East Asiatic Company, Genting Bhd, INTAN, NEC, MISC, and the Renong Group from Malaysia;

PT Salim Corpora, Ciputra Group, Kalbe Group, Ongko Group, and Lippo Group from Indonesia; DHL International, American Express (Singapore and Malaysia), Standard Chartered Bank, Telecoms (Singapore, Malaysia and Australia), Holiday Inns Asia Pacific, ITT Sheraton (Asia and the US), PGR (India), Northern Telecom Asia Pacific, United Overseas Bank (Singapore and Malaysia), Hewlett Packard (Singapore and Finland), MeCrastor Corporation (Finland), Japan Airlines, IBM (Singapore), Motorola (Singapore, Europe and the US), Dell Computers, Sundstrand Corporation (US), China Hotel, and Xian-Janssen (China) and Inchcape Motors (Singapore, Malaysia, Brunei and Hong Kong).

He has been appointed by the Government of Hong Kong to be a Member of the University Grants Committee and is currently Board Director of Neptune Orient Lines, the Telecommunication Authority of Singapore (TAS), Singapore Communication Investments Pte Ltd (SingCom), and Apollo Enterprises Ltd. He is presently Chairman of the Promote Mandarin Council. His extensive involvement also sees him contributing as a member of: the Defence Procurement Division Supervisory Board (MINDEF), the Board of Trustees of the Institute of Southeast Asian Studies, the Advisory Committee of the Lee Kuan Yew's Distinguished Visitor Programme, the Singapore Institute of Labour Studies, the Marketing Advisory Panel of the National Arts Council and the panel of advisors for the National Reference Library's Chinese Collection.

Dr Wee is a much sought-after speaker on marketing and strategic management. In particular, his lectures on Sun Tzu's Art of War as applied to strategic thinking and management have received increasing attention from many organisations around the world. He has written numerous articles on the subject and is the senior author of *Sun Tzu: War & Management* published by Addison-Wesley in July 1991, and has since been translated into Bahasa Indonesia, Chinese and Korean. In 1996, he published *Practical Marketing: An Asian Perspective*, also by Addison-Wesley, which has been translated into Chinese and Bahasa Indonesia.

LAN LUH LUH, LL.M (COMMERCIAL LAW) (CAMBRIDGE), ADVOCATE & SOLICITOR (SINGAPORE)

Lan Luh Luh is a Lecturer in the Department of Business Policy, Faculty of Business Administration at the National University of Singapore.

She was a former Overseas United Bank scholar (1985-1989) and graduated with an LL.B. (Hons) from the Faculty of Law, National University of Singapore in 1989. In 1993-94, she proceeded to do her Master of Law at the University of Cambridge, England and obtained a First Class award in Commercial Law. For that, she was also awarded a Book Prize in 1994 by her college, Magdalene College of Cambridge University.

Ms Lan is an Advocate and Solicitor of the Supreme Court of Singapore. Prior to joining NUS, she worked for a major law firm in Singapore as a corporate lawyer practising commercial and banking law. Presently, she teaches company law and corporate law and finance to the undergraduate and MBA students of the Faculty. She publishes extensively, both in professional and academic journals. She is presently the Associate Editor of Singapore Management Review published by the Faculty. In addition, she is involved in Faculty executive training programs.

Ms Lan is proficient both in the English and Chinese languages. Besides her career in the academia, Ms Lan is a regular contributor of literary works to the local Chinese newspaper and magazines. She has held personal columns in the leading Chinese newspaper *Lianhe Zaobao*.

CONTENTS

OFFENSIVE STRATEGIES (攻 战 计)

CONFUSION STRATEGIES (混 战 计)

DECEPTION STRATEGIES (并战计)

DESPERATE STRATEGIES (败战计)

INTRODUCTION

BACKGROUND

Historians today have still been unable to establish the exact time period and the authors of the famous "Thirty-six Strategies". The most commonly used strategy, Strategy 36, "Escape — the best strategy" (三十六计, 走为上计), was first mentioned in "The Biography of Wang Jingze" (王敬则传), a chapter appearing in *Nan Qi Shu* (南齐书) which writes that among "the thirty-six strategies of Master Tan, escape is the most supreme strategy" (檀公三十六策, 走是上计). The details of the escape of Master Tan or Tan Daoji (檀道济), a famous Song General, from the State of Wei were narrated in the fifteenth chapter of *Nan Shi* (南史), "The Biography of Tan Daoji" (檀道济传). The same phrase regarding the supremacy of the art of escape also appears in "Yuan Cai" (渊才), a chapter in *The Night Tales of Leng Zhai* (冷斋夜话). Judging from records, the "Thirty-six Strategies" should have a history of near two thousand years.

Although the "Thirty-six Strategies" is a summary of some of the war strategies used by the ancient Chinese warriors, the name "Thirty-six Strategies" may have come from Yi Jing's (or *I-Ching*) (易经) "Yin Yang Theory" (阴阳学说) which uses the *Tai Yin* number of 66 (太阴六六之数) to mean "many tricks". The main statement which sums up the "Thirty-six Strategies" writes:

> Six multiplied by six is 36. The word "calculation" (数) conceals another word, namely "strategy" (术). In the application of a strategy, careful calculation is required. Once one is able to calculate the pattern of how situations develop, he will find the required strategy. A strategy cannot be detached from an objective assessment of a situation. It cannot work by subjective imagination.

六六三十六, 数中有术, 术中有数。
阴阳变理, 机在其中。机不可设, 设则不中。

The strategist holds the key to the appropriate application of a strategy to each situation. As situations (like war conditions) change, so must the strategies. Thus, how well a strategist assesses a situation determines how good he is in applying the right strategy. The process is dynamic and the strategist is the guru. There is no single answer to any problem or situation; the answer depends on the strategist.

CLASSIFICATION OF THE 36 STRATEGIES

Generally, the Thirty-six Strategies are grouped under six categories. Each category contains six strategies. The six categories in turn can be used in two types of situations. The three categories, the "Advantageous Strategies" (胜战计), the "Opportunistic Strategies" (敌战计) and the "Offensive Strategies" (攻战计) are used in a winning situation. The other three categories, the "Confusion Strategies" (混战计), the "Deception Strategies" (并战计) and the "Desperate Strategies" (败战计) are used in a disadvantageous situation. However, the application and usage of these strategies can be mingled in various combinations. They are not intended to be used singly, nor are they only applicable in either a winning or losing situation. The possible combination and application of these strategies are limited only by the imagination and creativity of the strategist.

Other than Strategy 36, nobody can be certain of the content of the other thirty-five strategies. The most commonly-used version is that by an Anonymous author (无名氏). Nevertheless, over the years, these strategies have been commonly cited and used by many Chinese businessmen.

ADVANTAGEOUS STRATEGIES (胜战计)

The "Advantageous Strategies" are used in situations when time and resources are to one's advantage, when there is no need to rush, and detailed planning can be carried out. The six strategies in this category include the following:

1   "Deceiving the heavens to cross the sea"
    瞒天过海 (*Man tian guo hai*)

2   "Besieging Wei to save Zhao"
    围魏救赵 (*Wei wei jiu zhao*)

3   "Killing with a borrowed knife"
    借刀杀人 (*Jie dao sha ren*)

4   "Conserving energy while the enemy tires himself out"
    以逸待劳 (*Yi yi dai lao*)

5   "Looting a house on fire"
    趁火打劫 (*Chen huo da jie*)

6   "Making a feint to the east but hitting out in the west"
    声东击西 (*Sheng dong ji xi*)

OPPORTUNISTIC STRATEGIES (敌战计)

The "Opportunistic Strategies" thrive on situations where vulnerabilities can be exploited. The idea is to capitalise on all opportunities so as to gain the advantage. The strategies include:

7   "Creating something out of nothing"
     无中生有 (*Wu zhong sheng you*)

8   "Secret escape through Chen Cang"
     暗渡陈仓 (*An du chen cang*)

9   "Observing the fire from the other side of the river"
     隔岸观火 (*Ge an guan huo*)

10   "A dagger sheathed in a smile"
     笑里藏刀 (*Xiao li cang dao*)

11   "The plum dies in place of the peach"
     李代桃僵 (*Li dai tao jiang*)

12   "Stealing a goat along the way"
     顺手牵羊 (*Shun shou qian yang*)

OFFENSIVE STRATEGIES (攻战计)

Like the Advantageous Strategies, the "Offensive Strategies" are used in situations when time and resources are not constraining factors. However, these strategies seek to gain victory through direct attack. The six strategies include:

13   "Hitting the grass to startle the snake"
     打草惊蛇 (*Da cao jing she*)

14   "Borrowing a corpse to resurrect a soul"
     借尸还魂 (*Jie shi huan hun*)

15   "Luring a tiger from its lair in the mountain"
     调虎离山 (*Diao hu li shan*)

16   "Releasing the enemy to recapture him later"
     欲擒故纵 (*Yu qin gu zong*)

17   "Tossing out a brick to get a jade"
     抛砖引玉 (*Pao zhuan yin yu*)

18   "Disband the bandits by arresting their leader"
     擒贼擒王 (*Qin zei qin wang*)

CONFUSION STRATEGIES (混战计)

The "Confusion Strategies" aim to confuse a pursuing enemy to throw him off his guard. In this way, valuable time can be gained in making one's escape. These strategies include:

19 "Pulling out the firewood from beneath the cauldron"
    釜底抽薪 (*Fu di chou xin*)

20 "Catching a fish in troubled waters"
    混水摸鱼 (*Hun shui mo yu*)

21 "Making an unnoticed escape like a golden cicada shedding its skin"
    金蝉脱壳 (*Jin chan tuo ke*)

22 "Shutting the doors to catch the thief"
    关门捉贼 (*Guan men zhuo zei*)

23 "Befriend the far and attack the near"
    远交近攻 (*Yuan jiao jin di*)

24 "Borrow a passage to attack Guo"
    假途伐虢 (*Jia tu fa guo*)

DECEPTION STRATEGIES (并战计)

Deception is commonly used in war to create advantages for oneself, and to handicap the enemy. Such strategies are designed to mislead the enemy. They include the following:

25 "Replace superior beams and pillars with inferior ones"
    偷梁换柱 (*Tou liang huan zhu*)

26 "Pointing at the mulberry but scolding the locust tree"
    指桑骂槐 (*Zhi sang ma huai*)

27 "Pretending to be insane but remaining smart"
    假痴不颠 (*Jia chi bu dian*)

28 "Remove the ladder after the enemy ascends to the roof"
    上屋抽梯 (*Shang wu chou ti*)

29 "Deck the tree with flowers"
    树上开花 (*Shu shang kai hua*)

30 "The guest takes over as host"
    反客为主 (*Fan ke wei zhu*)

DESPERATE STRATEGIES (败战计)

In a desperate situation, one may have to resort to unconventional and unorthodox methods and means. As such, some of these strategies can be quite dramatic and "tragic". However, when used appropriately, such strategies can be very effective. Thes include:

31   "Beauty scheme"
     美人计 (*Mei ren ji*)

32   "Empty city scheme"
     空城计 (*Kong cheng ji*)

33   "Double agent ploy"
     反间计 (*Fan jian ji*)

34   "Self-injury scheme"
     苦肉计 (*Ku rou ji*)

35   "A series of interconnected ploys"
     连环计 (*Lian huan ji*)

36   "Escape — the best scheme"
     走为上 (*Zou wei shang*)

There are other version of the "Thirty-six Strategies". Some authors have instead incorporated alternative strategies to replace some of the strategies as highlighted above. However, they still stick to a total of thirty-six strategies. These other strategies include:

1   "Killing two vultures with a single arrow"
     一箭双雕 (*Yi jian shuang diao*)
     This is used to replace Strategy 2, "Besieging Wei to save Zhao"
     (围魏救赵).

2   "Pretending to be ignorant though knowing the answer"
     明知故昧 (*Ming zhi gu mei*)
     This is used to replace Strategy 9, "Observing the fire from the other side of the river" (隔岸观火).

3   "Gaining the initiative by striking the first blow"
     先发制人 (*Xian fa zhi ren*)
     This is used to replace Strategy 10, "A dagger sheathed in a smile"
     (笑里藏刀).

4   "Throwing a rock down when the enemy is in the well"
     落井下石 (*Luo jing xia shi*)
     This is used to replace Strategy 20, "Catching a fish in troubled water"
     (混水摸鱼).

5   "Making a deceptive show of strength"
虚 张 声 势 (*Xu zhang sheng shi*)
This is used to replace Strategy 22, "Closing the doors to catch the thief" (关 门 捉 贼).

6   "Shifting the blame to someone else"
移 尸 嫁 祸 (*Yi shi jia huo*)
This is used to replace Strategy 24, "Borrow a passage to attack Guo" (假 途 伐 虢).

7   "Stealing the dragon and replacing it with the phoenix"
偷 龙 转 凤 (*Tou long zhuan feng*)
This is used to replace Strategy 25, "Replace superior beams and pillars with inferior ones" (偷 梁 换 柱).

8   "Pretending to be a pig to prey on the tiger"
扮 猪 吃 虎 (*Ban zhu chi hu*)
This is used to replace Strategy 27, "Pretending to be insane but remain smart" (假 痴 不 颠).

9   "Pulling down the bridge after crossing it"
过 河 抽 板 (*Guo he chou ban*)
This is used to replace Strategy 28, "Remove the ladder after the enemy ascends to the roof" (上 屋 抽 梯).

10   "The provocation scheme"
激 将 计 (*Ji jiang ji*)
This is used to replace Strategy 29, "Deck the tree with flowers" (树 上 开 花).

Most of these alternative strategies have meanings similar to the original ones proposed by the Anonymous author and can be used interchangeably. Interestingly, no author has ventured beyond arguing for more than 36 strategies. Perhaps they have adhered to the figure "36" so as not to diminish the popularity and wide acceptance of the strategies. As the Chinese saying goes, there is no need to add legs to an already completed painting of a snake (画 蛇 添 足).

As these thirty-six strategies are merely a summary of the many methods used by ancient Chinese military strategists, there is no authoritative version of it. For the sake of our discussion, we will adopt the popular version by the Anonymous author. The explanations the Anonymous author provided for each strategy were adapted from Yi Jing's theory on the balance between Yin and Yang. The name of each strategy, however, came from various sources. These include historical examples such as *Wei wei jiu zhao*

(围魏救赵), *An du chen cang* (暗渡陈仓), and *Jia tu fa guo* (假途伐虢); ancient military phrases such as *Yi yi dai lao* (以逸待劳), *Sheng dong ji xi* (声东击西); ancient poetry such as *Li dai tao jiang* (李代桃僵) and *Qin zei qin wang* (擒贼擒王); popular Chinese phrases known as *cheng yu* (成语) such as *Jing chan tuo ke* (金蝉脱壳), *Tou liang huan zhu* (偷梁换柱) and *Zhi sang ma huai* (指桑骂槐).

COMMON USAGE OF STRATEGIES

While few Chinese systematically study the 36 strategies, many are able to cite and apply these strategies to their daily lives. Some of these have been adapted to suit the purpose of the user. For example, it is commonly acknowledged among the Chinese that no matter how great a hero is, he is no match for a beauty (英雄难过美人关). This, in essence, refers to Strategy 31, "Beauty scheme" (美人计).

Other strategies often cited include:

1   Strategy 1, "Deceiving the sky the cross the sea" (瞒天过海). This is commonly used as a ploy to create distraction.

2   Strategy 3, "Kill another with a borrowed knife" (借刀杀人). This is used as an indirect means to accomplish one's purpose. It reflects the reluctance of the strategist to be the bad guy who does for the "kill" himself.

3   Strategy 5, "Looting a burning house" (趁火打劫); Strategy 12, "Stealing a goat along the way," (顺手牵羊) and Strategy 20, "Catching a fish in troubled waters," (混水摸鱼). These three strategies reflect the opportunistic nature of the Chinese.

4   Strategy 6, "Making a feint to the east but hitting out in the west" (声东击西). This strategy demonstrate the Chinese preference to use the indirect approach to accomplish the objective.

5   Strategy 7, "Creating something out of nothing" (无中生有) and Strategy 32, "The empty city scheme (空城计). These two are used to highlight the craftiness and entrepreneurial spirit of the Chinese.

6   Strategy 9, "Observing the fire from the other side of the river" (隔岸观火). This is commonly associated with taking an apathetic and indifferent attitude. It reflects the Chinese mentality of avoiding trouble, and taking a distant view of things.

7   Strategy 10, "A dagger sheathed in a smile" (笑里藏刀). This is used to describe a scheming and dangerous person.

8   Strategy 13, "Hitting the grass to startle the snake" (打草惊蛇). This strategy is often used in the reverse sense, that is, "not to startle the snaker" so as to avoid trouble.

9   Strategy 15, "Luring the tiger to leave its lair in the mountain" (调虎离山), is used as another way to avoid direct confrontation, especially when the other party is much stronger.

10   Strategy 17, "Tossing a brick in return for a jade" (抛砖引玉), is used to describe an unfair exchange or transaction, but typically for a noble purpose. It reflects the ability of the strategist to extract much more out of the exchange.

11   Strategy 22, "Shutting the doors to catch the thief" (关门捉贼). This is a common tactic used to surround the culprit so that he has no escape. It is similar to another strategy called, "*Si mien chu ke*" (四面楚歌) which means to surround the enemy completely.

12   Strategy 34, "Self-injury scheme" (苦肉计). This strategy is usually used to illustrate the need to make sacrifices in order to achieve the greater goals.

Undoubtedly, the "Thirty-six Strategies" are familiar to the Chinese. Thus, it is not surprising to find that these strategies are foundational in the conduct of business. In fact, the Japanese, Korean and Taiwanese businessmen are known to apply these strategies.

It is instructive therefore, to understand these strategies and to learn how one can benefit from their applications to business.

A WORD OF CAUTION

In applying the "Thirty-six Strategies" to business, one must remember that these are *military strategies*. As such they are based on a very different set of assumptions and value system.

The differences between battle and business are varied enough for you to take exception to certain principles. For example, in war, it is imperative to win, because war is a zero-sum game. Your gain is the enemy's loss, and if you do not destroy the enemy, he will destroy you. Thus, it is inevitable that some questionable tactics such as espionage, deception, bribery and ruthless killings are employed. Though modern warfare is guided by an international code of conduct, aberrations are not uncommon.

In contrast, business competition need not result in a zero-sum outcome. In fact, win-win outcomes are common. The code of conduct governing business practices is rigid and transparent. Violators are forced to face the consequences of the law.

Besides regulatory restraints, businesses have moral and social dimensions as well; they are expected to bear social responsibility and to adhere to professional codes. Even if they escape the law for unethical practices, businesses will still be subjected to public scrutiny and sanction. Deceptive advertising and pricing techniques are heavily frowned upon. Similarly, while market studies, surveys and research are definitely accepted, industrial and business espionage would definitely incur the wrath of industry players and may result in severe sanctions.

So, in applying these "Thirty-six Strategies" to business, the strategist must consciously factor in legal and moral dimensions. While the business world may resemble a battlefield (商场如战场), it is not one without rules and censorship.

One must not be too carried away when applying military strategies to business practices. In the case of war, it is not surprising to find the aggressor pursuing territories in a relentless manner to occupy an increasing number of territorities. In business, this translates to the ceaseless pursuit of *market share.* Many Japanese and Korean companies that are known to practise military strategies in business have indeed adopted such an approach. Unfortunately, in the realm of business, relentless pursuit of market share (which indirectly results in the elimination of competitors) can only be successful when accompanied by attainment of profits. In other words, the success of a business, is not measured by market share alone but by profits (whether in absolute or relative terms). Without the profits, the company cannot be kept going!

The failure of many large companies in Japan and Korea that began in the mid-1990s bear testimonies to the severe consequences of paying too much attention to market share alone. Many of these Japanese and Korean companies were highly geared and used substantial borrowings to finance their expansion. As they paid little attention to profits and cash flow matters, it was only a matter of time before they had to "face the music" when the economic growth rates of their nations slowed down. With the Asian currency crisis that began in July 1997, the problems faced by the

Japanese and Korean companies are likely to escalate for the next few years.

For example, Japan's largest bank, Hokkaido Takushoku Bank, announced on 17 November 1997 that it would be out of business. Its closure was expected in view of its massive problem loans amounting to 937.7 billion yen (representing more than 13% of its total loan outstanding) as of November 1997. Closely following the failure of Hokkaido Takushoku Bank, Yamaichi Securities, the fourth largest securities house in Japan also announced its collapse on 24 November 1997. Yamaichi's failure was considered the biggest in Japan since World War II. It incurred massive debts amounting to three trillion yen (S$37.6 billion).

In fact, earlier in 1997, several Japanese financial institutions also collapsed under the weight of heavy debts. These include Nissan Mutual Life Insurance (April), Ogawa Securities (May), Kyoto Kyoei Bank (October), and Sanyo Securities (early November). Like many other Japanese firms, these companies were all known to pursue market shares aggressively. Thus, prior to the collapses of Hokkaido Takushoku and Yamaichi Securities, there were already signs of the inevitable failure of relentlessly pursuing a market share strategy without attention to profitability. This is because to increase market share, more and more marginal clients are taken in, resulting in a significant increase in risks. Thus, when the clients default as a result of poor business conditions, the "melt down" could be very serious.

The problems faced by the Japanese companies had spread to Korea in late November 1997. Already, Kia Motors, one of the largest conglomerates in South Korea, had filed for bankruptcy. With the Korean government seeking financial assistance of at least US$20 billion (S$31.8 billion) from the International Monetary Fund (IMF) in late November 1997, signs became abundantly clear. More Korean companies, including the *chaebols*, are likely to face severe financial strains in the days ahead. In fact, it would not be surprising to find more Korean *chaebols*, Japanese *zaibatsus*, and Asian financial institutions going bankrupt before the end of this century. Already, 16 Indonesian banks had been ordered by their government to shut down by November 1997, and Tokuyo City Bank (a second tier regional bank of Japan) went out of business on 26 November 1997. With the International Monetary Fund (IMF) coming into the rescue of Indonesia, Thailand and South Korea as of the end of 1997, more financial institutions in these countries may be asked to close down or to merge with other companies. Indeed, these institutions are paying a hefty price for ignoring basic market rules and forces.

In contrast, many American and European companies do not pursue market share blindly. In fact, they guard their bottom-line (profits and cash flow) very carefully. For example, American companies like Microsoft, General Electric and Motorola do not hesitate to expand market shares. However, they are also very profit-driven. As a result, they have maintained a very balanced and healthy approach in handling their businesses. Similarly, European conglomerates like Shell and Philips also watch their bottom-line carefully when they expand their market share. As a result, many of these American and European companies have survived decades of business upheavals.

In sum, it is not true that what works in the military realm will be equally applicable in business. The user of the strategies must learn to adapt and adjust them according to the situation at hand. The last thing that he wants to do is to apply the strategies blindly. If anything, the late 1997 currency and stock market turmoils in Asia that resulted in the financial failures of some governments and many companies serve to illustrate very clearly that the pursuit of a market share strategy cannot be sustained forever. A price has to be paid! It is only a matter of how big and painful it would be, and how soon it would befall the "victim."

STRATEGY 1

瞒天过海

DECEIVING THE HEAVENS TO CROSS THE SEA

备周则意怠, 常见则不疑。
阴在阳之内, 不在阳之对。太阴, 太阳。

EXPLANATION

"Deceiving the heavens[1] to cross the sea" (瞒天过海) is a literal translation of the strategy. It means to create a false impression to distract the target and so achieve one's goal without his knowledge. This strategy works on the assumption that people take extra precautions when faced with new or difficult situations, but tend to let their guards down in more familiar situations.

Every one expects a secret to be hidden, so if one conducts an important plan openly, it may not be noticed (备周则意怠, 常见则不疑). As the saying goes, "An open situation hides a dark secret" (阴在阳之内, 不在阳之对).

HISTORICAL BACKGROUND

This strategy was mentioned in the thirteenth chapter of *Discourses on Tang* (说唐) where a man named Jing De asked, "What is the meaning of 'Deceiving the heavens to cross the sea'?" (第十三回有云: 敬德道: "何为瞒天过海之计?")

The historical example most commonly cited as an illustration of this strategy is the story of how the emperor of Tang Dynasty, Tang Tai Zong (唐太宗), was deceived into crossing the sea by Xue Ren Gui (薛仁贵).

In the year of 643 BC, the Emperor of Tang Dynasty, Tang Tai Zong, was asked to send his troop to help a small country in the East. Emperor Tang Tai Zong decided to lead his men personally. His loyal subjects tried to dissuade him from going as the trip required them to cross the sea, but to no avail.

---

1   *The Emperor was known as the Son of Heaven. Hence the use of the term "heaven" to represent the Emperor.*

The Emperor Tang Tai Zong, however, lost heart when he saw the immensity of the sea. He summoned his subjects to come up with a good plan to cross the sea but when they saw the heavy waves and huge tides, they did not dare offer any advice.

Among the subjects was one named Zhang Shi Gui (张 士 贵). He had a soldier named Xue Ren Gui, a man well known for his strength and intelligence. Zhang Shi Gui consulted Xue Ren Gui for a solution. After some thought, Xue Ren Gui came up with a plan. "I have a plan which will make the sea disappear. The emperor and his troop will be able to cross the sea as if they were on land," he said. Zhang Shi Gui was delighted.

When the emperor next asked for a plan to cross the sea, a follower reported that an old but rich peasant living by the sea had requested to see him. The old man claimed that he would be able to supply food for the 300,000-strong troop for their journey across the sea. When the emperor saw the old man, he was impressed by the latter's manner and took an immediate liking for him. Therefore, when the old man invited the emperor to his house for drinks, Emperor Tang Tai Zong happily agreed and took all his men with him. After travelling for a few miles, Emperor Tang Tai Zong and his men were led into an enormous tent.

The tent was beautifully decorated and had hundreds of servants. The old man entertained Emperor Tang Tai Zong and his subjects with a sumptuous feast and beautiful dancers. Everybody was very impressed and enjoyed themselves wholeheartedly amidst the fine food and music.

The feast went on for a few days. One day, while Emperor Tang Tai Zong and his subjects were enjoying the food and wine, they suddenly heard strong winds blowing and the thundering roar of waves. The Emperor began to suspect that something was amiss and ordered his followers to rip the tent open. He was shocked to find that they were not enjoying a royal feast in the house of a rich peasant but were actually travelling on the sea! Emperor Tang Tai Zong panicked and immediately asked where he was. Zhang Shi Gui wanted to claim the credit for himself and said, "This is my plan for crossing the sea. We were lucky to be able to have a smooth journey so far and we will be reaching the east shore very soon." Emperor Tang Tai Zong finally realised that he and his subjects were actually on board a huge ship. To his great relief, he sighted the eastern shore.

The ship finally reached the east shore safely. When Xue Ren Gui saw that his plan was successful, he immediately bowed before Emperor Tang Tai Zong and asked for pardon. Emperor Tang Tai Zong discovered that the old man was Xue Ren Gui in disguise and was the originator of the plan. Xue Ren Gui was thus rewarded handsomely and given an official title.

COMMENTS & APPLICATIONS

This strategy requires that the **target is not alerted** to what might happen. So even if the scheme was uncovered, it would be too late for him to take counteraction. This was the case with Emperor Tang Tai Zong; he and his army were too deeply entrenched in Xue's plot to react. The person employing this strategy must also **offer distractions** that are non-threatening. In the story, Emperor Tang Tai Zong was too engrossed with the food and wine to realise that the enormous tent was used as a camouflage to distract him from his fear of the sea. His perception of reality was temporarily distorted by artificial means created by the strategist. The following are examples of how this strategy is applied in business.

MANAGING CHANGE

People typically resist change, more so if they have been operating within their comfort zones or in a stable environment. To lure them out of their comfort zones, their defence mechanisms must be lowered through the use of non-threatening situations, and by introducing gradual changes. The person in charge of implementing changes must be aware of potential hindrances. These obstacles could be caused by the organisation, the environment, the nature of the technology, resource constraints, or human factors. These blockages often create strong resistance to change and must be identified so that effective counter measures can be developed. In the case of Emperor Tang Tai Zong, the hindrance was clearly the fear of the sea. Once the cause was identified, Xue Ren Gui applied the appropriate strategy to overcome his fears.

A good example of this is the effort put in by Singapore Telecoms in its privatisation efforts. It began preparing its whole organisation at least six years before the company was listed.

Changes were introduced gradually so as to minimise any negative impact on the morale of the personnel. Policies were explained and senior management was heavily involved in implementing the changes. Dialogues with the rank-and-file were also conducted to allow them to appreciate the need for change and the implications involved. In addition, extensive and intensive training and consulting were carried out to ensure that employees would perform competently in a deregulated and competitive environment.

Their efforts paid off. Today, despite operating in a highly competitive domestic and international environment (the Singapore government has deliberately injected more competition in the industry by issuing out more licenses for telecommunication operations), Singapore Telecoms has remained a highly productive and profitable company. Among other reasons for success, one key factor is the time and effort (almost ten years) it used to prepare for the new competitive environment. Interestingly, it has also been successful in retaining many of its key personnel after the privatisation.

Singapore Telecom's experience gives us some worthwhile lessons. Firstly, *communication* is essential in facilitating change. The what, when and why of change should be explained. Secondly, *employees should be involved* in the plan for change. This can be done by encouraging them to provide ideas and suggestions. In this way, their commitment can also be induced. Thirdly, *adequate feedback mechanisms* must be established to counter fears and defuse rumours. Fourthly, changes made must *be acceptable*. Incremental changes are less painful and more acceptable especially in situations where time is not a constraint. Fifthly, a *climate of trust* is crucial (note how Emperor Tang Tai Zong trusted the old man in the story related earlier). This is where, in the context of a business organisation, sensitive and caring leadership is needed. Good internal relations also facilitate the building of a climate of trust. Finally, the *involvement of top management* will speed up the process of change and increase its effectiveness.

In sum, managing change is never an easy task. However, when skilfully done, it can achieve results that far exceed expectations. The key is to introduce them in ways that are not noticeable and do not incur great effort. Of course, time has to be on one's side. A *proactive* approach is often desired as it enables better control over the time, pace, direction and intensity of the change.

ADOPTION OF PRODUCTS AND SERVICES

This strategy applies to marketing too. A market may be resistant to new and radical products, especially if these are high-ticket items or items that are difficult to operate. To overcome resistance, marketers may use one or a combination of the following methods:

1 **Free trial period with money-back guarantee**
An increasing number of marketers advertise their products through the mass media and direct mailing using this technique. While few customers would actually send the product back for a refund, the free trial and money-back guarantee are very appealing as they project a risk-free purchase. The money-back guarantee also projects the seller's confidence in the product, boosting the customer's confidence.

2 **Free or low-cost lessons on usage of the products/services**
For example, sellers of archery and golf clubs in Asia typically conduct low-cost lessons to lure potential participants. After tasting the joy of archery or golfing, participants may be tempted to "invest" by joining the club and to purchase the expensive equipment. Similarly, marketers of expensive cookware like Frissler and AMC provide free cooking lessons to entice buyers.

3 **Allowing the product to be bought piecemeal**
IKEA furniture uses this strategy very well as buyers can literally build a whole household of furniture over time without worrying about changing designs. This approach appeals tremendously to young married couples with tight budgets.

4 **Selling a basic unit with options for upgrading or add-ons**
Microcomputers and home entertainment systems are good examples. Once the consumer is "hooked" on to the product, the potential future sales is enormous.

5 **Special offers/packages**
The sale of foreign properties to the more affluent Asian consumers provides a good example. Recently, an increasing number of developers from New Zealand, Britain, and Canada started to market their properties aggressively in Asia. To increase the attractiveness of their properties, they promise guaranteed rental yields and professional management services. These attractions, plus the lure of owning a property in these highly developed countries, tend to distract the buyer from other considerations. These include the higher than usual prices, the probability that there is an over supply (which is why these properties are marketed overseas), and that prices may drop.

PRODUCT/SERVICE BUNDLINGS AND TYING CONTRACTS

The marketing of a group of products and services provides a good illustration of the application of the strategy, "Deceiving the heavens to cross the sea". Known commonly as product or service bundling, the marketer attempts to sell a wide variety of products or services together, pricing the whole bundle lower than the sum of the individual prices of each product/service. Bundling has been exploited by marketers to make a product or service appear more attractive.

Packaged tours, set lunches and dinners and personal (priority) banking services are examples of product or service bundles. Marketers like Noel Hampers even highlight the detailed breakdown of the price of each individual item in the hamper to bring home the message that the value of the hamper is more than its cost.

As products get more sophisticated, they are sold more and more as bundles. Yet, after paying so much for the complete product bundle, many consumers do not fully use all the benefits or features offered. It is not surprising to find that owners of luxury cars rarely use the cruise control, that the capabilities of a personal computer are never fully exploited, that the sophisticated features in a Canon EOS 1N camera have rarely been used, and the state-of-the-art features of a home-video-karaoke set have hardly been tried out. Yet, all these features are paid for in the bundle.

A consumer may, in fact, forgo parts of the bundle without feeling any loss. For instance, after paying for a tour package, the consumer may not mind not visiting certain tour sites or attractions even though he has already paid for them. To him, the overall price is still cheap even if he does not consume everything in the package. In the same way, it is not uncommon to find a passenger forgoing meals on board the plane, a subscriber of cable television not tuning in to every programme, a car owner not capitalising on all the "free" maintenance services that come with purchase of the car, a tourist not using all the hotel facilities, and so on.

Interestingly, the consumer does not perceive the non-usage of these features as losses! These examples illustrate the success of the marketer in applying the "Deceiving the heavens to cross the sea" strategy.

Bundling is widely used by Japanese manufacturers of cars, consumer electronics, watches and appliances. They bundle all conceivable product options and price it attractively. Japanese car makers have used this approach with great success in their market penetration of Europe and America since the late 1960s. Then, car makers in Europe and America tended to sell only the basic car with other options sold separately. These options could add 50% more to the price of the car! In contrast, the Japanese cars were sold as a bundle, with all the options included as standard items. By pricing them competitively, Japanese cars gained a strong foothold in these markets, especially in America. Today, the Japanese strategy in product bundling has been copied not only by other car makers, but by many other product manufacturers as well.

For the marketer, product bundling is a creative way of marketing more products and services. This strategy is particularly appealing when the products contained in the bundle are complementary. Using this approach, the marketer can use a fast moving item in the bundle to help move the sales of the slower moving items, thus increasing sales.

Another prominent example is Microsoft. In an attempt to corner a bigger share of the market, Microsoft distributed its browser, the Internet Explorer, free with Windows 98. Microsoft was thus able to proliferate its browser on millions of personal computers as most PCs use Microsoft Windows as the operating system. In doing so, Microsoft prevented competitors such as Netscape from building market share. The practice by Microsoft, unfortunately, attracted the attention of its rivals as well as the US Justice Department. Microsoft was slapped with several antitrust charges for tying its Internet products to its operating·system.

FINANCING FOR EXPANSION

Occasionally, a company may need funds for expansion. Funds can be obtained by borrowing from the banks or from shareholders. Borrowing from the banks may push up the gearing ratio of the company. Besides incurring higher risks (as interest has to be paid regardless of the volume of business), the credit ratings of the company would also be affected. Thus, borrowing from the shareholders may be the better option.

A common approach used to entice shareholders is the issue of rights. This could be done in two ways. First, the company could deliberately price the rights below the market price of the share so as to make them very attractive. Alternatively, it could declare a bonus issue to shareholders, to be followed by a rights issue. More often than not, either of the two approaches would result in over subscription. Shareholders will perceive this exercise as a sign that the company is doing well, while the company benefits from this creative and effective way of raising additional capital without over leveraging. Risks are generally lower as the impact is only on the earnings per share, and the company is not compelled to pay a fixed dividend annually. These issues are less likely to be fully understood by the average investor. The rights issue utilises the logic behind the strategy of "Deceiving the heavens to cross the sea". The company is able to meet its financial needs while making shareholders happy.

MANAGEMENT OF SERVICES

In the service operation businesses, there are many examples in which the "Deceiving the heavens to cross the sea" strategy has been applied effectively. The way in which Singapore Airlines (SIA) strives to create an enjoyable experience for its passengers is fascinating. While flying is not exactly crossing the sea, the experience encountered by passengers is not much different from what Xue Ren Gui did to Emperor Tang Tai Zong.

SIA is well-known for its inflight service (one which "other airlines talk about"). For years, it has been voted the best airline in the world. Travelling by air can be stressful, boring and sometimes scary, as the passenger is confined within a very limited space. However, SIA manages to turn the hours spent into a delightful experience. It keeps passengers well-fed and well-entertained with food, unlimited flow of wines and liquor, and the best and most current movies. Magazines, newspapers and other reading material are also easy to hand. For those who want more excitement, cards and computer games are also available. To top it off, the SIA cabin crew display charm, good-looks, enthusiasm and warmth. With so much to do, passengers often find that time passes quickly. Before they know it, they have arrived at their destination!

SIA's success has led other airlines, especially those in Asia to adopt similar strategies. Some have tried to outdo what SIA has to offer on board. However few have surpassed the success enjoyed by SIA because SIA had a head start. The SIA girl has achieved an image that approximates a myth status, as evidenced and embodied in the wax form of an SIA girl at Madame Tussaud's Wax Museum in London, Britain.

In the luxury cruise business, too, operators literally apply the "Deceiving the heavens to cross the sea" strategy. With nothing but the sea and sky to look at, passengers can become really bored. Yet these luxury cruise companies have been able to occupy the attention of their passengers with an unlimited plethora of activities and programmes. Besides the high quality accommodation of various grades to suit the budget, cruise liners come equipped with state-of-the-art facilities like the gymnasium, exercise rooms, swimming pools, saunas, theatres, cinemas, games arcade, shops, dining rooms, restaurants, discotheques, night clubs, casinos, etc. They actively plan programmes and events to occupy the passengers so passengers are kept busily entertained till they arrive at their next port of call, where more excitement awaits.

The successful application of this strategy is demonstrated by the boom in this industry. With the screening of the movie Titanic in early 1998, the luxury cruise business received a further boost. There are no shortage of takers even for tour packages costing over US$100,000!

The casino city of Las Vegas adopts a similar strategy. The moment a person lands at the airport, he is assailed by thousands of gambling machines to excite his senses. The temptation is reinforced when he checks in to his hotel. No hotel in Las Vegas is void of gambling machines. The best casinos are built within posh and large hotels, some equipped with over a thousand rooms, and a multiplied range of services and facilities.

The entire atmosphere is carefully designed to ensure that the gambling experience is enjoyable, even if one loses money! Gambling is made very accessible and non-intimidating – all you need to play is a dollar, and a finger to press a button. In this titillating atmosphere, one easily loses track of time. Besides extensive gambling opportunities, Vegas offers enough sights and sounds to preoccupy a visitor for days with excellent shows, exhibits, shopping, rides, arcades and even circuses.

One final example of this strategy is the management of hospital wards. Better-run hospitals have cleverly applied the "Deceiving the heavens to cross the sea" strategy. A patient of higher-priced wards is provided services to occupy his time and make his stay more pleasant. Newspapers, a wider food selection, flexible visiting hours, in-house videos, and channel surfing opportunities all serve to occupy and distract the patient.

The strategy of "Deceiving the heavens to cross the sea" revolves round the use of distractions to lure the target from his main concerns. These non-threatening distractions can take many forms, and are created to appeal to the desire for creature comforts. In the case of airlines and cruise liners, it is to bring passengers to their destinations in the greatest comfort without fear or boredom. For casinos, it is to ensure that visitors will enjoy the visit despite spending huge amounts of money. And hospitals seek to ensure that patients do not feel trapped in an unproductive situation. The operator achieves his goals by using activities to distract and occupy his audience.

Strategy 2

围魏救赵

Beseiging Wei to Save Zhao

共敌不如分敌，敌阳不如敌阴。

Explanation

Instead of attacking a cohort of strong enemies (共敌), one should try to diffuse the concentration and to attack each enemy separately (分敌). Instead of a head-on attack (敌阳), one should wait for the best opportunity when the enemy is at his weakest point to launch an ambush (敌阴).

Historical Background

This strategy was explained in *Shi Ji*'s (史记) chapter on Sun Zi's biography (孙子吴起列传) as follows:

> Waging war is like controlling a flood. The best way to handle a strong enemy is to avoid a head-on confrontation and try to diffuse his strength, just like draining a flood. The best way to handle a weak enemy is to seize the opportunity to destroy him totally, just like building dams to block the flow. Therefore, when the state of Qi (齐) decided to rescue the state of Zhao (赵), Sun Bin[1] (孙膑) told Tian Ji (田忌), " To handle a bundle of entangled ropes, one has to tease it and not destroy it. Similarly, to settle a fight, one has to use the mouth to mediate and not to get involved physically. Divert the strong and hit the weak and let the enemy suffer some setbacks. He will not progress and the threat will be reduced."

治兵如治水：锐者避其锋，如导流；弱者塞其虚，如筑堰。故当齐救赵时，孙子谓田忌曰："夫解杂乱纠纷者不控拳；救斗者不搏击。批亢捣虚，形格势禁，则自为解耳。"

The story regarding how Zhao was saved by Qi follows.

During the period of the Warring States (战国时代) between the fifth and fourth centuries BC, many small states jockeyed each other for position. Among these, the Han (韩), Zhao (赵), Wei (魏), Qi (齐), Chu (楚), and Yan (燕) emerged as the stronger ones. In 353 BC, the state of Wei launched a full-force attack on the state of Zhao and besieged the Zhao capital Han Dan (邯郸). In response to a plea from the Zhao ruler for assistance, the King of Qi ordered General Tian Ji (田忌) to lead an army of 8000 to the rescue.

General Tian Ji contemplated using the Qi army in direct confrontation with the Wei army but was advised against this by his adviser, Sun Bin (孙膑)[1]. Instead, Sun Bin reasoned, "Right now, all of Wei's finest men are attacking Han Dan and the defence in Wei state, including its important city, Da Liang (大梁), is weak. If we were to attack Da Liang now, we would not only be able to defeat the state of Wei with ease, but would also convince the state of Zhao of the strength of our state."

Tian Ji took Sun Bin's advice. Sure enough, when the Wei army heard of the attack on their home town, they ceased the attack on Han Dan and began a forced march back to Wei. Meanwhile, a troop of the Qi army hid themselves at Gui Ling (桂陵) along the return path of the Wei army and ambushed them there. The Wei army was completely annihilated in the battle. Qi earned the gratitude of Zhao and the fear or Wei, and turned out to be the winner.

COMMENTS & APPLICATIONS

This strategy advocates that to win, one need not go head-on against the enemy. An indirect approach can sometimes be more effective. In the historical example, by attacking Wei's important city Da Liang, Tian Ji caused greater damage to the Wei army. With this approach, Tian Ji was able to achieve more.

The strategy, "Besieging Wei to save Zhao", also illustrates another important principle of winning in war — the *relative superiority at the point of contact* is more important than the absolute size of the army. In the words of Sun Zi, the famous Chinese military strategist:

---

[1] *Sun Bin (孙膑) was rumoured to have been a descendant of the famous war strategist, Sun Wu (孙武).*

If the enemy prepares for a frontal attack, his rear will be weak;
If he defends the rear, his front will be fragile.
If he strengthens his left, he will weaken his right;
If he strengthens his right, he will weaken his left.
If he tries to prepare in every area, he will be weak everywhere!

故备前则后寡, 备后则前寡,
备左则右寡, 备右则左寡,
无所不备, 则无所不寡。

Despite Wei's military superiority, its full-force attack on Han Dan opened its rear. The Qi army exploited this opportunity. In essence, the Qi army attacked *an area that was completely ignored* by the Wei army. This gave them an even greater chance of victory. This again, can be aptly captured by Sun Zi's words:

To ensure success, attack the enemy where his defence is weakest.

攻而必取者, 攻其所不守也

CHANGING THE POINT(S) OF CONTACT

Examples abound for the use of this strategy in business. When Citibank entered the markets in Asia, it aimed to corner a large share of the retail loan market. Unfortunately, being a foreign bank and faced with restriction on the number of bank branches allowed, it was unable to obtain a large pool of local funds (deposits). Thus, it had to use foreign funds which inevitably cost more. This meant higher loan rates which would then render it less competitive in the retail loan market. Instead of competing directly against the big local banks on the basis of price (loan rates), Citibank chose to compete indirectly on the basis of service. In particular, it focused on offering *convenience* by allowing telephone application for loans and *speed in approving the loan.* In economies like Hong Kong, Singapore and Malaysia where business opportunities come and go very quickly, speed and convenience are important *benefits* to consumers. Today, Citibank has become a major player in the retail loan market in Hong Kong and Singapore despite high loan rates!

The success of Citibank illustrates its ability to *change the point of contact.* Instead of following the rest of the industry by competing on *price*, it changes the point of contact to *speed* and *convenience.* Not only were these factors ignored by many local banks, they were also Citibank's greatest strengths. Thus, Citibank created their own victory by dictating where and how it wanted to compete, and was not hemmed in by competitors. The lesson from the Citibank's example is that it is possible to win even in a homogeneous service like retail banking. This can be done by developing one's own advantages. One can always attempt to "change the rules" that would "derail" competitors.

CHOOSING AREAS IGNORED BY COMPETITORS

Similarly, when American fast food chains entered the market in Asia, they chose to set up outlets in urban cities and tourist areas and avoided residential areas. They did not compete head-on on price nor tastiness of food, focusing instead on providing quality services and comfortable eating environment. They also relied heavily on advertising and promotion. They only made their onslaught into suburban areas after establishing strong footholds in the urban cities. In this way, they avoided the initial backlash from the local operators who tended to concentrate in the suburban areas where most residents live.

The strategy adopted by these fast food chains is similar to that of Citibank. By choosing areas ignored by the local food operators — quality services, comfortable eating environment, and heavy advertising — they achieved considerable victories. Today, fast food has become very much a part of life in many Asian cities.

Large supermarket chains and departmental stores like Carrefour, Isetan and Seiyu have adopted similar stategies. These large foreign players chose to exert their presence in urban cities first to avoid competing head-on against the smaller local players in the suburban areas, and to capitalise on the more affluent and "Western-oriented" consumers in the larger cities. Indeed, there is much wisdom in adopting such an approach. When these large chains tried to make inroads into suburban areas, they encountered serious resistance and backlash. In Indonesia, demonstrations and isolated cases of rioting were staged against these large stores for threatening the livelihoods of the local merchants.

CREATING ONE'S OWN ADVANTAGES

In business, as in war, absolute advantages do not last. Advantages and disadvantages are relative. One cannot be strong in all areas at one time. No matter how a company defends itself, it is bound to have weak spots that can be exploited by competitors. The business environment is dynamic and competitive edges enjoyed by a company can be eroded overnight by new competitors or new technology. So a company must proactively create advantages for itself. Choosing areas ignored by competitors in markets, products or service ranges or features is one way.

Interestingly, a company need not be the strongest in the playing field to use this strategy. A smaller competitor can win if it chooses its arena carefully. Opportunities are ample and ready to be exploited. So one should study the market to identify these specific opportunities. This is the essence of *niching*. The success story of Creative Technology, manufacturer of Sound Blaster, is a good illustration. Mr Sim Wong Hoo, its chairman, managed to pick a product ignored by the bigger players and chose to sell it in the largest market of the world (the United States). Over the years, it continued to innovate and make improvements to its product. By doing this, it created its own advantages.

These organisations sought to develop areas of advantage and created their own victories. Such competitive postures can perhaps be appropriately summed up by the following remarks by Sun Zi:

> Therefore, those who are skilled in warfare will always bring the enemy to where they want to fight, and not be brought there by the enemy.

故善战者, 致人而不致于人

PROPERTY PRICES IN SINGAPORE

The property market in Singapore in the 1990s is a good illustration of how some big players used the strategy of "Besieging Wei to save Zhao" to shore up prices significantly. In 1990, property prices in Singapore increased by a mere 3%. However, in the following few years prices rose by double-digit figures to 17.8% for 1991, 17.5% for 1992, 41.0% for 1993 and 33.6% for 1994.

The market went into a frenzy as many plunged in blindly, speculating with life-savings. There were countless calls for the government to intervene in the market. Meanwhile, the big property developers were capitalising on the greed of the unwary speculators. In the frenzy, developers jacked up the tender prices of land put up for sale. By pushing up the land prices, the developers created the impression that prices would be on the upward trend for some time. This, in turn, allowed them to sell their properties at much higher prices. Through this artificial price mechanism, they created the impression that prices were unlikely to drop.

These developers benefitted from this in that the value of large land banks that they had bought at much lower prices previously has now appreciated. Through this, they earned bumper profits. This spiralling effect went on despite warnings by the government. Finally, after another 11.4% increase of prices in 1995, the government decided to step in. It introduced a package of anti-speculation measures on private housing in May 1996 which then bought down prices by 2.6%.

This insignificant drop in price of only 2.6% is amazing, considering the fact that prices more than tripled between 1990 and 1995. The price drop was expected to be much higher considering the severity of the anti-speculation measures imposed.

Possible reasons why property prices did not fall significantly after the imposition of the tough anti-speculation measures are many. Firstly, there was tremendous liquidity in the market. Many buyers had learned from the bitter experience in the 1984/1985 economic recession, and had taken precaution in managing their money. In particular, many of them were using their savings in the Central Provident Fund which thus significantly cushioned their cash-flow problems. Secondly, mortgage rates were low, and this allowed speculators to hold their investments longer. Indeed, they had become more of "specuvestors" than pure speculators. In other words, they were willing to speculate for capital gains, but had the means and resources to hold for the longer term if needed. Thirdly, the big developers, having made bumper profits over the past few years, were able to hold on to the prices. This was particularly true when their mark-ups had been incredible (owing to land bought earlier at lower prices) and the break-even number of units that were needed to be sold to recover the project had been as low as 40% to 50% in some cases.

However, one of the most subtle ploys used by these big-time developers was the "Besieging Wei to save Zhao" strategy. After the May 1996 curbs, they continued to display a very confident front to the public by not adjusting their prices significantly downwards. Instead, they chose to absorb the legal fees and stamp duty which were more subtle. While they continued to put in ambitious bids for new land plots that were released for sale. They hoped that by keeping the bid prices for land tenders high, they could continue to prop up the prices of property. Potential buyers might then have the impression that prices were unlikely to fall, given the optimism displayed by the developers. In fact, this strategy of theirs worked very well for more than a year. The property market became a cat-and-mouse game during this period, and buyers and sellers were in a deadlock situation. Each was waiting for the other party to cave in.

At the end of July 1997, the developers began to show some signs of weakness. In a letter to the Minister for National Development, the president of the Real Estate Developers Association of Singapore (REDAS), Mr Heng Chiang Meng urged the government to slow down land sales. He commented that the local property market was sick, and given the uncertain economic conditions in Singapore and the region, property prices might be heading for a much greater fall if nothing was done to help it. Thus far, while prices appeared to hold firm, the volume of transactions had declined tremendously. With increased supply of new housing units coming onto the market for between 1997 to 1999, Mr Heng's fear was well-founded. However, for a fairly long period, the strategy of "besieging Wei" (pushing up the prices of new land sales) to "save Zhao" (prevent downward correction of property prices) worked to the advantage of the developers.

STRATEGY 3

借刀杀人

KILLING WITH A BORROWED KNIFE

敌已明，友未定，引友杀敌，
不自出力，以损推演。

EXPLANATION

This strategy works on the premise that while the enemy has clarified its stand (敌已明), the position of the alliance is still equivocal (友未定). In this situation, the best way is to entice the alliance to destroy the enemy (引友杀敌) on one's behalf (不自出力). This is an adaptation of the logic in Yi Jing's "Harm Theory" ([易：损]卦): "Harm the bottom to benefit the top" (损下益上).

HISTORICAL BACKGROUND

Historical examples of this strategy abound. In the ninth chapter of *Chang Duan Jing* (长短经), "Ge Xing" (格形):

> When the enemy has made his stand and another force is also increasing its strength, one should take advantage of this other force to destroy the enemy. As in the case where Zi Gong (子贡) defended the state of Lu (鲁国) by creating confusion within the state of Qi (齐国), destroying the state of Wu (吴国) and saving the state of Jin (晋国).

敌象已露，而另一势力更张，将有所为，应借此力
以毁敌人。如子贡之存鲁、敌齐、破吴、强晋。

The story of how Zi Gong saved the state of Lu (鲁国) was recorded in *Shi Ji*'s "Biography of the students of Confucius" (史记·仲尼弟子列传).

STORY 1

Confucius (孔子) was born during the Spring and Autumn period (春秋时期) in the state of Lu (鲁国). When he received news that the powerful state of Qi (齐国) was preparing to attack his homeland, he sent his rhetorically gifted disciple Zi Gong (子贡) to talk to the rulers of the surrounding states.

Zi Gong first went to the state of Qi and pointed out to the military generals the flaws in the decision in attacking Lu. He then succeeded in persuading the generals to attack the state of Wu (吴国) instead. Zi Gong subsequently went to Wu and instigated the king of Wu to attack Qi in order to protect Lu. When war broke out between Wu and Qi, Zi Gong hurried to the state of Jin (晋国) and advised its ruler, Jin Ding Wang (晋定王) to prepare to defend his state from an attack from Wu. In the fierce battle that ensued between Wu and Jin, Jin emerged victor. Thus, Zi Gong managed to save Lu.

STORY 2

During the period of the Warring States (战国时代) (403 - 221 BC), when Chu Zhao Wang (楚昭王) first became the ruler of the state of Chu (楚国), he appointed Xiang Wa (襄瓦) as his Chief Minister, and Que Yuan (却苑), Yan Jiang Shi (鄢将师) and Fei Wu Ji (费无极), to help in the running of the state. Once, Que Yuan was sent to lead an army against the state of Wu (吴国). He got a resounding victory and captured many soldiers. Emperor Chu Zhao Wang was very pleased with him and awarded him half of the captives and took him into his confidence. Fei Wu Ji was jealous of the Emperor's favour on Que Yuan so he instigated Yan Jiang Shi to plot against him. Yan Jiang Shi told the Chief Minister, Xiang Wa, "Que Yuan intends to hold a banquet. He sent me to present an invitation to Your Honour. Would Your Honour care to attend the banquet?"

Xiang Wa accepted the invitation. On the other hand, Fei Wu Ji went to Que Yuan and said, "The Chief Minister intends to drink at your place. Would you agree to be the host and let us all have a good time together?" Unaware that this was a trap laid for him, Que Yuan replied, "I am his subordinate. It is such an honour to be able to invite the

Chief Minister to my place. Let's make it tomorrow. I shall prepare a big banquet. Please inform His Honour."

Fei Wu Ji then asked, "Since the Chief Minister is coming to your place, what gift have you prepared for him?" On this, Que Yuan hesitated, "This is a problem. I do not know what His Honour likes." Fei Wu Ji took this opportunity to lure Que Yuan into his plot.

"Well, according to my sources," Fei Wu Ji deliberately paused for a while, then continued, "His Honour is the Chief Minister. He has everything from beautiful ladies to riches. However, he is very interested in powerful armours and strong weapons. He has hinted to me that he is envious of the Wu armours and weapons that you obtained. His main intention of coming to your house is to have a look at your possessions."

"This is too easy," replied Que Yuan. He then ordered his men to bring out the possessions he obtained from the battle with Wu. To show his enthusiasm, Fei Wu Ji even helped him to pick a hundred of the best and most powerful armours and weapons. Fei Wu Ji then told Que Yuan, "These should be sufficient. You place all these outside your door. When His Honour comes, he would ask you about them and you just show them and present them to him. I do not think he would accept other gifts."

Que Yuan believed Fei Wu Ji's words and ordered his men to place the selected weapons and armours, covered with a huge sheet of cloth, outside his door. The next day, Que Yuan prepared a grand banquet and requested Fei Wu Ji to invite Xiang Wa. Xiang Wa was all prepared to go but Fei Wu Ji said to him, "Recently, Que Yuan has become very arrogant. He did not state the reason for this banquet. We should not under estimate this person. Let me go and have a look at the preparation of the banquet first. Your Honour would then proceed. This will be safer for Your Honour."

"All right. You shall go and have a look first," said Xiang Wa. Fei Wu Ji went to the street outside and dallied for a while. He then staggered back to the Chief Minister's home. He pretended to have some difficulties in breathing and said in a worried tone, "I thought I could not return in time! I have found out that Que Yuan has an ulterior motive for this banquet. He intends to kill Your Honour! I saw that he

has hidden a lot of weapons outside his house. If Your Honour attends the banquet, you would fall into his trap."

When Xiang Wa heard this, he was suspicious and said, "I am on friendly terms with Que Yuan. He has no reason to plot against me." Fei Wu Ji tried to sow discord by saying, "Ever since Que Yuan's successful battle with Wu, he has gained favour with the Emperor. Everybody, except Your Honour, knows that he has always been eyeing the Chief Minister's position. Yan Jiang Shi and I have been guarding ourselves against him. Think of this: during the battle with Wu, Que Yuan could have fought till the end and destroyed the whole of Wu. However, he only captured some soldiers and returned home. It was rumoured that the state of Wu offered him a hefty sum of money and thus there was a conspiracy that he would only return with some captives. Therefore, he may have other plans. When he finally seizes some power, he will endanger the state of Chu."

Fei Wu Ji spoke with such conviction that even the Chief Minister was confused. However, he still did not trust Fei Wu Ji completely and he sent his own man to Que Yuan's place to spy at the latter. Xiang Wa's man came back and reported that it was true that a lot of weapons were hidden outside of Que Yuan's door. Xiang Wa was furious and sent for Yan Jiang Shi for the latter's advice. Yan Jiang Shi had conspired with Fei Wu Ji. He told the Chief Minister, "Que Yuan is planning to revolt against Your Honour. He has conspired with three powerful families to stage a revolution. It is lucky that we saw through his plan today."

"Damn!" cried Xiang Wa as he slammed table, "I will kill him." Xiang Wa immediately reported to the Emperor and ordered Yan Jiang Shi to lead a troop to surround Que Yuan's house. Que Yuan finally realised that he had been betrayed by Fei Wu Ji. He sighed heavily, drew his sword and took his own life.

COMMENTS & APPLICATIONS

This is a popular strategy and has been mentioned in other books of war strategies like **Han Fei Zi** (韩 非 子) and **Hou Han Shu** (后 汉 书). Essentially, it advocates making use of another person or party to one's own gains. This strategy is used when one lacks the resources to accomplish his goals. Thus, he manipulates a stronger party to unknowingly carry out his plan.

In the first historical example, Confucius had limited power to protect his hometown, Lu, from Qi's attack, so he "borrowed" the "knife" of Wu to curb Qi, and eventually Jin to curb Wu. In the second episode, Fei Wu Ji would not have been able to kill the powerful Que Yuan as the latter was the Emperor's blue-eye boy. Therefore, he had to make use of the power of the Chief Minister Xiang Wa to rid his enemy. In using this strategy, one is also attempting to "Shift the blame to someone else" (移 尸 嫁 祸).

OPERATING THROUGH SURROGATES

"Killing with a borrowed knife" is commonly used by a company or organisation to implement drastic policies or actions. If the company carries them out directly they would incur the wrath of its employees or concerned parties. Thus, one of the most effective ways is to employ *consultants* to be the scapegoat, to suggest the changes needed. Often, a company may even supply the "solutions" for the consultants to incorporate in their reports. The consultants become the buffer for negative responses. More importantly, they are the surrogates of the company. In doing so, the company can achieve its aims without confrontation. In fact, it can even push all blame to the consultants and relinquish all responsibility when things go wrong.

This strategy is also used by a company which intends to take over another firm without disclosing its own identity. One reason for not revealing its intentions to either its competitors or the firm to be bought is so that prices will not be pushed up significantly. *Surrogate companies* or third parties are used also when the buyer wants to dissociate himself from the purchase. In fact, the practice is commonly used in business acquisitions and investments (by using nominees and trustees). It can also be used by individuals, for example, in the purchase of exclusive art pieces or antiques. For privacy and other personal reasons, these buyers chose to conceal their identities. However, the best way for them to build their collections is through the "borrowed knife" approach.

The application of such a strategy can also be found in the *use of an established brand* to enter foreign markets. This was what Japanese companies did in the 1950s. After World War II, many Japanese companies were still weak and did not have any brands of international repute. To penetrate overseas markets, these companies marketed their products through established American and European brands. By operating through surrogates, they achieved their objectives without expending resources on brand development which could be very expensive. Once these Japanese manufacturers mastered the skills of distribution in these overseas markets, they developed their own brands in the 1960s. But in the infancy of their economic development, Japanese companies borrowed the "strengths" of its allies to attack overseas markets.

Due to intense business and economic competition, companies from more developed economies have found it increasingly difficult to market their products in developed markets like the United States. Without preferential treatment, and with heavy taxes and restrictive trade quotas, it can be a daunting task. In a creative bid to beat these odds, companies shifted their factories and manufacturing operations to less developed economies. By doing this, they not only enjoy lower production costs, but are also able to use products made in these less developed economies as "camouflage" to export to developed markets. Thus, through *overseas operators*, they are able to get around the trade quota problem. These products may even enjoy preferential treatment if they originate from economies that have the most favoured nation (MFN) status. For these reasons, multinational corporations (MNCs) prefer to set up operations in economies like China and Vietnam. So beneficial is this arrangement that when the United States threatened to cancel China's MFN status, MNCs lobbied against it.

Relying on Foreign Investments to Stimulate Growth

Singapore's success was created by borrowing from other's strengths. When the British pulled out of Singapore in the early 1960s, the country was in near disaster. As an island state with a small population base, it had neither natural resources nor local expertise. Unemployment was high, and social and racial disorder threatened to tear it apart. Instead of giving up, the political leaders sought foreign investments from multinational corporations to help in its economic development.

The heavy reliance on foreign multinational corporations allowed Singapore to achieve several objectives. Firstly, the MNCs ensured that there would be *ready markets* for the products made in Singapore. Secondly, the MNCs created the *much needed jobs* for Singaporeans. Thirdly, they helped to *impart training* to

Singaporeans. Fourthly, the MNCs generously *transfered technology and management skills*. In sum, not only did the MNCs help to earn the much needed foreign exchange for Singapore, they were also instrumental in stimulating the domestic economic growth. Indeed, by creating jobs and wealth, they provided social security for Singaporeans.

Singapore may not have developed at the rate it had to achieve its present success had it not borrowed the strengths of foreign MNCs. Today, the same strategy of capitalising on other's strengths is still in use, except that the focus is now on seeking out MNCs in the arena of high technology.

Another country which has successfully sought and promoted foreign investments is China. Despite China's late opening to the rest of the world, it has now out-paced some other Asian economies who have chosen to not pursue foreign investments.

The Malaysian government has also undertaken pragmatic approaches in courting foreign investment. It took pains to relax the application of its pro-local (pro-Bumi) policy and waived its policy requirement that a certain quota of Malays be employed in each company. This ensured an influx of trained personnel. It also permitted the setting up of private foreign universities, in which English is used as a medium of instruction. The relaxation of the requirement for using Bahasa Malaysia as the medium of instruction allowed local universities to follow suit in using English for the conduct of technology-related courses.

The Malaysian government aligned their sights to maximise the benefits of foreign investments, to achieve its ambition of becoming a developed nation by 2020.

India, however, has chosen to not rely on foreign investors, slowing down its economic development. In one situation, Tata's efforts to set up a joint-venture with Singapore Airlines was halted when Indian politicians yielded to domestic pressures to stall it.

LICENSING, FRANCHISING AND JOINT-VENTURES

At the corporate level, licensing, franchising and joint-ventures are examples of borrowed strengths. On its own, the local operator may not have the marketing power to dominate a market. However, by "borrowing" an established brand name, the market becomes wide open. Excellent examples can be supported by the many success stories of how local operators have secured the licenses and franchises of business like McDonalds, Haagan Daz, Pizza Hut, Planet Hollywood, Hard Rock Cafe and Club Med to open up vast business opportunities in many Asian cities. Similarly, many Asian manufacturers have entered into joint-ventures with American, European and Japanese partners in order to benefit from their marketing skills, management expertise and technological advancements.

One of the problems encountered by using the "borrowed knife" approach, especially in licensing and franchising, is that the licensee or franchisee may become so comfortable that he may not develop his own knife! In other words, local talents may not make significant developments when they have a strong fall-back position. This is one of the strongest criticisms against licensing and franchising as they may hamper the development of local industries. For example, the advent of fast food chains has robbed the livelihood of local food operators in Asia. Few of the local food operators have been able to challenge the onslaught of the fast-expanding franchised outlets of these large chains. Similarly, there are few Asian companies that can rival Coca-Cola, Pepsi-cola and even Western brands of beer. Instead, many of them are content to borrow these foreign brands (through licensing arrangements) to attack their own markets!

Recognising the importance of franchising, the Singapore government has encouraged it among local companies, going so far as to position itself as the franchising capital of the region with considerable success. Some local companies have developed franchising as a means of expanding their businesses to the rest of the world. Successful examples include Old Chang Kee (curry puffs), Noel Gifts International (corporate gifts and flowers), Bee Cheng Hiang (barbequed sweet meat) and Informatics Holdings (computer training schools). Franchising, like investment overseas, are part and parcel of the Singapore government's efforts to build its external, second wing. In a sense, this is Singapore's way of developing a "knife" good enough to be borrowed by others.

In sum, it is important to bear in mind that when one is weak, it is not advisable to go head on against stronger competitors or attempt to enter highly competitive markets. Instead, one should actively seek out stronger partners and borrow their strengths to help achieve one's goals and objectives. This can be done through franchising, licensing and joint-ventures. However, borrowing someone else's knife can only be a temporary solution. In the long run, it is important to develop one's own knife.

STRATEGY 4

以逸待劳

CONSERVING ENERGY WHILE THE ENEMY TIRES HIMSELF OUT

困敌之势, 不以战; 损刚益柔。

EXPLANATION

One does not need to always make a direct attack to subdue the enemy. Sometimes, one can use the theory of "using the mild (or weak) to control the strong" (损刚益柔) to delay and exhaust the enemy and strengthen one's position.

HISTORICAL BACKGROUND

The phrase "Conserving energy while the enemy tires himself out" is taken from Sun Zi's military chapter (孙子 . 军争篇) where it is written:

> Use the near to await the far, conserve energy while waiting for the enemy to tire himself out and strengthen oneself (with food) while waiting for the enemy to go hungry. These are the best ways to subdue a strong enemy.

以近待远, 以佚(同逸) 待劳, 以饱待饥, 此治力者也

This strategy is also mentioned in *The Hundred War Strategies* (百战奇略致战), *The Discourse of the South-North Army* (南北筹兵论), *Zuo Zhuan* (左传), *The Book of History* (史记) and *The Book of Han* (汉书).

There are many historical examples illustrating this strategy. One tells of how Cao Gui (曹刿) helped the weaker army of Lu (鲁国) to defeat its stronger enemy, the state of Qi (齐国).

During the Spring and Autumn Period (722 - 468 BC), the ruler of the state of Qi appointed Bao Shu Ya (鲍叔牙) as a General to launch a battle against the state of Lu. The ruler of Lu, Lu Zhuang Gong (鲁庄公), had suffered a bitter defeat during the last battle with Qi and thus when he heard of the attack, he was anxious and did not know what to do. He consulted his subject Shi Bo (施伯) for a plan. Shi Bo could not come up with a solution, so he suggested that they seek the advice of Cao Gui, a hermit.

Shi Bo said, "Although Cao Gui is a hermit and has never been a government official, he knows many strategies and has the calibre of a General." Lu Zhuang Gong then sent Shi Bo to invite Cao Gui to the palace. When Cao Gui learned of Shi Bo's intentions, he laughed and replied, "Are there no capable men in the palace suitable for the job that you have to come to this deserted place to look for an insignificant person like me?"

"Honestly, the attack from Qi has driven everybody in the palace into a state of panic and nobody knows how to tackle the problem. You are a man of great wisdom and know many strategies of war. We have thus come to seek your advice. If you can defeat the enemies, you will be given a post in the palace," said Shi Bo. Cao Gui considered this response and then replied, "I will go with you to the palace, not because I want an official post but because it is every citizen's duty to ensure the safety of his nation."

When they came before Lu Zhuang Gong, the latter asked Cao Gui, "What are your plans for defeating the enemies?" Cao Gui said, "In a war, the situation is ever-changing, so it is difficult to conclude on a plan unless one is at the scene of the war. I request that Your Highness send me to the war front with the soldiers so that I can come up with a solution appropriate for the circumstances."

Lu Zhuang Gong realised that Cao Gui was indeed the right man and immediately appointed him adviser to the army. The two armies met at Chang Shao (长勺). When the Qi General, Bao Shu Ya, saw the army of Lu, he immediately called for a full attack. Bao Shu Ya did not consider defeating the Lu army difficult since his army had defeated them before. The Qi army was fully prepared and at the signal, they came forward like huge tidal waves.

Lu Zhuang Gong panicked when he saw the strength of the Qi army and wanted to call a full attack as well. Cao Gui immediately stopped him and said, "Hold it! The enemies are in a high spirit and we should only keep a strong defence. We must not be too impatient."

After the first wave of attack, the Qi army sounded their drums for a second attack. However, the Lu army remained in a defensive position and refused to respond with a head-on attack. The Qi army was thus unable to engage them in battle. General Bo Shu Ya smugly told his subordinates, "The army of Lu is afraid of us. We have made two challenges but they dared not retaliate. I am sure they will flee before us at our third attack, like defeated dogs."

When the war drums of the Qi army sounded for the third time, the Qi army marched forward, but this time, they had relaxed their guard against their enemy as they thought that the latter would not retaliate. Cao Gui said to Lu Zhuang Gong, "Now is the time to retaliate! Give signal to attack."

When the Lu army heard their war drums signalling an attack, they charged forward like hungry animals and caught Qi army off guard. The surprised Qi army realised too late to raise a defence and was bitterly defeated. The survivals of the Qi army beat a hasty retreat.

Lu Zhuang Gong was overjoyed and wanted to give chase. Cao Gui again stopped him and said, "There is no hurry. Let's wait a while." Cao Gui came down from his carriage to observe the horse trails left by the Qi army. He then went back to his carriage to take a look at the scrambling Qi army, after which he told Lu Zhuang Gong to order the Lu army to give chase and annihilate the enemies. The Lu army did and captured many soldiers.

At the celebration banquet, Lu Zhuang Gong happily asked, "When we first met with the Qi army, why did you wait for the enemy to sound their war drums thrice before ordering an attack?"

Cao Gui said, "In warfare, the fighting spirit is most important. The sounding of the war drums is the signal for the charge. At the first sounding of the drums, the fighting spirit of the army peaked, like a troop of hungry tigers descending from the mountains. One should never go for a head-on attack at this time. When the drums sounded the second time, the defences of the enemy slackened when they still could not provoke an attack from us. At the third sounding of the drums, the enemy exhausted their fighting spirit and this was the perfect time for an attack. Our army was all prepared and we took them by surprise. The Qi army was thus easily defeated."

"Yes, but when the enemy retreated, why did you have to look at the tracks and the sky before you advised me to order them to give chase?" Lu Zhuang Gong asked again. Cao Gui explained further, "It's an old saying that we have to be aware of our enemy's traps. The Qi army is well known for their tricks. It might have been a scam for them to retreat to lure us into their traps. If we were not cautious, we might have been ambushed and totally destroyed. Therefore, I came down from the carriage to look at the horses' trails and the carriages' tracks. They appeared messy which meant that they were genuinely trying to escape and it was not a planned retreat. However, to be doubly sure, I went up the carriage to look at the escaping enemies from a distance. I saw that they were very disorderly and even their army flag was down. This confirmed that they were taken by surprise and there would not be any reinforcement. So I advised you to give chase."

"You are truly an excellent expert of warfare!" Lu Zhuang Gong said and offered him a cup of victory wine.

COMMENTS & APPLICATIONS

This strategy advocates winning by waiting patiently for the enemy to exhaust himself before launching an attack. To do that, one has to be in the advantageous position and be sufficiently prepared in case the enemy springs a surprise attack. Instead of confronting the enemy when they are prepared and ready, the strategy teaches one to sit and watch the enemy, and to bring him down at his weakest. This saves energy, time and resources.

STRIKE WHEN THE TIMING IS RIGHT

In the business arena, the Japanese are masters of this strategy. They demonstrated this in the way they handled their Western competitors. In the 1960s and 1970s, many Japanese companies were weak in comparison with the Western giants. Instead of taking their competitors head-on, the Japanese manufacturers waited and chose to compete in product areas in which the competitors were weak or where there was no competition.

Take the automobile industry for example. Japanese automobile makers avoided taking the American competitors head-on, focussing instead on making smaller and cheaper cars that were sold to other markets. They were awaiting the right time, and for their companies to gain sufficient strength. But when oil prices rose in the late 1970s and 1980s, Japanese cars, which were by then known for their fuel efficiency, high quality and reliability, made significant inroads in the American market. Today, Japanese brands like the Lexus command a commendable share of the American luxury car market.

Japanese companies are not the only ones known to wear down their competitors. In the commercial property market, companies in Hong Kong and Singapore have been able to bag fantastic bargains at basement prices by applying this strategy. Mr Kwek Leng Beng, CEO of City Development Limited (CDL), is one such example. One notable approach he took was to wait for his competitors to tire (due to business downturns or poor management) before making his move. Between 1989 to February 1997, CDL Hotels grew from six hotels to 62! Among Mr Kwek's prized catches are The Plaza in New York bought jointly with the Prince of Saudi Arabia, Al Waleed, for US$325 million from American billionaire Donald Trump. He also acquired the Copthorne chain of 17 hotels in Europe and launched the brand name, Millennium and Copthorne Hotels (M&C) for his overseas hotels in 1995. By September 1997, the M&C chain was listed on the London Stock Exchange, with 24 hotels in Britain (16 hotels), France (3 hotels), Germany (2 hotels) and the US (3 hotels), with a total of 7,064 rooms. It was voted favourite hotel group in Britain in 1997 by frequent business travellers in a survey conducted by the Executive Travel magazine. By timing his moves in the shrewdest manner, Mr Kwek built CDL and M&C into a hotel empire that spanned 13 countries in less than ten years!

CDL is not the only company that has succeeded. A number of other Asian companies have used a similar strategy. They waited for property prices to bottom out in Australia, Europe and America before making their purchases. Being cash-rich, they out-manoeuvred their European and American competitors. Up till 1997, Asian corporate and individual investors are known to be the major property buyers in Britain, Australia, New Zealand and Canada. In the hotel industry, Singapore-based companies are known to have become the biggest owners of hotel properties in New Zealand as of 1997.

Significantly, some Singapore companies have acquired properties from Japanese owners. Singapore's DBS Land is one example. Through its subsidiary, Raffles Holdings, DBS Land bought the world-famous Four Seasons Hotel in Hamburg for 80 million deutsche-marks (about S$64 million) in July 1997. The price was only one-third what its previous owner, the Aoki group of Japan had paid. The Japanese paid DM215 million to buy the 161-room hotel in 1989. The hotel started operation in 1987, and has now become a historical landmark with 100 years of history. It is well-endowed with antiques and art collections. The purchase was definitely a great bargain.

In June 1997, Raffles Holdings purchased Brown's Hotel in London for £45 million, also a bargain. It is a hotel with a history that dating back to 1837. With these purchases, Raffles Holdings, like CDL, has built a good portfolio of grand historical hotels that include the Raffles Hotel in Singapore, the Hotel Le Royal in Phnom Penh and the Grand Hotel d' Angkor in Cambodia.

CAPITALISING ON FALLING PRICES

When prices are falling, it pays to wait. This applies to both the stock and property markets. In the case of the stock market, it is important to not rush in when share prices begin to fall. This is because they may plummet further! To quote a phrase from Peter Lynch's "Beating the Street": "Buying on the bad news can be a very costly strategy, especially since bad news has a habit of getting worse." One never knows when prices have hit rock bottom. It is more prudent to wait, and buy on the strengths of recovery.

Property prices operate the same way except that the indicators are even more tangible, making it easier to determine if the market is heading up or down. Supply of housing units, interest rates, general economic conditions and liquidity are major factors that determine property prices. The principle of what goes up must come down also applies. Thus, after the bull run that began in 1986, the property market slowed down in 1996 when tough anti-speculation measures were introduced. Prices fell by 2.6% in 1996.

Historical data shows property prices in Singapore fell by 15.3% in 1984 during recession. Had someone bought a property then, he would be disappointed as the prices fell by another 15.4% in 1985. In fact, a more appropriate time to buy would have been in 1986 when the Singapore economy was coming out of recession. That year, property prices went up by an average of 8.8%. Similarly,

1997 may see property prices in Singapore falling by more than 2.6%. Hence, better bargains may be picked up after 1997. (*Note: This assessment is made as of 1 August 1997.*)

Interestingly, the Malaysian property market underwent similar challenges over the past few years. As an attempt to check speculation in the property market, supposedly fueled by strong purchases by foreigners, the Malaysian government imposed severe restrictions on the market. In 1995, it banned foreigners from buying properties below M$250,000 and imposed a hefty levy of M$100,000 on foreigners buying properties costing over M$250,000. Effectively, the price of a property valued at M$300,000 would increase by 33%, while a M$400,000 property, would increase by 25%! In addition, all capital gains would be taxed at 30%.

It came as no surprise when foreigners ceased buying Malaysian properties. With the sudden withdrawal of foreign demand, there was an overnight glut of unsold properties, especially condominiums. During this period, shrewd investors concluded that these policies would not last for long. Foreigners have ample alternative options for investing in properties in other Asian economies. So, they could afford to wait for a better time to enter the Malaysian property market. Expectedly, the Malaysian government had to ease the property rules barely two years after implementing them, in order to attract foreign investments. The M$100,000 levy on foreigners who bought Malaysian property was waived in 1997. Those who had waited, were likely to have secured great bargains.

ENTERING FOREIGN MARKETS

It also pays to wait when markets are chaotic and rules and regulations undefined. Particularly so for smaller companies with limited resources. Costly mistakes is something such companies can ill afford.

When China first opened its doors, companies which rushed in immediately encountered much frustration. Gradually, the Chinese authorities learned how to manage foreign investment, so companies that entered later enjoyed better benefits.

Companies' preference for a wait-and-see approach has prevented them from entering economies like India and the East European countries. Torn by political rivalry, and hampered by inefficient and bureaucratic civil services, these countries' efforts to attract foreign investment have met with limited success.

To minimise risks and conserve a company's resources, a gradual approach in entering foreign markets is preferred. If a company is uncertain about the potential of an overseas market, they could start with indirect exporting (for example, going through a local trading company) before moving towards direct exporting with its own agents or branches marketing the product. It can gradually increase its involvement either through joint venture or direct investment, when it is better able to ascertain the market and prospects.

趁火打劫

L O O T I N G   A   H O U S E   O N   F I R E

敌之害大，就势取利。刚决柔也。

E X P L A N A T I O N

When the enemy is in a big crisis (敌之害大), that is the time to destroy him (就势取利). This will enable the strong to conquer the weak (刚决柔也) as mentioned in Yi Jing's chapter on "Jue" ([易经:决]卦).

H I S T O R I C A L   B A C K G R O U N D

This strategy came from Sun Zi's chapter on "Planning" (孙子:计篇) which mentioned taking advantage of confusion (乱而取之). The most often quoted historical illustration of this strategy is how the Emperor of Yue (越王), Gou Jian (勾践) avenged his defeat against the Emperor of Wu (吴王), Fu Chai (夫差).

In 498 BC, when the Emperor of Yue, Gou Jian heard of the impending attack from the Emperor of Wu, he led a troop to meet the enemy against the advice of his General Fan Li (范蠡). Gou Jian suffered a bitter defeat as they were outnumbered by the stronger enemy. He finally surrendered at the Mountain of Ji (稽山). To save his army and his state, Gou Jian agreed to become Fu Chai's slave.

For three years, Gou Jian, his wife, his adviser and some men, served as Fu Chai's slaves. Gou Jian worked as a groom in Fu Chai's stable. As Gou Jian appeared very respectful, Fu Chai thought that he had become a loyal subject and he permitted Gou Jian to return home after three years. Gou Jian wanted to ensure he did not forget his dream of vengeance, so he slept on a bed of straw and brushwood and tasted a piece of gall before each meal (卧 薪 尝 胆). For over ten years he gradually rebuilt and strengthened the state, nurturing all the while their determination to avenge their humiliation at Mountain Ji.

But Gou Jian continued to pay homage to Fu Chai. He sent gold and money, and, under the advice of Wen Zhong (文 种), Gou Jian also sent beautiful women. One of these was the famous Xi Shi (西 施), one of the four great beauties of ancient China. While Gou Jian schemed to deplete the state warehouses of Wu, he awaited the right moment to strike.

Finally, the opportunity came. First, the state of Wu met with a fierce drought and the storage in the warehouses had insufficient food for the people. Then, Fu Chai, under the influence of corrupted officials, executed his most loyal and intelligent adviser Wu Zi Xu (伍 子 胥). Finally, in 482 BC, Fu Chai led his best men to Huang Chi (黄 池) to meet rulers from the surrounding states, leaving behind the old and the weak. The state of Yue took this opportunity to "loot a burning house". Gou Jian led 50,000 men to war and bitterly defeated the army of Wu. The state of Wu was finally taken down by Yue ten years later.

COMMENTS & APPLICATIONS

The direct translation of the phrase 趁 火 打 劫 means to loot a burning house. This strategy suggests taking advantage of the enemy when he is in danger. The best time to exterminate the enemy is when he is in chaos. In the historical example, Fu Chai had a chance to kill Gou Jian when the latter was his refugee but he let his opportunity slip, and this led to his eventual downfall. Gou Jian, however, fully utilised his opportunity. In the crisis created by the serious drought and the execution of the loyal Wu Zi Xu, the state of Wu was like a house on fire. Gou Jian exploited the chaotic situation to destroy Fu Chai completely.

VULNERABILITY CREATED BY INTERNAL SQUABBLES

The case of Yeo Hiap Seng (YHS) is a good illustration of how vulnerable a company can be in times of crisis. YHS is a well-known household brand name in the food and beverage business in Singapore. Its products are sold in many markets in Asia and even in America. A publicly listed but largely family-owned business, it had operated successfully for several decades. Unfortunately, it was embroiled in bitter family squabbles that resulted in legal suits and countersuits among members of the family. In the midst of the chaos, Fast East Organisation (FEO) swooped in and bought YHS. Three generations of hard work and empire building fell into the hands of a smart buyer who was able to strike at the right time.

YHS is not the only company that fell victim as a result of internal chaos. Other successful Asian companies have met the same fate at the hands of the third generation corporate leaders, either because of family squabbles or because they failed to employ professional managers to boost the quality of management.

A company can also become vulnerable when major shareholders are at odds. But it does not take major differences to bring a company down. A weak alliance is just as damaging, for instance, where one of the parties wants to cash out its investment. These cracks provide opportunities for others to exploit.

One clear case of this was when DBS Land of Singapore entered the healthcare business in 1997 by buying over the stakes of one of the three major shareholders of Parkway Holdings. The move significantly weakened the other two major shareholders. In fact, after the successful purchase, the market was rife with rumours that one of the two remaining major shareholders of Parkway Holdings might even sell out his shareholdings to DBS Land if the price was right.

In the corporate world, some "predators" thrive on the woes of others. In the United States, these *professional predators* actively seek out ailing or dying companies. After buying over a company, these professional predators would do one of two things. If the company's business is not promising, they would strip its assets and sell them for cash. They are able to amass sizeable profits from the sale of these assets as these "predators" are specialists in this area. If the business shows potential, they would trim the excess "fat" (head-count) and focus on turning the company around. Once this is done, they would quickly sell it as a viable going-concern and make a handsome margin in the process. These corporate predators or raiders thrive on "looting a house on fire".

Exploiting Chaotic Business Situations

From a business perspective, chaotic situations may provide ample opportunities for the shrewd investor or businessman. For example, when prices in the stock and property markets fluctuate significantly, they represent high risks and signify chaotic situations. But one can still make a fortune with well-timed purchases or sales. In fact, many Asian corporate and individual investors have succeeded in picking properties at basement prices in Australia, Canada and Britain in the late 1980s and early 1990s when these markets were in chaos.

In the same way, opportunistic companies and businessmen will not hesitate to exploit chaotic situations created by temporary market distortions or political uncertainties. The following are some examples:

1   When tickets are sold out for premier events such as sports, theatre or concert, touts appear to re-sell tickets at much higher prices. Basically, these ticket touts exploit the vulnerabilities of those who turn up at event sites without tickets.

2   Prices of food and drinks at shows, exhibitions and tourist attractions are also marked-up substantially. Vendors capitalise on the fact that visitors to such events want convenience over price. Moreover, being "locked" into a confined space, they have few alternatives. The more entrepreneurial vendors would even market various souvenir items (like mugs, T-shirts, sweaters and caps) at premium prices. Thus, customers become vulnerable to "looting" by these opportunistic vendors.

3   Scarcity of a product may also provide opportunities for the "looters". This occurs in the demand for collectibles like coins, stamps and other souvenirs. Typically, commemorative issues of stamps and coins are priced at a very high premium.

4   When the demand for private condominiums in Singapore was at its peak in 1993 and 1994, people reportedly sold their places in the queue for thousands of dollars. These opportunists cashed in on others' desperation to purchase property.

5   Nature sometimes plays a part in creating situations for looters. For example, in times of food shortages caused by floods, drought or other natural disasters, unscrupulous businessmen jack up prices of essential commodities. Sadly, even in war, opportunists seek to benefit from the woes of others. In times of crisis and confusion, people are prepared to pay a high price to stay alive.

CURRENCY AND STOCK MARKET RAIDERS

The currency crisis that began in July 1997 in the ASEAN region (the Association of Southeast Asian Nations) is a good illustration of how speculators tried to benefit from chaos. The crisis was triggered after the Thai baht was floated on 2 July 1997. Suddenly, there seemed to be relentless attacks on the baht and the other currencies of the ASEAN countries. Within two weeks, the Thai baht fell by 15%, the Indonesian rupiah hit historic low, while the Malaysian ringgit and Philippine peso also dropped significantly against the US dollar. Even the traditionally strong Singapore dollar sunk to a three-year low against the greenback. By mid-January 1998, many of these currencies hit historic lows, and the market was rife with opportunists and speculators. On a fair number of occasions, the Indonesian rupiah fluctuated in value by more than 10% from one day to the next.

As of early 1998, the end was still not in sight for the ASEAN currency crisis. The turmoil was worsened because of speculators who went all out to cash in on the crisis, and were determined to push the ASEAN currencies down. To counter the speculative attacks of these currency "looters", the governments and their central banks had to intervene on numerous occasions to prop up their currencies.

Speculators also pursued the Latin American currencies. A fortnight after attacking the ASEAN currencies, the Brazilian reai, the Mexican peso and the Argentine peso began to feel the heat. At the same time, the Brazilian stock market plunged significantly in mid-July 1997 on fears of the domino effect from ASEAN. The Mexican and Argentine stock markets were shaken too.

These currency raiders thrived on others' crises. They therefore incurred the wrath of the respective governments. The Malaysian government responded most strongly, threatening speculators with severe punishment. Malaysian Prime Minister Dr Mahathir Mohamad went as far as to name Mr George Soros, multi-billionaire and financier, as the main culprit responsible for the currency attacks. Mr Soros was a well-known currency speculator who reportedly made more than one billion pounds when he speculated on the British pounds in 1992. With a fortune estimated at over US$12 billion, he has the financial clout to influence any market. In fact, within two years (1995 to 1996), he became the largest landowner in Argentina. In the process, he out-gunned and out manoeuvred the big boys.

While George Soros or his associates might be involved in the ASEAN currency crisis, their actions alone would not have created so much havoc. Obviously, other smaller and camouflaged speculators were out to make quick profits too. These people probably include local companies and individuals, some of who were based in Malaysia. Ironically, Malaysia had become a victim of its own past behaviour. The Malaysian central bank (Bank Negara) had been an aggressive speculator of foreign currencies right up to the early 1990s. Despite warnings by the US Federal Reserve and the Bank of England that excessive speculation of foreign currencies could destabilise international financial markets, Bank Negara persisted, claiming it was an active manager of foreign exchange reserves policy. It was when it lost billions of dollars in 1993 that Bank Negara refrained from playing the market.

The currency turmoil affected the stock markets of ASEAN as well as other Asian markets (for example Hong Kong, Taiwan and China). Within barely six months, the market capitalisation of several ASEAN stock markets went down by almost two-thirds! Many company's shares became penny stocks, and overnight, they became vulnerable to corporate takeovers. The International Monetary Fund's (IMF) intervention resulted in some of these economies (for example South Korea, Thailand and Indonesia) having to open up their markets to foreign investors. This effectively made many of the companies easy targets for foreign takeovers and buy-outs. Expectedly, a fair number of foreign corporate raiders, especially those with large investment funds, stood to benefit from current chaotic situations. With their huge funds and the opportunity to purchase Asian companies at basement prices, it would be very easy for these foreign investors to make significant inroads within a short time.

THE 1997 HANDOVER OF HONG KONG

One good example illustrating how a major occasion could create opportunities for "looters" involved the 1997 handover of Hong Kong to China. Prior to the handover on 1 July 1997, the Chinese government had on several occasions accused the British government of trying to run down the large foreign exchange reserves of Hong Kong. These accusations were not without justification as the Hong Kong government, under Chris Patten, embarked on several mega projects, including the building of a new airport which cost billions. Lucrative projects were reportedly awarded to British companies. Not surprisingly, such moves incurred the wrath of other companies with lower bids.

Closer to the date of handover, hoteliers began to double and triple room rates to exploit visitors who wanted to witness the historic event. Banquet prices were also increased significantly, especially for the evenings of 30 June and 1 July 1997. Auspicious numbers and phrases were used as prices and names for menu items. All kinds of souvenirs were put on sale. Enterprising tour operators organised packaged tours to coincide with the handover. Shopping centres in Hong Kong organised sales to lure overseas visitors too.

While the handover of Hong Kong to China in July 1997 is not strictly a situation of a "burning house", the significance of the event presented tempting opportunities for shrewd businessmen. The more enterprising businessmen and corporations in China also capitalised on this opportunity. The number of souvenirs and commemorative items that were produced for the occasion numbered in the thousands.

声东击西

MAKING A FEINT TO THE EAST BUT HITTING OUT IN THE WEST

乱志乱萃, 不虞, 坤下兑上之象。
利其不自主而取之。

EXPLANATION

When the enemy is in a state of confusion, like grass growing wild (萃), he will not be able to clearly assess a situation. Neither will he able to cope with sudden and unexpected changes in circumstances (不虞). This is the confusion (坤下兑上) described in *Yi Jing*'s "Cui" chapter ([易经:萃]卦). A good strategist defeats the enemy by taking advantage of him when he has lost control.

HISTORICAL BACKGROUND

"Making a feint to the east but hitting out in the west" (声东击西) means pretending to launch an attack to the east while targeting to take the west. This strategy works by creating a false impression before launching the crucial attack. Many ancient texts by Chinese military gurus, such as Sun Zi's chapter on "Momentum" (孙子:势篇), Zhun Nan Zi's teaching about training soldiers (准南子兵略训) and Tong Dian's discourse on military affairs (通典 兵六), have included this as an important strategy.

There were times when this strategy failed, as shown in Story 1 where Zhou Ya Fu (周亚夫) avoided the the trap set by the Wu army (吴). Other times, the strategy worked perfectly, as in the case where Liu Bang (刘邦) escaped from his arch rival Xiang Yu (项羽) as documented in Story 2.

STORY 1

In the Han Dynasty (汉朝), during the reign of Emperor Jing (景帝) riots broke out among the seven states, including the states of Wu (吴) and Chu (楚). Famous Han General

Zhou Ya Fu (周 亚 夫) was tasked with capturing the rebels. General Zhou Ya Fu built a strong high wall in the path of the Wu army, preventing the rebels from moving northward and cutting off food supply.

The Wu army was trapped and had no other choice but to fight their way out. They pretended to attack the Han army at the south-east end of the brick wall, but General Zhou Ya Fu did not fall for their trick. Instead, he ordered that troops be stationed at the east end of the wall. When the Wu army made a fierce attack at the east end, the Han army was well-prepared and beat the enemy into a quick retreat. General Zhou Ya Fu seized this opportunity and ordered his best men to launch an attack. By then the Wu army was exhausted and was easily defeated.

STORY 2

In 207 BC, the Qin Dynasty (秦 朝) fell at the battle of Yu Lu, when the army of Xiang Yu (项 羽) won decisively. Subsequently, power struggles broke out between Xiang Yu and other rebel leaders, in particular, Liu Bang (刘 邦).

In 206 BC, Liu Bang and Xiang Yu, set out to attack the city, Xian Yang (咸 阳), by separate routes. The Emperor of Chu, Chu Huai Wang (楚 怀 王) promised that the first person to pass the gate of the city would become the next Emperor. Liu Bang was the first to go through the gate but as Xiang Yu had more men, he forced Liu Bang to concede.

After Xiang Yu became Emperor, Liu Bang was made ruler of a province called Han Zhong (汉 中). Xiang Yu's capable subject Fan Zeng (范 增) was wary of Liu Bang and had tried to eliminate him a few times. He suggested that Liu Bang should be kept in the palace in Xian Yang and not be permitted to resume his post at Han Zhong under the pretext that he was required to assist the new Emperor.

Liu Bang was anxious to escape from this trap. He sought advice from Zhang Liang (张 良) who in turn asked Chen Ping (陈 平) for suggestions. Chen Ping's wise plan so delighted Zhang Liang that he agreed to it immediately.

The next day, Chen Ping requested an audience with Xiang Yu to propose that Fan Zeng be sent to the city of Peng (彭 城) to persuade the former emperor Chu Huai Wang to move to the state of Bin (彬 州). Before he left, Fan Zeng cautioned Xiang Yu with three pieces of advice, one of which was to never allow Liu Bang to return to Han Zhong.

After Fan Zeng had left, Chen Ping then proposed that rulers of each province be allowed to return to their provinces to cut down the nation's expenses. Xiang Yu granted all the newly appointed rulers, except Liu Bang, to return to their provinces.

When Liu Bang realised that Xiang Yu was out to harm him, he met with Zhang Liang to devise a plan. Zhang Liang asked Liu Bang to request leave to return to his home town Feng Pei (丰 沛), to visit his parents. Xiang Yu read Liu Bang's request and asked, "Are you really being filial when you request to return to your home town to see your parents? I am afraid that is not your real intention. Is it because I want you to stay in Xian Yang that you came up with this plan?"

Liu Bang sadly said, "My father is very old and there is no one to take care of him. I have been thinking of him. In the past, I saw that Your Highness had been very busy with the work of the state and so I dared not make such a request. Now all the newly appointed rulers have all returned to their respective provinces to be with their families. I wonder when my turn will come?" And Liu Bang began to cry.

Zhang Liang then said, "We cannot let him return to his home town. We should send him away to Han Zhong and order men to bring his family from Feng Pei to the palace as hostages, so he will serve Your Highness wholeheartedly." Xiang Yu agreed, "You are right. The reason why I refuse to let him return to Han Zhong is because I fear that he has a dissident mind."

Chen Ping took this opportunity to say, "Your Highness has conferred Liu Bang the title of the Ruler of Han Zhong. The whole nation knows this. If we refuse to let him assume his post, the people would think Your Highness is a man who does not honour his words. They may refuse to obey your orders in future. Why not take Zhang Liang's suggestion and send Liu Bang to Han Zhong while holding his family hostage. In this way, Your Highness will honour your word and prevent Liu Bang from taking action against us."

Xiang Yu gave it some thought and then said, "Since everybody is of this opinion, I think it is reasonable to send you to Han Zhong and not to Feng Pei. You shall start your journey tomorrow." Liu Bang was of course very pleased but he acted very sad and refused to get up until he was given permission to return home. Xiang Yu felt sorry for him and consoled him, saying, "Go to Han Zhong. I will send for your family and will take good care of them here until you have settled everything in Han Zhong. You can send for them later." Liu Bang got up reluctantly and thanked Xiang Yu for his magnanimity. Liu Bang returned to his camp and sent for all his generals. They took off like tigers returning to their mountains at Han Zhong.

COMMENTS & APPLICATIONS

This strategy is based on the principle of *diversion*. Without doubt, Liu Bang planned to retreat to Han Zhong to escape Xiang Yu's clutches. However, to make a direct request would arouse Xiang Yu's suspicion as he was specifically reminded by Fan Zeng to not let Liu Bang return to Han Zhong. Thus, Liu Bang collaborated with Zhang Liang and Chen Ping, in a ruse of wanting to return to his hometown to be with his father. In the absence of his capable adviser, Fan Zeng, Xiang Yu was unable to see through the "making a feint to the east but hitting out in the west" ploy used to distract him. He fell for the trick. Liu Bang, subsequently, became the Emperor of China around 200 BC (see story in Strategy 8 on "secret escape through Chen Cang").

This principle of diversion is commonly used in warfare. When the enemy's attention is diverted, and his defences relaxed, one can then launch a successful attack. The party using this strategy often releases false information about its intended plan. The enemy, believing the information, would concentrate its resources on tackling the decoy. The company then carries out its actual plan unhindered. The enemy's discovery usually comes too late to do anything.

CONCEALING ONE'S TRUE INTENTIONS

In the business world, rumours are often used to distract and mislead competitors and the market. Stock markets in Asia are often affected by rumours, causing havoc among uninformed investors. In marketing, a company often announces heavy price cuts as a promotional ploy to attract customers and to increase sales. These are diversion tactics used to conceal the real intention — the sale is necessary to make room for new stocks.

A good example is the strategy employed by Cycle and Carriage, authorised distributor of Mercedes in Singapore. In 1995, it not only slashed the price of its old "E" series, it also augmented its features by naming it the "Masterpiece" model. They did this because the new "E" model was substantially different from the old model in design. Its arrival would greatly affect the sale of the old model as it may make the latter look obsolete. However, with the clever "Masterpiece" label, Cycle and Carriage was able to clear off old stock.

Another illustration of this strategy is when Far East Organisation (FEO) bought over Yeo Hiap Seng (YHS). FEO is a major property developer with hardly any experience in manufacturing. Yet, it paid a fairly high price premium to acquire YHS. FEO's interest in YHS was not confined to manufacturing. In reality, it was more interested in the land bank held by YHS. As it turned out, after its acquisition, YHS diversified into property development. It was thus not surprising that FEO was prepared to pay a premium for this purchase.

Similarly, when Edaran Otomobil National (EON), Malaysian manufacturer of Proton cars, decided to acquire Lotus, its intention was not to add another brand to its cars, but rather, to allow EON to access the latest design and technological knowledge of Lotus — a well-known British sports car manufacturer. By doing this, EON hoped to leap-frog forward in manufacturing technology.

The strategy of "making a feint in the east but hitting out in the west" is often applied in the acquisition of business. Genuine intentions for acquisitions are often not disclosed so that the seller will not increase the asking price or jack up the premium. By concealing the real intention, the buyer also avoids the attention of competing companies, and at times, regulatory bodies.

A good example was the acquisition of the American President Lines (APL) by the Neptune Orient Lines (NOL) of Singapore. There were many advantages sought by NOL in its acquisition of APL. However, it chose not to over-disclose its intentions. Instead, it worked quietly behind the scenes to ensure a smooth takeover. This was because the acquisition was a very complicated exercise that required the approval of many parties in the United States. After all, APL was almost a national icon of the US shipping industry and it was the oldest shipping firm with strong governmental links. Thus, it was important not to startle the snake while hitting the grass (打草惊蛇) as illustrated in Strategy 13.

The strategy adopted by NOL worked. By keeping a low profile, it received support from many concerned parties in the United States. The wide ranging support came from unions and other professional groups. Most importantly, it also obtained the approval of the various government agencies by early November 1997. This potentially problematic acquisition was completed very smoothly. After the successful acquisition of APL, NOL decided to use the brand name of APL for all its container shipping business. By this, it hoped to receive favourable response from the American public and lobby groups. Because APL is a national icon of the United States, any attempt to retain it would help reduce negative perceptions about NOL.

In the Property Market

In property development, the major and shrewd players are often known to bid high prices for new but smaller plots of land to create the impression that property prices are likely to increase. With that, their existing land bank would also increase in value. The large number of unsold units they hold will also be made to look cheaper by comparison. Thus, by bidding high on new and smaller land plots, the developer is able to move sales on his existing stock! In fact, the developer could even ask for higher prices. Large developers in Singapore and Hong Kong often practice this strategy.

An interesting example of the use of the "Making a feint to the east but hitting out in the west" strategy in the property market in Singapore occurred at the end of July 1997. Mr Heng Chiang Meng, president of the Real Estate Association of Singapore (REDAS) made a public call to the government to slow down its sale of land. He argued that the property market was very sick and on the verge of collapse. Claiming that the economic prospects in Singapore and the region were far from encouraging, Mr Heng cautioned that excessive land supply would cause hardships to developers and could even affect the other sectors of the economy.

Unfortunately, Mr Heng's views were not shared by the smaller developers, the academics, the general public and the government. The smaller developers, in particular, were very upset by the remarks. To them, Mr Heng and REDAS only represented the interests of the large developers who were more interested in enlarging their profit margins. According to the smaller developers, the market had shown signs of consolidation and transactions had been gradually increasing. More significantly, price decreases were minor; the market did not appear to be heading for a collapse.

The position of small developers were supported by statistics and survey data produced by some academics from the Real Estate Department of the National University of Singapore. In a public forum held in early August 1997, these academics stood by their view that the property market in Singapore was not heading for a major downturn. Mr Heng's remarks generated a lot of letters to the media. Members of the public expressed great displeasure in these letters. To them, REDAS acted to enlarge their bottom line, rather than out of genuine concern for consumers. Some questioned the logic of his argument, claiming that REDAS did nothing

It would seem that the strategy of "making a feint to the east but hitting out in the west" did not work for REDAS when Mr Heng made his remarks in July 1997. What was interesting, however, was that barely two months later, the government announced a cutback of land sale for private property development for 1998. While the cutback was part of the government's plan to regulate the long term supply of land for private property development, and upward pressure on property prices were unlikely, it was nonetheless received very enthusiastically by property developers. It was the psychological boost they were hoping could avert further decline of property prices.

In November 1997, the Singapore government announced that it had met with major developers and was monitoring the property market closely. There were concerns that a severe downward correction of property prices might be unhealthy for the Singapore economy, especially since many Singaporean companies were suffering from the effects of depreciating and volatile currency and stock markets in Southeast Asia. Some property companies had also suffered from exposure to the regional market. They could be hit with a "double whammy" if they should suffer setbacks in Singapore. So, Mr Heng's original call might be valid afterall!

STRATEGY 7

无中生有

CREATING SOMETHING OUT OF NOTHING

诓也，非诓也，实其所诓也。
少阴、太阴、太阳。

EXPLANATION

The strategy advocates using a false front (诓), not to deceive the enemy totally (非诓也), but to make what is false seem real (实其所诓也). If one can use false fronts to conceal the truth, the enemy will have a misconception about a situation. That is the time to launch an attack. This aligns with the theory in *Ling Qi Jing* (灵棋经：发蒙卦) which expresses this in terms of changes between Yin and Yang (阴变阳来、阳极阴生).

HISTORICAL BACKGROUND

This strategy came from Yu Liao's *War Power* (尉缭子·战权：战权在乎道之所极。有者无之，无者有之。). It has also been mentioned in ancient Chinese classics like *The Story of the Stone* (脂评石头记：俗谓冷中出热，无中生有也). The two stories below illustrate the usage of this strategy. The first story is taken from the chapter on General Zhang Xun (张巡) from the *Book on New Tang* (新唐书：张训列传).

STORY 1

In 755 AD during the Tang Dynasty (唐朝), military governor An Lu Shan (安禄山) revolted against the Emperor. Under An Lu Shan's command was General Ling Hu Chao (令狐潮), who led an army and besieged the city of Yong Qiu (雍丘). Defending the city against the rebels was General Zhang Xun (张巡) who had only a small troop and limited weapons. Zhang Xun ordered his soldiers to make many dummies of straw, each the size of a man. The dummies were then dressed in black, fastened with ropes and lowered down the outside of the city walls in the night. When Ling Hu Chao's army saw the straw dummies, they thought the enemies were scaling down the city wall and immediately unleashed a volley of arrows against them.

By the time Ling Hu Chao's army realised that it was a scam, they had already "given" millions of arrows away. Subsequently, General Zhang Xun commanded 500 real soldiers to scale down the city walls during the night. Ling Hu Chao's army ignored the move, thinking that Zhang Xun was up to his old trick in order to obtain more arrows using straw dummies. The 500 "dare devils" stormed Ling camp, setting the tents on fire. Ling Hu Chao's army, caught unaware, was bitterly defeated.

STORY 2

During the period of the Warring States (战 国 时 代), Zhang Yi (张 仪), a politician, persuaded some men to follow him to the state of Chu (楚 国) to seek a fortune. However, he could not find favour with the ruler of Chu and so he lived in great poverty while in Chu. His followers could not bear with the poverty any longer and threatened to leave him.

Zhang Yi assured his followers that he would be able to bring them riches if they would give him a few more days to obtain an audience with the ruler of Chu. Zhang Yi managed to see the ruler but the latter did not like him. Zhang Yi said, "I have been here for quite a while and Your Highness has not given me anything to do. If Your Highness really does not find me useful here, I beg your permission to leave Chu. I plan to go to the state of Jin (晋 国) to seek my fortune."

"All right. You may leave," the Emperor of Chu was only too glad to see him leave. "Of course, whether I am of any use there, I will still come back here. Does Your Highness have anything that you wish from Jin?" asked Zhang Yi. The Emperor of Chu looked at him coldly and said, "There are plenty of gold, pearls and ivory in Chu. I do not think that there is anything Jin can offer me."

"Does Your Highness not like beautiful women?" Zhang Yi pursued. These words struck the Emperor like lightning and with revived interest he asked, "What did you say?"

"I am speaking of the beautiful women in Jin," Zhang Yi said with mock seriousness. *"The women in Jin are as lovely as goddesses, with their rosy cheeks, pearly white skin and black silky hair. When they walk, they resemble supple willows and their voices are clearer than crystal bells."*

This got the Emperor excited and he said, *"Yes. Our state is a remote land. I have not seen the women of Jin. You shall go to Jin and bring some back for me."*

"But, Your Highness..." Zhang Yi hesitated. *"Of course, you will need some money to travel,"* the Emperor of Chu gave him many pieces of gold and silver and ordered him to proceed with the plan. At that time, the Emperor of Chu had two favourite concubines: Nan Hou (南 后) and Zheng Xiu (郑 袖). Zhang Yi deliberately disseminated the news so Nan Hou and Zheng Xiu came to know of the mission. When the latter heard the news, they feared that their positions might be replaced by foreign women. Each quickly sent someone to Zhang Yi, offering the latter a lot of money to ensure that he would have their interest at heart.

Before his departure, Zhang Yi came before the Emperor of Chu to take his leave. Zhang Yi pretended that he was reluctant to leave and said, *"Your Highness, the roads to Jin are long and communication is difficult. Please allow me to drink a farewell toast to Your Highness and at the same time, it will help to boost my morale."*

"That will be fine," the Emperor said and ordered someone to bring him wine. Zhang Yi drank a few cups and requested that he could be toasted by those closest to the Emperor so as to give him further encouragement.

"That is not a problem, as long as you can accomplish your mission promptly!" The Emperor was eager to send Zhang Yi off so he could get his *"beauties"*. He then ordered his favourite concubines Nan Hou and Zheng Xiu to take turns to toast to Zhang Yi. When Zhang Yi saw the two women, he dropped his cup and threw himself before the Emperor, saying, *"Please kill me, Your Highness. I deserve to die since I have lied to you."*

"But why?" the Emperor of Chu exclaimed. Zhang Yi said, *"I have travelled much but I have not come across any women more beautiful than your two ladies. In the past, I had claimed*

that I could bring back beautiful maidens for Your Highness was because I had not yet met these ladies. Now that I have seen them, I realise that I have lied to Your Highness."

The Emperor of Chu then said to Zhang Yi, "I was wondering what the matter was. Well, in that case, you need not proceed with the plan. I have always been convinced that nobody under the dome of the heaven is prettier than my two favourite concubines, am I not right?" The Emperor winked to his left and his right where the two happy ladies were. From that day onwards, the Emperor of Chu had a change in his attitude towards Zhang Yi and Zhang Yi flourished in his courts.

COMMENTS & APPLICATIONS

The scheme of creating something out of nothing is based on deception. Although deceit works temporarily and is not a long-term measure, it is a good plan when one is at wit's end. Zhang Xun used this strategy (Story 1) to create a false front, trick his opponents and win the battle. Zhang Yi (Story 2) was able to manipulate the situation to his advantage by creating false impressions, gaining himself riches and gold from the Emperor of Chu and his concubines as well as recognition.

BIDDING OF FAVOURITE/POPULAR NUMBERS[1]

One of the most interesting applications of Strategy 7 in the context of Asian businesses has to be in the bidding for auspicious numbers for car license plates, telephone numbers, and other products. In reality, these numbers have to be distributed anyway. But, by playing to the cultural peculiarities of Asian consumers, the authorities and agencies concerned have been able to reap handsome rewards by using this strategy to "create something out of nothing". The following are some fascinating examples.

On 27 July 1994, a Hong Konger offered to sell a car license plate, HK 1997 for HK$5 million (about S$990,000)! Ten years earlier, the same owner had bought it for only HK$21,000. This may seem very ridiculous to non-Chinese, but it is perfectly understandable to Asian Chinese. In 1993, an official car number plate "2" of the Hong Kong government was sold to a businessman for HK$9.5 million (about S$1.98 million). To the Cantonese-speaking Hong Kongers, "2" is an auspicious number. It sounds like "easy" and is believed to bring easy good luck and fortune. At the same time, the shape of "2" resembles a rooster. In Chinese astrology, the rooster symbolizes decisiveness, alertness, and adaptability. Thus, to the superstitious Hong Kong business community, this number is worth a fortune! Notably, HK$9.5 million is not the highest price paid for a car number plate. On 19 March 1994, the car number plate "9" (which sounds like "forever" in Mandarin or "surely" in Cantonese) was bought for a record price of HK$13 million (S$2.7 million) by Hong Kong businessman Albert Yeung Sau-ching.

The desire – and corresonding prices paid – for auspicious numbers are not confined to car number plates. In Shenzhen, a city in southern China, a telephone number, "908-8888" was auctioned off for RMB655,000 (about S$120,000) on 21 April 1994. The number sounds like "surely prosper forever" in Cantonese. Other high prices at the same auction included RMB39,800 (about S$7,300) for number "908-9168" and RMB67,000 (about S$12,275) for "908-8999". It is amazing that even businessmen in China are prepared to pay big bucks for sheer numbers!

Apart from the cultural preference for auspicious numbers, the other reason for the high prices paid is the consideration of "face". Chinese businessmen are generally very "face" or status-conscious and do not like to be seen as losing out to competitors. This fuels the bidding process, with prices pushed quickly to ridiculously high levels — all for the sake of social recognition. This was the case with Shenzhen's auction of telephone numbers.

In Hong Kong, well-established companies also vie for auspicious telephone numbers. These include Hong Kong Telecoms (telephone number: 888-2888), Jardine Fleming Securities (telephone number: 843-8888), Vickers Ballas Securities (telephone number: 878-8888), Cathay Pacific Airways (telephone number: 747-1888).

The same fixation for "lucky" numbers is also found in Singapore. Singapore Telecoms cleverly exploits this by allowing public bidding of telephone numbers which it calls "Golden Numbers". Similarly, the Singapore's Registry of Vehicles also allows public bidding of car license plate numbers with a minimum bid of S$1,000. While prices paid in Singapore have not equalled Hong Kong's, they are nonetheless hefty sums.

Though these telephone or car license plate numbers have to be distributed anyway, regulators have been able to capitalise on the cultural peculiarities of the consumers, "creating something out of nothing".

The impact of culture can also be seen in pricing of residential property in markets like Hong Kong and Singapore. Similar properties located on the same street can command different prices owing to the difference in house numbers. A house number like "12" (which sounds like "definitely easy"), "18" (which sounds like "definitely prosper"), or "26" (which sounds like "easy to do") would easily command a price premium over "14" (which sounds like "definitely die")! A number like "28" ("easily prosper") would fetch an even higher price. So prevalent is this fixation with auspicious numbers that even non-Chinese are influenced. While they themselves may not be concerned about numbers, the future buyers of their properties do!

The developers benefited tremendously from these superstitions by cleverly pricing houses/apartments with auspicious numbers higher. Condominiums on some floors (such as 18, 19, 28, 29) fetch higher prices as the buyers are willing to pay a premium for them. In fact, they can cost much more than similar units on higher floors!

Auspicious numbers was something that many Australian, New Zealander, Canadian and British developers failed to understand when they first tried to market their properties in the Asian market. They could not understand why the Chinese paid so much attention to a house number when they should be concerned about other details! They were puzzled as to why some land plots and houses were quickly snapped up when they were obviously in inferior locations. It took these westerners some time to figure out the intricacies. However, once they mastered the meanings of numbers, these western developers began to play the game too. They too have learned how to "create something out of nothing"!

Actually, cultural perceptions of numbers is not unique to Asians. In the West, "13" has always been considered an unlucky number (interestingly, to the Cantonese, 13 sounds like "definitely multiply"). Similarly, "666", the number of the anti-Christ is eschewed. So, idiosyncrasies about numbers are not confined to any society, though in Asia, they have more prominence.

ADVERTISING AND SALES PROMOTION

Advertisers often practise the "creating something out of nothing" strategy. A coke is a coke. Yet, amazing drama and excitement have been injected into television commercials promoting coke. Though beverages are "commodity-like" products, marketers create desire for them through creative marketing.

Companies often offer the "sale of a lifetime". Some even claim that the offers would never be repeated again. Excessively marked-down prices are deliberately displayed. Ironically, in Asia, the laws governing pricing are rather loose. In fact, there are no requirements stipulating that a product must be sold at the normal price for a certain duration before it can be marked down. Marketers have exploited such loopholes to their advantage. Thus, no one can be sure what the original price of a product is. Small wonder then that some stores can have sales throughout the year!

Product or service bundling is another good example of creative marketing. The marketer would price a bundle of products lower than the sum of the individual items. In doing so, the consumer would think that he is getting a great bargain. However, more often than not, the bundle would include items the consumer may not need. In bundling the products, the marketer cleverly include some slow-moving items (often they are old stock). Gift hampers, set lunches and buffet are marketed in this manner.

Service bundling operates on the same principle. Package tours, comprehensive service contracts, priority banking services and insurance policies offer a wide range of benefits of which only a few are really needed.

TARGETING AND POSITIONING

One of the most fascinating functions of marketing is its ability to create demand for products and services through creative targeting and positioning.

Take the example of Chinese paintings and calligraphies. If the works of great masters like Wu Guan Zhong (吴 冠 中), Chen Yong-Yu (陈 永 玉) and Qi Gong (启 功) remained in China, their value would remain in the doldrums. The value of their art rose tremendously because art dealers and auction houses cleverly positioned them on the international market. In so doing, art dealers have created a larger market with greater purchasing power. Consequently, demand increased, pushing up prices, while the quality of work has remained static. The price of a painting sometimes escalate as a result of muliple transactions from one collector to another. The increase in premium paid each time is due largely to the art dealer's ability to "create something out of nothing". In fact, the margin/commission earned depends entirely on the art dealer's ability to exploit this strategy.

Interestingly, auction houses like Christie's, Sotheby and Victor Morris operate on the same principle of "creating something out of nothing" in how they generate a high demand and price. While it is true that each product comes with a price, auction houses are able to manipulate the asking price of the same product each time it is auctioned. This is indeed "creating something out of nothing" as the product has not changed!

Today, auction houses deal in a wide spectrum of products and antiques. These include such things as paintings, calligraphy, jewellery, furniture, carpets, chinaware, jade, precious stones, carvings, coins, stamps and ceramics. With the increasing affluence of Asian consumers, international auction houses like Christie's, Sotheby and Victor Morris, have also set up offices in cities like Hong Kong and Singapore. They obviously recognise that with an effective marketing strategy, they can create value in a product or antique and generate *benefits* to the consumer. Collector's items and antiques are valued subjectively according to the eyes of the collector, that is, they are *perceived value and benefits.* The upper limit to their worth depends on how deep the pockets of the collectors are. This is where collectors can become vulnerable to the exploitation of professional auctioneers who are experts in the art of "creating something out of nothing".

Whenever a marketer repositions his products and services or targets a new market, he is applying some aspect of this strategy because marketing is a creative discipline which *creates value and benefits* to the consumer.

Singaporean cars have a 10-year lifespan after which they must be scrapped. However, many of these cars are still in good condition. So, instead of scrapping them, entrepreneurial second-hand car dealers will re-export them cars to countries with demand, such as Indonesia, India and Sri Lanka.

"Creating something out of nothing" is possible when one is innovative, entrepreneurial and willing to think beyond normal boundaries of possibility.

SHARE BUY-BACK SCHEMES

In corporate finance, companies can increase the value of their shares by buying these shares back from the open market. Under this arrangement, a company may buy back its own shares traded on the stock exchange if they consider it a better investment than other alternatives. The company's share capital is thus reduced, and its earnings per share increased as corporate earnings are then divided over fewer shares. Accordingly, the price-to-earnings (P/E) ratio are lowered, pushing up market price. Thus, shareholders stand to gain more.

In countries where there are no capital gains tax, such a strategy will benefit shareholders more. This is a scheme that "creates something out of nothing" for shareholders. It is even preferred to paying out more earnings in the form of dividends as the latter is taxable.

In the US and some countries in Europe (for example, Britain), share buy-back schemes are legal. They are used as a means to return surplus funds to shareholders, especially when these funds cannot be used in other ways. By buying back the shares, the company is also indicating that its shares are under-valued. Hence, the act of buying back the shares will create a demand that pushes share prices higher — a double bonus for shareholders. At times when the stock market is not performing well, the share buy-back scheme can be a very tempting proposition. This was evident during the August-September 1997 currency and stock crises in Asia.

In August 1977, in an attempt to shore up the Malaysian stock market, the Malaysian government passed a bill to allow companies to buy back their shares. Prior to this, share buy-back schemes were not allowed in Malaysia. Since the bill was passed, several Malaysian companies have indicated strong interest in the scheme. These companies include Lion Land, Amsteel Corp and EON (manufacturers of the national Proton vehicle). The Malaysian move is likely to trigger similar moves among its neighbouring countries whose stock markets have also been severely hit.

Singapore had also begun to re-examine the share buy-back scheme in September 1997. In fact, several blue-chip companies, including Singapore Telecom and Singapore Airlines (SIA) openly supported such a scheme. Singapore Telecom's share prices did not perform well between 1996 to 1997. Meanwhile, it had more than S$4 billion in cash reserves which it could not effectively and expediently invest in high-yield projects. Thus, the share buy-back scheme was an attractive means for boosting share prices, and returning some of the surplus funds to shareholders. For SIA, the problem is slightly different. Despite trading at a very favourable P/E ratio of 8 to 12 times between 1996 to July 1997, its share price had not increased significantly. This was an issue worth noting in view that the average P/E ratio on the Singapore Stock Exchange was about 16 to 17 times during the same period. Thus, buying back the shares from the market would have been a good investment decision for SIA, helping to increase its share price.

THE BUSANG GOLD HOAX

One of the most visible cases illustrating the strategy of "creating something out of nothing" is the Busang gold hoax. The original dreams of finding the largest deposit of gold in the world turned into dirt when it was discovered in May 1997 that the samples sent for testing were doctored.

Bre-X Minerals, the company responsible for the find, and listed on the Toronto Stock Exchange, not only managed to fool novice investors as well as the big guns, including Barrick Gold (the second largest gold miner in the world), Placer Dome but also the Indonesian government! The extent of the damage is yet to be fully realised. One thing is certain — the reported US$20 billion in gold reserves caused much misery to investors.

The scale of the hoax was incredible. Among the parties deceived were experts, consultants and even investment bankers. Amazingly, almost every broker in the Canadian broking industry recommended a must-buy on Bre-X shares right up to March 1997. The price of the share was chased to an all-time high of C$280 per share before a 10-for-one split. Finally, the hoax had to end. Strathcona Mineral Services Ltd, a Toronto-based company, discovered that the gold in Busang was an extensive and elaborate scam. It found that samples sent for testing were manipulated. In fact, gold was deliberately inserted into the crushed core samples. According to Strathcona, the tampering was so well done that it escaped the eyes of the experts and the testing company. It was not surprising therefore that it took a while before the fraud was discovered.

Bre-X shareholders subsequently sued three investment banks connected to the company. These highly reputable banks were JP Morgan & Co, Lehman Brothers Inc and Nesbitt Burns Inc. In addition, they also sued the management of Bre-X and their mining consultant. Interestingly, it was the very bullish recommendations of the three investment bankers that lured investors into buying Bre-X shares. Prior to their recommendations, Bre-X was only a little-known company in Calgary, Alberta. Without doubt, the strong recommendations of these world-class investment banks lent credibility to these otherwise worthless shares. In fact, they claimed to have done detailed research and strongly advocated the purchase of Bre-X shares. How they had in turn been fooled by Bre-X management is a mystery.

The Busang gold hoax saga did not stop after the fraud was discovered. Months later, creative and opportunistic businessmen began to exploit it further. These included the sale of T-shirts, Bre-X stock certificates (though worthless, they had become collector's items), coffee mugs and other souvenir items.

Books on the saga were also published. More amazingly, songs were written and sold on compact discs. As of September 1997, there were plans to make a movie out of the scam as well.

Of course, the biggest gains will be made by lawyers handling the large number of class action suits on behalf of shareholders. Thus, while this hoax inflicted a lot of damage, it also yielded some winners. These winners were those who managed to "create something out of nothing".

---

[1] *This section is taken largely from Wee Chow Hou (1996), <u>Practical Marketing: An Asian Perspective</u>, Addison-Wesley Publishing Company, pp,184-187.*

暗 渡 陈 仓

SECRET ESCAPE THROUGH CHEN CANG

示之以动，利其静而有主，"益动而巽"。

EXPLANATION

The gist of this strategy is to hit the enemy at the point where he is least prepared, that is, his back. In battle, one should pretend to expose one's movement (示之以动), then launch a surprise attack at the enemy's weakest point, when he is ill-prepared to defend himself (利其静而有主). This is explained in *Yi Jing*'s "Yi" chapter ([易经：益] 卦) which advocates that one should be alert in warfare, and if possible, turn around to make ambush the enemy from the back in what appears to be a head-on battle. Thus, he will be able to penetrate all situations like the wind (巽).

HISTORICAL BACKGROUND

The full strategy is known as "Repairing the pathway in the open, but secretly escape through Chen Cang" (明修栈道, 暗渡陈仓). It is adapted from the story of how Liu Bang (刘邦) managed to escape from Xiang Yu (项羽) and launch an ambush against the latter, as described in the *Book of History* (史记).

> *In 200 BC, before Liu Bang became Emperor of China, he was at one time under the control of Xiang Yu and had to retreat to Han Zhong. (This story is found in the account of Strategy 6 – "Making a feint to the east but hitting out in the west.") Later, Liu Bang managed to break free from Xiang Yu's control and led a troop into Si Chuan (四川). To strengthen his defenses agains Liu Bang, Xiang Yu deployed General Zhang Han (章邯) and his troop to monitor his enemy's movements.*

Liu Bang's army was stationed at a place called Shu (蜀), surrounded by steep mountains. The main route out of Shu was through wooden bridges. Under the advice of General Zhang Liang (张良), Liu Bang ordered that all the wooden bridges be burnt. They did this firstly, to prevent an attack from Xiang Yu's men, and secondly, to assuage Xiang Yu's fears that he would ever return eastward.

In the days that followed, Liu Bang appointed Han Xin (韩信) his general and began preparing his army to retaliate against Xiang Yu. Just before they were ready to retaliate, Liu Bang ordered soldiers to repair the burnt bridges. Xiang Yu's general, Zhang Han, who had stationed his troops on the other side was aware of the move. So, while the wooden bridges were gradually restored, Zhang Han got ready for the attack from Liu Bang's army. However, there was no sign that Liu Bang's army was going to charge forward through the almost completed bridges.

General Zhang Han became suspicious and ordered some men to spy on Liu Bang's camp. The men brought back bad news for General Zhang Han. Liu Bang had left with all his men leaving behind empty tents. The truth was finally out. Liu Bang had used the restoring work as a decoy so that General Zhang Han would not suspect his main intention. Liu Bang had led his main force secretly out of Shu via a small road to Chen Cang, opposite where General Zhang Han was stationed. Li Bang's army then launched a surprise attack and defeated General Zhang Han's army.

COMMENTS & APPLICATIONS

This strategy is similar to the sixth strategy, "Making a feint in the east but hit out in the west". It suggests diverting the enemy's attention and then attacking from the direction he least expects. The difference is that this strategy emphasizes the interplay between the "open" (明) and the "dark" (暗). This is like the well-known ancient Chinese strategy which advocates a surprise ambush to complement a direct attack. Both of these elements are interdependent, one cannot exist without the other (奇出于正, 无正则不能出奇). This strategy has also been mentioned in Sun Zi's chapter on "Momentum" (孙子：势篇：凡战者，以正合，以奇胜) and "Hundred War Strategies" (百战奇略奇战：凡战，所谓奇者，攻其无备，出其不意也).

Contingency Planning in Business

The use of this strategy in business can be likened to contingency planning. In contingency planning, one always hopes that the original plan will work well. However, in the event that the plan fails, an equally effective alternative must be in place. This alternative can turn out to be the more effective.

A good example of effectiveness in contingency planning is Coca-cola's attempt to replace the "old" coke with a "new" coke. Several years ago, Coca-cola was losing market share to Pepsi-cola in the North American market. In an attempt to arrest this loss, Coca-cola decided to replace its old coke with a new product to be called New Coke. As it turned out, many Americans protested strongly against dropping the old coke. Lobby groups were formed to petition against the move. In fact, this "fiasco" generated much worldwide publicity for Coke. It became a major news item in many newspapers around the world, and even made it to the cover page of many major magazines, in particular, the Time magazine. This was significant because Time magazine typically features personalities on its cover page, and had never permitted the use of a corporate logo. The exception was made for Coke.

This publicity blitz, worth millions of dollars, placed Coke in the limelight. To cushion the backlash, Coke decided to revive the old coke with a new name – Classic Coke – within a short three months. A company that size could not have turned the crisis into an opportunity so quickly if it did not have a contingency plan in place. They obviously had a Plan B that was ready to roll out should Plan A fail.

In this instance, Plan B provided the best escape route for Coca-cola. In fact, its success far exceeded that of Plan A! Not only did it recapture lost market share, it succeeded in launching another brand into the market as well. It was also a plan that caught all its major rivals, especially Pepsi-cola, by surprise. In essence, Coca-cola was able to develop a "secret escape through Chen Cang" without arousing the suspicion of its competitors.

Use of "Shell" and Project-based Companies

One tactic commonly used by companies to escape government detection is to set up "shell" companies. These "shell" companies are usually set up to escape taxes. In fact, some countries have developed a reputation as safe tax havens for such companies. These include the Virgin Island and Cayman Island. At other times, "shell" companies are used for investment (for example, acquiring other companies without disclosing the buyer's identity) and international transfer pricing.

Interestingly, Hong Kong was used heavily by Taiwanese companies as a base to conduct business with China. Prior to July 1997, it was estimated that there were more than 10,000 Taiwanese "shell" companies in Hong Kong. Many of these companies were registered entities with no manufacturing facilities. They were used as *conduits* for business with mainland China with the main objective of evading tax. Using these "shell" companies in Hong Kong also desensitived political differences between China and Taiwan. Many Taiwanese companies did not want to miss out on the immense opportunities in China. At the same time, they did not want to be perceived being unsupportive of their government's China policy. The best way out, therefore, was to trade through Hong Kong. "Shell" companies were thus used as "secret escapes".

After the Hong Kong handover in July 1997, the Chinese government began investigations on "shell" companies to weed out tax evasion activities, requiring them to declare linkages with companies on the mainland. Since July 1997, the Beijing government required foreign companies to declare earnings from holding companies in Hong Kong.

Besides tax evasion issues, the Chinese government may also have a hidden agenda. Taiwanese companies had used "shell" companies in Hong Kong to move their low-technology, labour-intensive industries into China to enjoy the lower production costs there. In addition, the Taiwanese government did not allow their companies to invest directly in China in high technology industries and major infrastructure projects. Thus, the move by the Chinese authorities could be a means of forcing the Taiwanese government to lift curbs on major investments in China. Besides sealing the escape route through Hong Kong, the Chinese government was applying the strategy "Making a feint to the east but hitting out in the west".

In the construction industry, developers commonly set up a separate company for each project. This company will oversee the entire project from ground-breaking and construction to marketing the housing units. Besides efficiency in accounting and control, project-based companies also steer clear of liabilities of the parent company. Unfortunately, this approach is subject to abuse. Small contractors or sub-contractors in Hong Kong, Singapore, China, Indonesia, Thailand and Malaysia would set up separate companies to bid for projects that include building the infrastructure and providing construction services. Some of them would even give warranties and guarantees on their services. However, upon completion of the project, they wind up the company, pack-up and simply disappear. When defects are discovered, complainants may find the warranties worthless. Allowing companies to liberally set up separate corporate identities to escape their legal liabilities are loopholes that provide "secret escape" routes for unscrupulous businessmen.

The shipping industry also has a similar practice. Typically, in the oil bunkering business, the owner will register each ship as a separate legal entity to ensure that the owner would not face unlimited liabilities should anything averse happen to the ship. At the same time, the owner will insure the ship and its cargo, a compulsory practice in this industry. Insurance provides owners with another "escape" against any potential liabilities.

BID FOR HONG KONG LAND

In August 1997, Li Ka-shing, a multi-billionaire based in Hong Kong made a noticeable 3% purchase each of Hong Kong Land (HK Land) and Jardine Matheson Ltd (JMH). Besides creating major headlines in Hong Kong and Singapore, Mr Li's move could also be used to demonstrate the use of the strategy "Secret escape through Chen Cang" with "Making a feint to the east but hit out in the west". Business analysts and newspaper editorials questioned the intention behind Mr Li's actions. Their concerns were not unfounded.

Nine years earlier and soon after the stock market crash of October 1987, Mr Li Ka-shing and his partners began to amass HK Land shares. At that time, the sensational takeover bid was foiled by JMH which owned 32% of HK Land. JMH negotiated for a settlement that included buying back Mr Li's shares at a huge premium. In addition, JMH won a seven-year moratorium on a fresh bid. Though the consortium led by Li Ka-shing (which included a Beijing company) lost their acquisition attempts, they reportedly made more than HK$1 billion from relinquishing their stakes. That indeed provided a "secret escape through Chen Cang" for Li Ka-shing and his partners.

Just when the market least expected, Li Ka-shing's flagship companies, Cheung Kong Holdings and Hutchinson Whampoa Ltd, made purchases of shares costing over US$370 million in HK Land and JMH (a company related to HK Land). Prior to the move, the market was filled with occasional rumours of another possible bid as the moratorium expired in 1995. The move by Mr Li kept the market alive with rumours and speculations.

This time however, the situation was somewhat different. The Keswick clan, the major shareholders of JMH and HK Land, might not resist takeover bids in view that Hong Kong was reverted to China. As the Keswick clan's relationship with China had not been very cordial owing to their linkages to London, HK Land had made very little progress in recent years, especially in the China market. Since transferring their listing to Singapore, HK Land also missed out on the biggest bull run on the Hong Kong stock market prior to July 1997. On the other hand, Mr Li has very strong connections with China. Thus, it was not surprising that the market responded very favourably to the announcement. There were even speculations that he might have the blessings and support of the Chinese government.

As of September 1997, events were only beginning to unfold. It is difficult to forecast if Mr Li is just aiming for another HK$1 billion extraordinary profits or if he is serious about making a bid for HK Land after a lapse of nine years. One thing, however, is for sure. Mr Li Ka-shing is not known to play second fiddle. He would always go for the commander's seat. In fact, on 25 September 1997, Mr Li raised his stake in JMH by US$50 million. This increased his holdings in JMH to 4.01%. Based on this purchase, it would appear that he is not going to stop at the 3% stake in HK Land either. In the months ahead, it would be interesting to observe how the corporate battle would be fought out. Of course, the Keswick clan may still hold the final say as to whether HK Land would be sold. The big question is the price that the Keswick are prepared to pay. More importantly, they must predict correctly whether Mr Li is using Strategy 6, "Making a feint to the east but hit out in the west" or Strategy 8, "Secret escape through Chen Cang" or a combination of both strategies.

隔岸观火

OBSERVING THE FIRE FROM THE OTHER SIDE OF THE RIVER

阳乘序乱，阴以待逆。
暴戾恣睢，其势自毙。
顺以动豫，豫顺以动。

EXPLANATION

When there are disorder and internal struggles amongst the enemy's forces (阳乘序乱), one should wait till the enemy's situation turns bad before attacking(阴以待逆). Arguments and unhappiness in the enemy's camp (暴戾恣睢), weaken the enemy's strength (其势自毙). This is when one should seize the opportunity and reap the benefits with minimal effort. The whole concept can be summarised by the phrase in *Yi Jing's* "Yu" (or "Pleased") Theory ([易经:豫]卦) which advocates using the smoothest method to achieve the best result (顺以动豫，豫顺以动).

HISTORICAL BACKGROUND

This strategy originates from Sun Zi's chapter on "Manoeuvre" (孙子:军争篇:以治待乱，以静待哗). It is similar to the strategy mentioned in the *Book of History* (史记:张仪列传) about sitting on a mountain to watch a fight between two tigers (坐山观虎斗，一举果有双虎之功).

The following story is adapted from *Tales of the Three Kingdoms* (三国志:魏书:武帝纪:袁绍传:郭嘉传).

During the period of the Three Kingdoms (三国时), around AD 200, the major forces in the region were divided between Yuan Shao (袁绍) and the famous warrior, Cao Cao (曹操). When Yuan Shao died, his wife, Liu (刘氏), divided his kingdom among his three sons, Yuan Tan (袁谭), Yuan Xi (袁熙) and Yuan Shang (袁尚). As Yuan Shang was borne by Liu, she gave him the power to control the more important cities. The eldest son, Yuan Tan, was unhappy and contemplated staging a war against his brother. He decided against this idea only for fear that Cao Cao might take advantage of the situation to conquer them. Nevertheless, the animosity amongst the brothers persisted.

Three years later, a fierce battle broke out between Cao Cao and the Yuan brothers. The latter were badly defeated and escaped to the state of Yi (翼 州). Most of Cao Cao's generals suggested that they should take this opportunity to destroy the Yuan brothers. However, Cao Cao's adviser, Guo Jia (郭 嘉) said, "Ever since the death of the old Yuan, his wife, Liu, has created animosity and strive amongst the brothers by giving the major power to the youngest son instead of the eldest. Now, they are united because of the external pressure exerted by our military power. However, once we retreat, the brothers will fight among themselves and we can take advantage of the situation then."

Cao Cao took Guo Jia's advice and retreated. As expected, Yuan Tan and Yuan Shang began fighting with each other. Yuan Shang emerged the better of the two and Yuan Tan had to escape. Subsequently, thinking that he might be able to trick Cao Cao into killing his brother for him, Yuan Tan pretended to surrender to Cao Cao and swore that he would assist the latter to fight Yuan Shang who was still in the state of Yi. Cao Cao, aware of his plan, decided to play along. Later Cao Cao led a troop against Yuan Shang who could not hold his position because his army had been weakened after the battle with his brother. Yuan Shang escaped to the state of You (幽 州) where Yuan Xi was. Yuan Tan now turned against Cao Cao and launched an attack, but he was no match for his adversary and was killed in battle.

When Yuan Shang and Yuan Xi learnt that their brother had been killed by Cao Cao, they knew that they were next on Cao Cao's hit list. They gathered their remaining army and left for Liao Dong (辽 东) with a view to seek the assistance of the governor, Gong Sun Kang (公 孙 康). Gong Sun Kang had not submitted to Cao Cao because he figured that Liao Dong was too far from the centre of Cao Cao's power. When Cao Cao's generals learned that the Yuan brothers sought assistance from Gong Sun Kang, they suggested that Cao Cao take this opportunity to kill the Yuan brothers and conquer Liao Dong.

However, Cao Cao smiled and said, "I will make Gong Sun Kang bring the heads of the Yuan brothers to me in a few days. We need not go to war." A few days later, as predicted by Cao Cao, Gong Sun Kang sent a messenger to bring the heads of the two brothers and a letter expressing his wish to surrender to Cao Cao. His generals were amazed and begged Cao Cao to reveal his insight.

Apparently, Gong Sun Kang had always been worried that the Yuan brothers would seize Liao Dong by force and he knew that the Yuans had not launched an attack against him because they were too busy defending themselves against Cao Cao. However, when the Yuan brothers decided to seek his assistance, he knew something was amiss. He had heard about the struggle amongst the Yuans and that they had no mercy even against their own flesh and blood. Therefore, if he were to take them in, it was very likely that they would stage a war against him at a later date. Also, by receiving them, he would be perceived as going against Cao Cao, an adversary he was no match against.

After consulting his advisers, Gong Sun Kang decided to play by ear. If Cao Cao were to launch an attack against Liao Dong, he would join forces with the Yuans to defeat the enemy. If there was no threat from Cao Cao, then the Yuan brothers were to be killed and their heads be presented to Cao Cao as gifts for peace. Therefore, when Gong Sun Kang realised that Cao Cao was not going to send his troops against Liao Dong, he killed his guests and presented their heads to Cao Cao. Gong Sun Kang himself was later made a general in Cao Cao's camp.

COMMENTS & APPLICATIONS

This strategy does not advocate merely watching for the enemies to annihilate themselves but waiting for the right moment to strike. In the above episode, both Guo Jia and Cao Cao were able to assess the situation and twice applied the strategy effectively. The Chinese have a similar story about how a fisherman benefitted from the fight between a sea bird and a large clam. The large clam, having clammed the beak of the bird, refused to budge. The bird refused to give in either. As a result, the clam could not move and the bird could not fly away. The commotion created by their bitter fight caught the attention of a passing fisherman. He simply picked up both the clam and the bird, two easy prey (鹬蚌相争, 渔翁得利). Another famous Chinese saying tells about how the preying mantis is so focused in poaching the locust (prey) that it forgets to guard against the preying sparrow behind it (螳螂捕蝉, 黄雀在后).

Strategy 9 can be used with Strategy 3, "Kill another with a borrowed knife," as illustrated when Cao Cao made use of Gong Sun Kang to kill the Yuan brothers. At times, it could also be used with Strategy 5, "Looting a house on fire". In this case, the strategist allows the enemies to exhaust each other, waits for the right moment, then moves in for the decisive kill. The strategy can be combined with Strategy 6, "Making a feint to the east but hitting out in the west" as illustrated by the following example on family businesses.

Squabbles within Family Businesses

A very good illustratration of this strategy was the acquisition of Yeo Hiap Seng (YHS), a beverage and food manufacturing company, by Far East Organisation (FEO). The third generation owners of YHS were engaged in rivalry and family feuds that resulted in expensive law suits. FEO watched the squabbles very closely and when it sensed that the timing was right, it moved in quickly by buying over the shares of some family members. To entice them into selling out, FEO offered attractive price premiums. FEO was thus able to seize board control with lightning speed.

The offer of a price premium by FEO was interesting. At that time, some analysts and sceptics even argued that FEO was paying rather a high price for a beverage and canned food business, especially one fraught with problems. In reality, FEO was not eyeing the manufacturing business alone. As explained in Strategy 6, its main intention was on the large land bank held by YHS. After acquiring YHS, FEO relocated its manufacturing facilities and redeveloped the old factory site, a freehold land title in a prime district, to build upmarket condominiums.

Bitter sibling rivalries and in-fighting have often been the "curse" of many successfully-run family businesses in Asia. Typically, the first generation would start and expand the business. The second generation of leaders would maintain it, and the third generation would ruin it! Hence, the Chinese saying "wealth seldom crosses the third generation" (富不过三代).

In 1997, the well-known Jumabhoy family, owners of Scotts Holding in Singapore, was also involved in complicated family squabbles and lengthy law suits. Fortunately, in this case, no "poachers" tried to buy out the company. However, many interested parties were "observing the fire from the other side of the river". If the Jumabhoy family remains disunited, it would only be a matter of time before their business empire becomes a target for acquisition.

EXPLOITING CONFLICTS IN INTERNATIONAL BUSINESS

At the macro level, the United States_had accused its allies of exploiting its difference with China to their benefit. While the United States tried to ensure China respects trade accords, copyright laws and human rights issues, its European and Japanese allies chose to "observe the fire from the other side of the river". Instead of joining the US in advocating tough measures against China, including reducing business contracts and investments, the European and Japanese allies remained on the sideline. At times, they even cashed in on the vacuum left by the United States. As a result of the conflicts between China and the US, Boeing lost a US$1.2 billion contract to supply aircrafts to China. The contract was awarded to Airbus Industrie in April 1996 instead.

European and Japanese manufacturers benefited significantly from this conflict. The stakes here were high and were not confined to the sale of aircrafts. In fact, the biggest beneficiaries of the US efforts to crackdown piracy of music and video recordings in China were not American companies but Japanese (Sony) and German companies (Bertelsman). Similarly, Japanese automobile makers exploited the 1996/97 trade and business tensions between China and the US to win approval to set up new plants in China. Other European and Japanese manufacturers did likewise.

The Japanese often demonstrated this ability to exploit situations to their advantage. When the Western allies joined to condemn China on the 4 June 1989, Tiananmen episode, a number of them pledged to boycott business in China. Instead of joining the rest, the Japanese government remained silent and merely "watched the fire from the other side of the river". Japanese businessmen quietly stepped up their business linkages with China during that period. Without doubt, the successes of many Japanese companies in China today can be explained in part by their skill in applying this strategy.

Another instance of this was when the US pulled out of South Africa because of apartheid. Japan moved in quietly after observing the situation for some time. The same approach was repeated in Vietnam. For years after the Vietnam war, the US and Vietnam were entangled in political problems and issues related to prisoners-of-war. While the US imposed trade embargoes on Vietnam, Japan moved into Vietnam in a big way.

To be fair, the US is not always the loser in international business. Its defence industries, for instance, have always thrived on the disputes and differences between countries. For example, having observed the bitter differences between China and Taiwan in the 1990s, the US defence industries cashed in by selling state-of-the-art military hardware to Taiwan. The US had been accused of fanning the fire so that it could benefit even more! One example of how the US added fuel to the fire was when they liberally granted visit visas to top Taiwanese politicians despite strong protests from the PRC government.

STAYING OUT OF UNCERTAIN SITUATIONS

"Observing the fire from the other side of the river" also implies staying out of situations with uncertain outcomes. In a battle among major shareholders, for example, minority shareholders will refrain from taking sides. In fact, it is wise to remain at a distance and observe the battle before deciding what to do. In the case of a takeover, minor shareholders should take their time to decide whether to sell out. They should wait to hear the advice of investment bankers and the offer made by the acquiring company before deciding what to do with their shares.

Similarly, when investing overseas, one should adopt a wait-and-see attitude if one is unsure of the investment climate. For example, when the property markets in Australia and the UK slumped in the late 1980s, some innovative developers marketed their properties in Asian cities like Hong Kong, Singapore, Jakarta and Kuala Lumpur. In an effort to market their properties, these developers hailed that it was the best time to invest in an overseas property in a developed country. They produced impressive statistics to show how these economies would rise. Their marketing gimmicks enticed many Asian investors who rushed into purchases.

Unfortunately, it took almost eight years before the UK market recovered. In the case of Australia, there was still no sign of recovery as of August 1997, ten years after the property market slump! Under such circumstances, investors who waited and only went in between late 1980s and early 1990s stood to lose as compared to those who invested during the 1996/97 period. This is because over the ten-year period, property prices in Australia hardly moved upward at all, and rentals had remained flat.

An inexperienced company planning to invest or operate overseas should also adopt a wait-and-see attitude. This is particularly so if the political situation contains unclear rules and conditions. For example, when China first opened its doors to foreign investors in the late 1970s and early 1980s, many Asian small and medium-size companies rushed in, hoping to exploit the immense opportunities. Unfortunately, a large number of them ended up as victims. With little experience in operating in China, they did not know how to develop the right business connections. As a result, they incurred heavy losses, with some going bankrupt.

Things, however, shaped up in China during the 1990s. The rules governing foreign investments became clearer and the Chinese government and organisations began to appreciate and better understand the mindset of overseas investors. They have also become aware that no one would be keen to invest heavily in China unless they were sure of reaping profits comparable to investing in other countries. Foreign investors now have more options, and China must promise as much to be attractive. Most importantly, the political succession after the death of Deng Xiao Ping went smoothly. President Jiang Zemin has demonstrated that he is solidly in charge. With the successful handover of Hong Kong to China in July 1997, uncertainties surrounding the future of China and Hong Kong appeared to be largely eradicated. Thus, to many multinational corporations, the period of "observing the fire from the other side of the river" is over. Many of them are likely to increase their stakes in China and Hong Kong.

On the other hand, uncertainty surrounds the situation in Indonesia. Under the leadership of President Suharto, Indonesia had developed greatly. Many Indonesians and companies have prospered under President Suharto and many multinational corporations have moved into Indonesia in a big way. However, in view of the uncertain economic, social and political climate as of mid-1998, foreign investors have become more cautious in increasing their stakes in Indonesia. It is very likely that they would adopt the wait-and-see attitude until the situation stabilises.

In fact, the dilemma faced by MNCs on investing in various countries is not confined to Asia alone. In the euphoria following the collapse of the Berlin Wall, analysts confidently predicted that former communist republics with their high level of technical skills, were set on the path of a new economic surge. Some scholars, like economist Lester Thurrow, even claimed that Eastern Europe would overtake Asia as the most exciting and attractive region for foreign investment in the 1990s and beyond. However, many of the former East European economies are still plagued with political, social and racial problems. Many MNCs, still cautious about moving into Eastern Europe, stand "observing the fire from the other side of the river".

In contrast, the initial hesitation about Asia, and especially China, has turned into confidence, as indicated by the foreign investments poured into China in recent years. In fact, China has become the world's largest benefactor of foreign investment in the mid-1990s.

笑里藏刀

A DAGGER SHEATHED IN A SMILE

信而安之，阴以图之；
备而后动，勿使有变，刚中柔外也。

EXPLANATION

One should win the trust of one's enemy so as to disarm him (信则安之) while preparing to launch an ambush (阴以图之). The enemy must not be alerted to the changes that have taken place (勿使有变) and the ambush must only be made when one is well-prepared (备而后动). This fulfils the saying, "What appears to be weak (or soft) on the outside may actually be strong (or hard) on the inside" (刚中柔外).

HISTORICAL BACKGROUND

Another saying parallel to this strategy is "The mouth is as sweet as honey but the stomach is as dangerous as a sword" (口蜜腹剑). It means to display two entirely different faces or intentions — the one on the surface is pleasing but the hidden intention is a questionable one. A common description for someone practising this form of deceit is "smiling tiger" (笑面虎).

This strategy has been recorded in the ancient Chinese classics, the *Book on Ancient Tang* (旧唐书·李义府传) where the story of a crafty man, Yi Fu (义府) is recorded. Yi Fu appeared to be polite and gentle, and would smile when he talked to anybody. But he would secretly destroy those who were against him. People therefore said that behind Yi Fu's smile was a knife:

义府貌状温恭，与人语必嬉怡微笑，而褊忌阴贼。既处权要，欲人附己，微忤意者，辄加倾陷。故时人言：义府笑中有刀。

Below are two historical examples where such a strategy had been used.

STORY 1

During the Spring and Autumn Period (春秋时期), the ruler of Wu, Zheng Wu Gong (郑武公) wanted to conquer the state of Hu (胡). Instead of using an open attack, he married his daughter to the Prince of Hu to signal that he wanted to maintain peace.

He gathered his ministers and posed the question, "Which state would be a suitable candidate for an attack by Wu?"

One minister suggested an attack on Hu and Zheng Wu Gong pretended to be furious and had that particular minister beheaded. When the ruler of Hu came to know of this incident, he no longer doubted Zheng Wu Gong's sincerity and treated the state of Wu as a close ally. However, when Zheng Wu Gong had strengthened his army, he mounted a surprise attack on Hu and destroyed it.

STORY 2

This episode is adapted from the **Words of Nations** (国语：越语). Part of the story has been mentioned under Strategy 5, "Looting a house on fire".

During the last days of the Spring and Autumn Period, at around 500 BC, the battle between the states of Wu and Yue (吴越之战) which had lasted half a century, finally ended with victory on the side of the ruler of Wu, Gou Jian (勾践). The ruler of Yue, Fu Chai (夫差) took his own life. Yue became a very powerful state and its influence extended to Chang Jiang (长江) and Huai He (淮河) and Gou Jian was acknowledged the Chief among the rulers.

Fan Li (范蠡) was one of Gou Jian's most capable men and was given the title, Supreme General. However, he intended to retire from politics as he thought, "It is not a good thing to be too famous. It is better if I retire soon and refrain from further involvement with the politics. Further, Gou Jian is one who is willing to share his problems but not his successes. The wisest thing to do is to leave this place."

He then wrote a letter to Gou Jian, saying, "A subject must always try his utmost to help his master to resolve problems.

If the master were humiliated by another, the subject should die to defend His Majesty's name. In the past, when Your Highness was humiliated at the Mountain of Ji (稽 山) [by Fu Chai], I did not die immediately because I wanted to help Your Highness to clear Your name. Now that we have achieved our goal, please allow me to resign from my post."

Gou Jian granted Fan Li his request and the latter left with his family and servants together with all his possessions, which included jade and gold. They settled down in the state of Chu (楚 国) and Fan Li changed his name to Chi Yi Zi Pi (鸱夷子皮). Fan Li subsequently became a multi-millionaire as a result of his superb business abilities. In fact, the revered writings on doing business by Tao Zhu Gong (陶 朱 公 商 训) are attributed to Fan Li.

After Fan Li left Yue, he wrote a long letter to another of Gou Jian's aid, Wen Zhong (文 种), saying, "When all the birds have flown away, there is no use for a fine bow and it will be laid aside. Similarly, when the rabbit dies, the hounds which have been used to hunt it would be killed. The ruler of Yue is a person who will share his problems but not his successes. If you do not leave the palace early, you may meet with an ill fate."

Although Wen Zhong knew what Fan Li said made sense, he could not bring himself to leave the riches and power he had as a general in the palace. One day, Gou Jian gave Wen Zhong a sword and said, "You used to tell me that there are seven ways to destroy Wu. I only used three of these methods. You still have the remaining four methods. Why don't you use one of them to end your life?" Wen Zhong heaved a sigh and took his own life.

COMMENTS & APPLICATIONS

This strategy suggests winning the enemy's trust and attacking him when his guard is down. To do so, one will have to pretend to be friendly and unarmed on the surface, even though he has a deadly scheme behind his smile. In the first example, the ruler of Wu went to the extent of sacrificing his own daughter's happiness and the life of a loyal subject in order to gain his enemy's trust. In the second example, Gou Jian had proven to be the master when it comes to using this strategy. Firstly, he demeaned himself to be a slave to Fu

Chai so as to win the latter's trust, and waited ten years to destroy him (*see story in Strategy 5*). Secondly, he made use of capable advisers like Fan Li and Wen Zhong to defeat Fu Chai, only to kill them later to prevent them from overthrowing him. His distrust for his advisers made him use the "gain the initiative by striking the first blow" strategy (先 发 制 人). However, it was not difficult for the brilliant Fan Li to see through his "murderous intention behind the smile".

The Art of Smiling in Winning Business

Among the various professions, sales people probably practise this strategy of "a dagger beneath one's smile" most frequently. In fact, the skilful salesman has probably perfected this strategy into an art. Of course, the "dagger" cannot be interpreted literally in the application to business. However, in the context of selling, behind the smile of the skilful salesman is the intent to make the biggest sale out of the customer. Indeed, the shrewd salesman uses the smile to his maximum advantage — to lure and charm the customer. The smile can be a very effective sales weapon. By smiling, the salesman also lowers the defences of the potential customer and causes him to be less agitated. Conveying warmth, confidence and courtesy, a pleasant and friendly smile definitely facilitates the sales process.

So important is the smile that professional companies conduct personal grooming lessons to teach salespeople the art of smiling. Among the major attributes of successful companies, one can easily spot that winning smile among their service personnel. Companies such as McDonalds, Singapore Airlines and Walt Disney World all use service personnel well trained in the art of smiling.

The power of a smile is so well-recognised that Singapore Tourist Promotion Board (STPB) actively promoted a smile campaign in 1996/1997 to lure a greater number of tourists. In a series of advertisements and television commercials, the STPB used prominent personalities to explain why it is so important to smile — it is one of the most effective ways to win the tourist dollar. STPB is one of the few organisations to openly acknowledge the power of the smile, and the need to use it to one's advantage.

Japanese Business Strategies

To some extent, the success of many Japanese companies in conquering world markets can be partially attributed to the application of this strategy. The Japanese would typically claim to be weak and vulnerable. They would seldom admit that they are, in fact, harbouring very ambitious business plans. By feigning weakness and vulnerability, they lower the defences of their major Western competitors and acquire much of their know-how while making significant inroads into the market. Before the Western corporate giants can respond, the Japanese manufacturers flood the world markets with countless brands of cameras, electronics, home appliances and cars.

This ability of the Japanese to humble themselves enabled them to outdo their Western competitors. Many Japanese companies are now occupying leading positions. Among the top 10 banks in the world, nine belong to the Japanese! The only non-Japanese bank is from China. Indeed the abilities of the Japanese companies are reflected very much in the following quotation from Sun Zi, the well-known Chinese military strategist:

> In the beginning of battle, be as shy as a young maiden to entice the enemy and lower his defences. When the battle progresses, be as swift as a hare to catch the unpreparedness of the enemy.

是故始如处女, 敌人开户 后如脱兔, 敌不及拒.

The Japanese had also been accused of "stealing" technology from the West under the pretext of learning and co-operation while being very unwilling to transfer their technology to other countries. This was particularly true in the 1960s and 1970s. Japanese companies are known to be reluctant to export their research and development activities. Despite being an economic superpower, the Japanese still avoid taking leadership and continue to classify themselves as being vulnerable and needing to learn from the Western world. In reality, they have much to offer to the rest of the world. Their ability to project a weak front can be captured by these words from Sun Zi:

> Therefore, when capable, feign incapability; when active, feign inactivity. When near to the objective, feign that you are far away; when far away, make it appear that you are near.

故能而示之不能, 用而示之不用, 近而示之远, 远而示之近.

This is possible largely because of the strict discipline of the Japanese. Japanese executives generally do not brag or gloat about their achievements, preferring instead to keep a low profile. This behaviour can best be summed up by Sun Zi:

Therefore, the victories won by a master of war never gain him
reputation for wisdom or courage.

故善战者之胜也, 无智名, 无勇功.

MICROSOFT'S INVESTMENT IN APPLE

In a move that shocked shareholders, market analysts, and
competitors, Microsoft Corporation announced in early August 1997
that it would be investing US$150 million in Apple Computer Inc.
This stunned the public for a number of reasons. Firstly, Microsoft
Corporation and Apple Computer Inc are traditional arch rivals.
They had competed very bitterly in the past for market shares.
Secondly, Microsoft Corporation had so dominated the software
market that Apple Computer Inc had been reduced to a non-threat.
As of August 1997, Apple had a less than 4% share of the market.
Thirdly, despite retaining a strong brand name and possessing some
excellent technology, Apple was losing money. It did not make
business sense to invest US$150 million into a money-losing
company. This whole episode evoked high drama when the move
was announced by Steve Jobs, co-founder of Apple, especially since
Steve was known to have great disdain for Bill Gates, founder of
Microsoft. In his announcement at the MacWorld Trade Show in
Boston on 6 August 1997, Steve justified the decision saying, "If we
want to move forward, we have to let go of a few things. We have
to let go of the notion that for Apple to win, Microsoft has to lose.
The era of us thinking that we can compete with Microsoft is over.
We need all the help we can get. We had better treat Microsoft with
a little gratitude."

Steve's comments were expectedly booed at. To die-hard users
of Apple, the move was a sell-out to a larger and greedier competitor.
They had good reason to suspect there was a "knife" behind
Microsoft's smile. Since Apple was no longer a threat to Microsoft
and was losing money, Microsoft's investment defied business logic.
Microsoft does not need Apple to prosper. To sceptics and cynics,
the investment was more than an altruistic gesture to save an ailing
company, despite the assuring words of Bill Gates, the founder of
Microsoft: "We think Apple makes a huge contribution in the
computer industry... And we think it's going to be a lot of fun
helping out."

To these sceptics, Bill Gates often gets more than his money's
worth of his investments. Some speculated that perhaps a software

or platform Apple had developed has great use to Microsoft. However, the greatest motivation behind the investment, in our assessment, is that Microsoft was basically trying to find a creative way to overcome the concerns of the anti-trust regulators. This is because Apple's Macintosh operating system was the only rival to Microsoft's MS-DOS. If this trend continued, Apple's operating system might be wiped out, which would present a bigger problem to Microsoft. Thus, it made sense to keep Apple alive to avoid the regulators. By buying into Apple, Microsoft can then dictate and control the strategic directions in which Apple develops its software. Thus, beneath this seemingly friendly gesture lies ulterior motives which will only be revealed in time.

Besides this "Knife beneath the smile" strategy, Bill Gates was also applying Strategy 5 ("Looting a house on fire"), Strategy 6 ("Making a feint to the east but hit out in the west") in not disclosing his real intention and Strategy 22 ("Closing the doors to catch the thief") in cornering the entire market for Microsoft.

Whatever the motives, this investment news benefited shareholders of Apple Computer Inc. Within a week of the announcement, its share price escalated by over 40%. Interestingly, among the biggest winners of the Microsoft-Apple tie-up was the Saudi Prince Al-Waleed Bin Talal. Known internationally for applying the "looting a house on fire" strategy, the Prince had bought a 5% stake Apple in March 1997 at the time when the company was losing money and besieged with management problems. When he invested that US$115.4 million, he stated openly that he liked the strong brand name of Apple and that he believed Apple would turnaround one day. Prior to his Apple's investment, he had also bought into other distressed companies, including Euro Disney and Citicorp. Barely four months after investing the US$115.4 million, the value escalated to over US$165 million!

The Microsoft-Apple deal suggests that not all offers of help will be perceived favourably. On one hand, the benefits of the deal appeared very straightforward and obvious – sharing of technology, economies of scale and a financial boast to an ailing company. The market, in fact, responded positively when the share prices of Apple rebounded strongly. Yet the motives behind Microsoft's moves were highly suspected. Altruism has been ruled out. If anything, many sceptics believed that the move was calculated to strengthen Microsoft's monopolistic position without "Hitting the grass to startle the snake" (Strategy 13) in addressing the concerns of anti-trust regulators. Most significantly, the pessimists feared that the alliance would kill the unique corporate culture of Apple Computer Inc, especially its maverick behaviour of defying all odds in order to survive and fight against market trends. Apple Computer Inc was to many Americans, the hero of the underdogs.

The suspicion behind the deal was further strengthened by the fact that Bill Gates was able to win over two of his former harshest critics and rivals. Besides Steve Jobs who openly embraced Bill Gates and expressed great appreciation and admiration for the management style of Microsoft, another former critic of Gates was also invited to join the new Apple Computer's board. He was none other than the Oracle Corp chairman Larry Ellison. Only time will tell if there was indeed "a dagger" behind Microsoft's friendly gesture.

李 代 桃 僵

THE PLUM DIES IN PLACE OF THE PEACH

势 必 有 损, 损 阴 以 益 阳。

EXPLANATION

Where losses are inevitable (势 必 有 损), one should be willing to make sacrifices (损 阴) to gain victory (益 阳). In warfare, this strategy is applied when the enemy has the upper hand. To turn the tables around and achieve victory, one needs to make sacrifices. It may be necessary to sacrifice a few battles to achieve the ultimate objective of winning the war.

HISTORICAL BACKGROUND

The phrase "The plum dies in place of the peach" (李 代 桃 僵) comes from a poem in *A Collection of Music and Poems* (乐 府 诗 集: 鸡 鸣). The original poem reads as follows:

> The peach blooms above the well,
> The plum tree grows next to the peach,
> When the worms gnaw the roots of the peach tree,
> The plum dies in the place of the peach,
> The trees are willing to sacrifice for each other,
> Should not brothers be more so?

桃 生 露 井 上, 李 树 生 桃 旁。虫 来 啮[1] 桃 狠, 李 树 代 桃 僵。树 木 身 相 代, 兄 弟 还 相 忘 ?

The original meaning of the poem is that the trees growing side by side have cultivated such close ties that one is willing to die for the other. Brothers should be all the more willing to sacrifice for each other, especially in times of danger. The meaning of the phrase

---

[1] *Pronounce "nie" and it means to bite.*

was later expanded to describe a situation where it is necessary to concede a battle to win the war.

Story 1, adapted from the ***Book of History*** (史记), tells of how Sun Bin (孙膑) helped Tian Ji (田忌) to win a horse race.

STORY 1

During the period of the Warring States (战国时代), General Tian Ji of the state of Qi (齐国) had a very good adviser, Sun Bin, with whom he would discuss all matters. One day, Sun Bin noticed that Tian Ji looked troubled and asked him why. Apparently, the royals and generals were very fond of horse racing and they would place heavy bets on their own horses. Tian Ji had horses participating in a number of races but they failed to win most of the time. Sun Bin consoled him saying, "It is only a small matter and you should not worry too much about it. Maybe you should bring me to the races one of these days and I may be able to help you to win what you have lost."

Tian Ji did bring Sun Bin with him to one of the races. Sun Bin realised that everybody was in the habit of categorising their horses into Upper Class, Middle Class and Lower Class according to how fast the horses would run, the Upper Class horses being the fastest. The rule of the game was that the winner needed to win two out of three classes. Sun Bin found out that Tian Ji's Upper Class horses were of no match for the other horses in that class. Similarly, his Middle Class and Lower Class horses were not comparable to the others' in the respective categories. However, the speed of Tian Ji's horses was not far behind that of the other horses. Therefore, with careful manipulation of the situation, Sun Bin was confident that he could help Tian Ji win his races.

When Sun Bin and Tian Ji went home, Sun Bin told Tian Ji that he should make heavy bets in the next race as he was confident that Tian Ji would win. Knowing that his adviser was more brilliant than himself, Tian Ji happily said, "If you can guarantee that I will win, I would like to invite the Emperor of Qi (齐威王) to participate and place a thousand pieces of gold as my bet." Sun Bin asked him to go ahead and make the necessary arrangements.

The Emperor of Qi's horses had out-run Tian Ji's horses many times in the past. The Emperor therefore gladly agreed to participate. Very soon, the whole nation came to know about this big race. On the day of the race, thousands of peasants and royal subjects turned up to view the competition. Just before the race started, Sun Bin told Tian Ji, "Please use your Lower Class horses to race against the Emperor's Upper Class horses. You will lose the first race. Then use your Upper Class horses against His Majesty's Middle Class horses and finally, your Middle Class horses against his Lower Class horses. You will win two races out of three and you will be the overall winner."

The first race ended with the Emperor's horses winning convincingly. The Emperor happily jeered at Tian Ji, but the latter was not discouraged and replied, "Well, I have only lost the first race. You can laugh at me if I lose all three matches." In the next two races, Tian Ji's horses miraculously beat the Emperor's horses and the Emperor was amazed. Little did he know that Tian Ji was using the "The plum dies in place of the peach" strategy of Sun Bin.

At this time, Tian Ji smiled and said to the Emperor, "My Lord, I won the race today not because there was a sudden increase in power in my horses but because I had listened to Sun Bin's strategy." He then told the Emperor about Sun Bin's plan. When the Emperor heard the plan, he was full of praise for Sun Bin and summoned for him. He then asked the latter to explain the use of this strategy in warfare.

Sun Bin replied, "The strategy is not new but its application is the most important thing. Where both parties are of equal strength, proper use of the strategy will guarantee victory. Where the enemy is much stronger, the strategy will reduce losses. That is the gist of the plan." The Emperor was deeply impressed.

Story 2

During the Spring and Autumn period, lived a high-ranking official, Tu An Jia (屠岸賈). Tu was jealous of the power of the Zhao clan (趙 氏) so he plotted to eliminate them all. One of his Generals, Han Jue (韓 厥), did not approve of this, and informed the son of Zhao Dun (趙 盾), Zhao Shuo (趙 朔), so he could take precaution. Zhao Shuo said, "There is no escape. Please save one of the members of our Zhao family and I shall die in peace."

Zhao Shuo had Cheng Ying (程 嬰), a guest, escort his pregnant wife, daughter of the ruler of the state of Jin (晋 国), back to the Jin palace. The next day, Tu An Jia came with a troop to the Zhao residence and exterminated them all. However, they could not find Zhao Shuo's wife.

When Tu An Jia learned that the princess had returned to the palace, he went there and asked the ruler of Jin, Jin Gong (景 公) to kill her. He reminded Jin Gong how his predecessor, Ling Gong (灵 公) was assassinated by one of the Zhaos and warned that the princess's child might take revenge. Jin Gong promised to have the child killed if the princess really bore a son.

The princess indeed gave birth to a son. When Tu An Jia heard the news, he immediately sent his men to the palace to search for the new-born boy. However, the men could not find the child. Tu offered a reward for the person who surrenders the child.

Meanwhile, Cheng Ying met up another loyal subject of the Zhao clan, Gong Sun Chu Jiu (公 孙 杵 臼) and conferred with him, "Although Tu An Jia's men failed to find the child the first time, they will return to the palace to search again. It is best to take the child and hide him in a faraway place."

Cheng Ying and Gong Sun Chu Jiu came up with a plan to disguise another new-born child as Zhao Shuo's son while Gong Sun Chu Jiu take refuge with the decoy at Shou Yang mountain (首 阳 山). Cheng Ying would pretend to reveal the hiding place to Tu An Jia. When Tu finds the child, he would think that he has killed the last of the Zhaos and give up his search.

At that time, Cheng Ying's wife had just bore him a son. In the middle of the night, Cheng Ying took his own son and gave him to Gong Sun Chu Jiu. He then went to the palace and told General Han Jue the plan.

Cheng Ying then went to Tu An Jia and lied to him that he and Gong Sun Chu Jiu were under the princess' orders to hide Zhao Shuo's child in the mountains. He claimed that he was afraid his family would be killed if the plan fell through, and that he thought the way to save his family and to receive a hefty reward was to tell Tu An Jia the hiding place.

Tu An Jia was overjoyed at this and followed Cheng Ying to the mountain of Shou Yang. When Gong Sun Chu Jiu saw

Tu An Jia, he turned to run. Tu An Jia ordered his men to seize Gong Sun Chu Jiu. Later, Tu An Jia's men found the decoy child crying. Gong Sun Chu Jiu pretended to condemn Cheng Ying.

Tu An Jia ordered that Gong Sun Chu Jiu and the child be beheaded. While Tu An Jia was out of the palace, General Han Jue smuggled Zhao Shuo's son out to safety. After fifteen years, the ruler of Jin learnt the truth and restored the Zhao clan. Zhao Shuo's child grew up safely and revealed himself to Jing Gong who permitted him to take revenge on Tu An Jia.

COMMENTS & APPLICATIONS

All parties suffer losses in the battlefield. This strategy advocates that where both parties are of equal strength, it may be necessary for one party to deliberately sustain some injuries to distract the enemy and win the war.

PRIORITISING THE USE OF LIMITED RESOURCES

In war, as in business, it may not be possible to win every time because of constraints of financial, human, technological resources. *Trade-offs are therefore inevitable* for gaining the upper hand. This is the essence of strategising, as illustrated by these two stories.

It is often not possible to pursue a strategy of market penetration (pricing a product cheaply to sell many) together with a strategy of market skimming (pricng a product to cream the top end of the market). The former implies a pursuit of market share, while the latter implies the pursuit of profit margins. Each strategy entails different marketing skills and resources. It is difficult for a company to use both strategies at the same time. Similarly, a strategy of product diversification requires very different resources than a market expansion strategy. The company has to decide which strategy to pursue. One will be a trade-off against the other.

Prioritising usage of limited resources applies even to large companies. American and European companies prefer to focus on what they can do best. Among the 1996 listings of the Fortune 500 companies, the most profitable ones are those which have chosen to concentrate on their own line of business. Some of these companies are shown in Table 11.1.

Despite the highly diversified businesses of the Japanese *zaibatsus* and the Korean *chaebols*, they are not among the most profitable companies in the world. American and European companies which stay focused on selected lines of businesses, appear to be doing much better than the Japanese and Korean companies, judging by their profit margins.

Rank	Company	1996 Profits	Main Business
1	Royal Dutch/Shell Group	US$8.89 billion	Petroleum
2	Exxon	US$7.51 billion	Petroleum
3	General Electric	US$7.28 billion	Electronics & Electrical equipment
4	Philip Morris	US$6.30 billion	Tobacco
5	AT&T	US$5.91 billion	Telecommunication
6	IBM	US$5.43 billion	Computers
7	Intel	US$5.12 billion	Computer chips
8	General Motors	US$4.96 billion	Automobiles

Table 11.1 The Most Profitable Companies (1996)

A company has to decide how best it wants to excel. This could be done by positioning its products and services, and focusing on areas where it has the competitive advantage. Unfortunately, some companies fail to realise this. Instead, they choose to defend "dying" products and services, or to support too many products and services, thereby wasting resources.

FOCUSING ON THE RIGHT MARKETS

The three categories of horse races can be likened to a scenario of competition in three types of market places — developed markets, developing markets, and less developed markets. To win in a developed market, one must have the "ingredients" or factors to compete. In the absence of these, the shrewd company would be better off forgoing the developed market and focusing its resources on the developing and less developed markets.

This is the tack taken by many companies in Singapore. Realising that it is difficult to win in the developed economies of the US, Japan and Western Europe, these Singapore-based companies focus their investments in the newly developing and less developed economies of Asia such as Malaysia, Indonesia, China, India, Myanmar and Vietnam. Thus far, this strategy appears to have worked well.

Many Japanese companies have been doing this for years, although in a different way. With rising production costs, it is not worthwhile competing at the lower end of the range. So, these Japanese companies shifted the production of the lower-end products such as televisions, refrigerators, hi-fi equipment and other household appliances to countries with lower production costs (for example, Thailand, Malaysia, China). They focus their efforts and resources on the higher end. By voluntarily conceding defeat in some areas in which they have no competitive advantages, many Japanese companies have been able to secure decisive victories in other areas. As a result, the Japanese economy prospered. In contrast, many developed economies in the West have declined because of their unwillingness to concede "defeats" in industries in which they are no longer competitive.

Even in heavy industries such as automobiles and shipbuilding, the Japanese have voluntarily yielded to Korean and Malaysian manufacturers. In the camera industry (where the level of technology is high) Japanese manufacturers have farmed out production of lower-end models to economies like Taiwan. By losing a battle or two in the business war, the Japanese corporate warriors have been able to score an overall victory! Indeed, Strategy 11 is consistent with what the great Chinese military strategist Sun Zi said, "Do not stay on desolate ground."

Sacrifices Needed

In the battlefields it is sometimes necessary to sacrifice people or things. There is a Chinese saying that goes: "Sacrifice the little things in order to accomplish the big plan" (牺 牲 小 我, 完 成 大 我). Chinese books on warfare write that:

> In order to get the enemy's flesh and blood, one will have to let the enemy peel his skin. In order to chop off the enemy's bone, one will have to allow the enemy dig his flesh from the body.

为了挖取敌人的血肉, 就要让敌人割自己的皮;
为了砍断敌人的骨, 要忍痛让敌人挖自己的肉。

While these sayings may appear morbid, they were practised by people like Cheng Ying and Gong Sun Chu Jiu. Amazingly, Cheng Ying sacrificed the life of his own son, while Gong Sun Chu Jiu gave up his life for Zhao Shuo's son. The extent to which they were prepared to make sacrifices for the ultimate victory over Tu An Jia was remarkable. Not only were they unquestionably loyal to the Zhao clan, but they were prepared to sacrifice life and limb for 20 years, waiting for Zhao Shuo's son to grow up.

In economic development, sacrifices must be made too. Often, these sacrifices take a time to bear fruit. For example, investment in education, infrastructure, technology, and research and development take many years before results are seen. In the spirit of making sacrifices for the future, Singapore implemented a compulsory scheme of savings, called the Central Provident Fund (CPF) for every working Singaporean, and compulsory military service for every able-bodied male citizen.

Over the years, the CPF system has enabled the new generation of Singaporeans to accumulate savings that can be used to purchase homes, shares and other investments. With high economic stakes, the average Singaporean is willing to work harder and to be rooted to his country. They have every reason to ensure that their assets appreciate in value. This gives them strong motivation to work hard and achieve more. In the earlier years, the CPF funds were also channelled toward the development of Singapore. For example, this large pool of available funds enabled the Singapore government to finance development of infrastructure.

Compulsory military or national service has also helped to build a strong defence force. More importantly, the training inculcates a sense of national pride and loyalty among national servicemen. Military training also lays a foundation for a disciplined workforce, essential for economic development.

Singapore took more than 20 years to reach its current state of affluence. For a country with no natural resources, and where everything, including water, has to be imported, its achievements are nothing short of an economic miracle. This would not have been possible without the sacrifices made in the earlier years. Many of the policies enacted by the Singapore government demanded various degrees of sacrifice from the citizens. Without these sacrifices, it would have been more difficult to maintain and improve the standard of living.

Sacrificing in business is equally necessary. Consider these examples:

1   Holding sales to get rid of old stock to generate cash for new products. Old stock may become obsolete (as in the case of fashion goods), and it also requires more money to carry it as inventory. In business, it is better to turn over the inventory as quickly as possible.

2   Giving away free product samples to lure the consumers. The free samples act as "baits" for the purchase of the actual

product. At times, the company may even allow trial periods.

3   "Buy-one, get-one free" is another business ploy used to secure larger sales volume and protect one's market share. This ploy takes various forms. For example, many sellers of cellular handphones and pagers offer several months of free subscription plus gifts. M1, the second cellular phone operator in Singapore, used this strategy when it launched its services. Within months, it secured thousands of customers.

4   Product/service bundling where the price of the bundle of products/services is less than the sum of the individual items. Bundling is a common ploy used in marketing gift hampers, banking services, package tours, wedding dinners, and photographic services.

5   Gifts with purchase are often used in the sale of high-ticket cookware, cosmetics and even encyclopaedias. The marketer lures the consumer to buy the major item by throwing in a number of other free items. The value of the "sacrificed" items can add up to a fairly substantial amount, often making the offer irresistible.

The idea behind sacrificing the little things to accomplish the big plan can be used in many areas of business, including negotiation of contracts. At times it is better to give away small benefits or perks to secure the big deal. The irony is that one can get caught or distracted by the small issues, and end up missing the main objective. This is the essence behind the "plum dies in place of the peach" strategy.

顺手牵羊

STEALING A GOAT ALONG THE WAY

微隙在所必乘，
微利在所必得，少阴，少阳。

EXPLANATION

No matter how small a hole may be, one should use it to one's advantage (微隙在所必乘). No matter how small the advantage is, one should obtain it for his benefit (微利在所必得). One should take advantage of the enemy's small weaknesses (少阴) for one's small gain (少阳). This is similar to the analogy that by gathering crumbs of bread, one can still get a full meal. However, if one is only interested in the full loaf, there may be none at all.

HISTORICAL BACKGROUND

This strategy came from **Cao Lu Jing Lue** (草庐经略：游兵：伺敌之隙，乘间取利). It has also been mentioned in other ancient Chinese war books like **Deng Tan Bi Jiu** (登坛必究：叙战：见利宜疾，未利则止，取利乘时，间不容息，先之一刻则太过，后之一刻则失时也) *San Lue* (三略．上略：察其天地，伺其空隙) and *Li Wei Gong Wen Dui* (李卫公问对．卷中：伺隙捣虚), where the meaning is similar: take advantage of the enemy's slightest negligence or carelessness to steal his goat. The story below demonstrates the usage of this strategy.

> *Cui Zhu* (崔杼) *had helped Qi Zhuang Gong* (齐庄公) *become the ruler of the state of Qi* (齐国). *As a result, he was promoted to Chief Minister. Qi Zhuang Gong would frequently visit Cui Zhu's residence for drinks, and Cui Zhu treated him as family.*
>
> *One day, Qi Zhuang Gong, after having one too many drinks, took the opportunity while Cui Zhu was out of the house to rape his concubine, Tang Jiang* (棠姜). *After this, Qi Zhuang*

Gong and Tang Jiang frequently committed adultery secretly. Cui Zhu eventually learnt of this and reprimanded his concubine. Tang Jiang admitted her affair with Qi Zhuang Gong, but in defence, she claimed that she, as a female, could not offend the ruler.

"But you should have told me earlier!" said Cui Zhu angrily. "I know I have done wrong, but the wrong has been done, what was the point of letting you know about it? If I had revealed the truth earlier, and if the ruler knew of your anger, he might have harmed you. It was all your fault, bringing him to our residence in the first place," defended Tang Jiang.

After some consideration, Cui Zhu sighed heavily, "Well, I can't blame you now. I can only blame myself for leading the wolf into our house (引 狼 入 室)." From then on, Cui Zhu was on his guard and did not allow Qi Zhuang Gong to get near to his wife. At the same time, he secretly plotted to kill the ruler.

Qi Zhuang Gong had a subordinate called Jia Jian (贾 监) who had once been heavily punished by Qi Zhuang Gong for a minor offence. Jia Jian therefore bore a grudge against him. When Cui Zhu learnt about this, he paid Jia Jian a hefty sum to be his spy in the palace.

Subsequently, the ruler of the state of Ju (莒 国), Li Bi Gong (黎 比 公) paid a visit to Qi. Qi Zhuang Gong was pleased and planned a banquet at a guest lodge in the northern territory near Cui Zhu's residence. When Cui Zhu was informed of this, he realised what Qi Zhuang Gong's real intentions were. He then pretended to be ill so that he absent himself from the banquet. At the same time, he sent Jia Jian to spy on Qi Zhuang Gong. Jia Jian then informed Cui Zhu that the ruler wanted to visit Cui Zhu after the banquet.

Cui Zhu thought, "That adulterer's real motive is to visit my wife." He summoned his wife and told her, "I am going to kill that good-for-nothing ruler tonight. You are to do what I ask you to do. If we succeed, I will make you my first wife and your son will be my direct successor. I will also keep your affair a secret. If you do not follow my instructions, I will kill you now."

"I am your wife. It is only right that I should listen to you. Moreover, you are doing this to take revenge for me. I will do as you say," replied Tang Jiang. "Good!" replied Cui

Zhu who then told her what she should do. Next, Cui Zhu had all his men hide inside his house and told Jia Jian the plan. The bait was ready to lure the fish to the hook.

Qi Zhuang Gong had been thinking of Tang Jiang lately and was overjoyed at this opportunity to see her. He came immediately after the banquet. "How is the Chief Minister?" Qi Zhuang Gong asked on arrival at Cui Zhu's house. "Your Highness, the Chief Minister is very ill. He has just taken his medicine and is asleep now," said the guard at the door.

"Where is his bedroom?" asked Qi Zhuang Gong. "At the East Room," came the reply. Qi Zhuang Gong was very happy and walked instead towards the West Room. His four bodyguards were held back by Jia Jian who hinted to them, "You know what His Highness intends to do. You should not follow him."

The guards then stayed behind. Qi Zhuang Gong went into the room together with Jia Jian. Qi Zhuang Gong was met by Tang Jiang as he entered the West Room. When he saw the beautiful lady, he was about to grab hold of her when a maid came to inform Tang Jiang that the Chief Minister was thirsty and wanted his concubine to make and send him a honeyed drink.

Tang Jiang smiled at Qi Zhuang Gong and said, "Please be patient. Wait for me while I take him the drink, and I will be back soon." After Tang Jiang left the room, Jia Jian excused himself. Qi Zhuang Gong was waiting impatiently in the room when all of a sudden, he heard soldiers shouting outside. He realised that something was amiss so he tried to escape by the back door. When he found that it was locked, he retreated to the attic. The soldiers surrounded the place shouting, "We are under the Chief Minister's order to capture the adulterer!"

Qi Zhuang Gong could not find a way out and through the window, begged, "I am Your Majesty. You are not to harm me." "We do not care if you declare yourself to be His Majesty. We are under strict orders to capture the adulterer," replied the soldiers. "Where is the Chief Minister? I want to have a word with him!"

"The Chief Minister is ill in bed and cannot see you." Qi Zhuang Gong knew that there was no way out and begged

again, "I know you want me dead. But can you grant me my
wish to return to the Royal Temple? I will take my life there."

"It is better you solve your problem now before you get
humiliated!" came the reply. Qi Zhuang Gong suddenly leapt
out of the window to try climbing over the walls. However,
his left leg was hit by an arrow and he fell to the ground. The
soldiers then killed the ruler and his four bodyguards.

COMMENTS & APPLICATIONS

This strategy suggests that one should not miss any opportunity, no matter how minor or insignificant. This strategy advocates an attitude of constant vigilance so one can exploit opportunities whenever and wherever they arise. In the above story, Qi Zhuang Gong took advantage of his position to have an affair with Cui Zhu's wife. He literally "stole a goat along the way". In return, Cui Zhu took advantage of Qi Zhuang Gong's weakness for his wife to kill him. He not only revenged his personal grudges but also benefited politically.

SEIZING EVERY BUSINESS OPPORTUNITY

In business, one must be on the constant lookout for opportunities. For example, in the 1950s and 1960s, American automobile makers paid little attention to the markets in Southeast Asia. They felt that the Southeast Asian market was too small, and the consumers too poor to afford large American cars, so they did not bother to market their cars there. In contrast, the Japanese automobile makers came in with their small, cheap cars. Today, Japanese car markets are reaping rich dividends from their attention to the "small fry" because the demand for automobiles in Southeast Asia has grown significantly.

European luxury car makers did not, however, ignore the small markets of Asia. Many of the luxury brands like Mercedes, Rolls Royce, BMW and Volvo have gradually built up their market shares in Asia. On a per capita basis, Hong Kong has the largest number of Rolls Royce, while Singapore holds the record for Mercedes owners. On the roads today, one out of ten cars in Singapore bears the Mercedes emblem.

In the courier business, United Parcel Service (UPS) and Federal Express concentrated their business activities in North America and

Europe. They did not consider Asia a market worth exploring. DHL, a much smaller company in the United States, decided to explore the relatively untapped Asian market. From a very humble beginning with small market potential, DHL has, over the years, substantially developed the Asian market. Today, DHL has become a major courier company in Asia.

Predictably, the more successful companies are those which capitalised on and exploited every available opportunity. In the fast growing economies of Asia, this attribute has become very important, because opportunities fade away quickly.

Markets in the newly opened economies of Asia such as Myanmar and Vietnam may seem small today but shrewd investors and businessmen can learn a few lessons from the Japanese. Like many Singaporean, Hong Kong and Taiwanese companies, they should go after the small business opportunities in these economies. Unlike the Western and American business giants who are only interested in large scale projects, these Singaporean, Taiwanese and Hong Kong businessmen have been nibbling away very effectively in Myanmar and Vietnam. Their successes have prompted many Malaysian and Indonesian companies to adopt similar strategies. They see the advantage of going after the small but certain victory rather than wait for the one ephemeral huge success.

GROWING A BUSINESS

The ability to seize every available business opportunity can be best illustrated by the success stories of two Asian business tycoons. Mr Robert Kuok, a Malaysian, has an estimated wealth of US$7 billion (*Forbes Magazine*, 1996). Known as a shrewd businessman, Mr Kuok's business empire now spans the globe with interests in property, hotels and manufacturing. Some of his prize catches include the license to bottle Coca-cola in China. The deal was reported to be worth over US$5 billion. In 1996, the value of his Shangri-La Hotel in Singapore had appreciated 300 times since he bought it in the late 1960s, while his 1988 purchase of the US$175 million luxury apartments in Hong Kong were valued in excess of US$1 billion in 1997.

Among his many superb qualities as a shrewd businessman, his ability to judge events far ahead of others is apparent. When the former President of the Philippines, Ferdinand Marcos, fled the country in 1986, the whole country was in chaos. Few businessmen would dare to spend their money in the Philippines. Yet Mr Kuok bought two Shangri-La Hotels in Manila. He has an uncanny judgement for when to "Steal a goat along the way".

Mr Kuok's ability to attract the best people to work for him has been one of the factors accounting for his success. He is always on the lookout for people smarter than himself to go into business with him. In his own words, "If there are smarter people — stronger, better horses running — then why aren't you putting some of your money on them?"

Mr Kwek Leng Beng from Singapore is an equally astute businessman. Although he inherited a great fortune from his late father, Mr Kwek Leng Beng has demonstrated his ability to multiply his family fortunes within the few years he has been in charge. He is well-known among the international hotel circles for his ability to pick up the choicest hotels at rock-bottom prices. A decisive and quick purchaser, he is able to seal a deal at lightning speed. Within less than ten years, his chain of hotels grew to 64 in 12 countries. In July 1997, his company City Developments Limited (CDL) was the hot favourite for purchasing the Radisson chain. A successful purchase would make CDL a global hotel player as it would more than double its existing rooms and cover new markets.

Besides hotels, Mr Kwek controls a still-growing US$16 billion business empire which includes property, finance and trade. Just like Mr Kuok, Mr Kwek has the acumen to lure capable people to work for him. He sees the development of entrepreneurial professionals a key priority for ensuring the continual success of his group of companies. Whether it is dealing with businesses or people, highly successful business tycoons like Mr Robert Kuok and Mr Kwek Leng Beng have been able to make full use of every available opportunity to enlarge their businesses.

Taking On More Than One Can Chew

This strategy also underlines another interesting point which is not to take on more than one can chew. Going after small opportunities may not be a bad business proposition. For example, one can expand steadily by acquiring smaller companies which can provide the synergy. The risks are lower and the certainty of success higher. In the same way, it is more prudent to pursue related businesses than to over-diversify. In the case of Mr Kwek Leng Beng, he made full use of his background and expertise in real estate to expand into the hotel business in 1989. Since then, he has remained very focused on expanding the hotel business.

A company can expand by borrowing, using internal funds, or by using a combination of both. Leveraging through bank borrowing may provide quicker growth. However, this entails higher risks as interests and bank loans must be repaid regardless of the level of earnings. The use of internal funds is a slower but steadier way to grow, entailing fewer risks as there are no compulsory financial obligations to be met. A company will need to find the right balance between these two means of financing so as to not over-extend itself.

An example of the high risks of over-leveraging is the case of Renong Berhad of Malaysia. For a number of years, it had borrowed heavily to finance its projects. These included projects like the North-South Highway, the RM3.3 billion Putra Light Rail project and the RM10.4 billion township project in Johore. While growth prospects continued to look good, Renong was able to maintain its stance. However, with the depreciation of the Malaysian ringgit and the stock market crash in July 1997, Renong Berhad was saddled with heavy debts which required a bailout. This happened on 17 November 1997 when United Engineers (M) Berhad (UEM), an associate company of Renong, paid a massive RM2.388 billion (S$1.13 billion) for a 32.6% stake in Renong.

Unfortunately, the move was not well-received by the stock market and the investing public. Analysts held the view that the bailout by UEM would not solve Renong's massive debt problem, but would instead worsen the debt servicing capability of UEM. Renong was not the only company trapped by taking on more than it could chew. Problems created by over-leveraged companies in Thailand sparked off the July 1997 currency turmoil in Asia. By end January 1998, recovery was still not in sight. The contagion spread to other countries in Asia such as Korea and Japan. Analysts and political leaders forecasted that the weak economic and business conditions of the ASEAN countries would persist for a further two to three years.

It is prudent to not attack too many markets at the same time. Rather, one should pursue markets with greater potential for success, those familiar to the company or where market conditions are similar to those of the home country. This strategy advocates that when in doubt, a more cautious and conservative approach is desired.

OPPORTUNITIES ARE NOT LIMITED BY SITUATIONS

As in Strategies 7 to 11, "Stealing a goat along the way" is an opportunistic one. This strategy relies on one's ability to seize opportunities and is not limited to particular situations. Opportunities may present themselves even in a crisis. Interestingly, the Chinese characters for *crisis* (危 机) consist of two words, namely, *dangers* or *risks* (危 险) and *opportunities* (机 会). The Chinese clearly acknowledge that embedded in any crisis there are both dangers and opportunities. The outcome depends on one's perspective.

If one is concerned only with the danger, then one is likely to see only the problems and respond reactively. If one is able to confront the crisis with the optimism to spot opportunities, one is likely to emerge a winner. Any crisis involves the need to manage and implement changes. This is where the opportunities lie. Leadership ability is often tested in times of crisis, hence the Chinese saying that heroes are borne out of crises (时 势 造 英 雄).

TRAFFIC MANAGEMENT IN SINGAPORE

The Singapore government is probably one of the most creative in its approach to developing policies for the benefit of the country and the people. One of the most innovative and unique public policies has to be its handling of the traffic problem. Unlike other Asian cities where traffic congestion and pollution are worsening, roads in Singapore have been spared the congestion and pollution because of the very proactive, and at times, tough policies adopted. These policies were also designed to generate revenue that can then be channelled to other uses in the development of Singapore.

To purchase a car in Singapore, potential owners must first bid for a Certificate of Entitlement (COE). This COE has a lifespan of only ten years, after which the car owner has to bid for another one. Prices of COEs are determined by bidders, therefore, the public has little ground to complain when COE prices increase. The COE system has become a very creative way of taxing those who can afford to own cars. It costs very little to the government but has generated hundreds of millions in revenue each year. Besides managing traffic congestion, the COE system allows the government to "steal a goat along the way" by raising government revenue.

The Singapore government used other creative ways to curb the car population such as heavy import duties and limiting the number of COEs issued. In addition, it imposes charges on cars entering the central business district during peak hours and on heavily used highways. With the electronic road pricing scheme, Singapore has become the first country with a comprehensive mechanism for controlling the number of cars on the road.

The Singapore government is not against the ownership of cars but is discouraging car owners from excessive road usage. It has concurrently developed a very comprehensive and affordable public transport system — buses, taxis, and a Mass Rapid Transit (MRT) system. Those who persist in car ownership and usage will have to pay for it.

打 草 惊 蛇

H I T T I N G T H E G R A S S T O S T A R T L E T H E S N A K E

疑 以 叩 实, 察 而 后 动; 复 者, 阴 之 媒 也。

E X P L A N A T I O N

An attempt should be made to clarify suspicious circumstances before making the next move (疑 以 叩 实, 察 而 后 动). To repeatedly probe and investigate a suspicious matter is the best way to discover the enemy's plot (复 者, 阴 之 媒 也。). This is in accordance with *Yi Jing's* "Fu" (meaning "repeat") Theory ([易 经: 复] 卦: 反 复 其 道, 七 日 来 复。复 小 而 辨 于 物).

H I S T O R I C A L B A C K G R O U N D

The title of the strategy "Hitting the grass to startle the snake" (打 草 惊 蛇) comes from an episode mentioned in *You Yang Za Zu* (酉 阳 杂 俎) about a corrupt official named Wang Lu (王 鲁) of the Tang Dynasty (唐 朝). One day, Wang received a letter of complaint from a resident under his jurisdiction about his corrupt accountant (主 簿). Wang was troubled by the complaint as he was worried that his own corruption would be exposed one day. He scribbled these words on the letter: "When you hit the grass, you startled the snake that is hiding in it." (汝 虽 打 草, 吾 已 惊 蛇).

Subsequently, the phrase was modified to bear a slightly different meaning, that is, that one should assess the enemy's situation before making the next move (观 彼 动 静 而 后 举 焉). These two stories illustrate this strategy.

S T O R Y 1

Once there lived a very intelligent 15-year-old orphan. After his parents' death, he stayed with his uncle. One day, he noticed that his uncle was unhappy and asked him what was bothering him. His uncle told him that he was worried because he had no son. He had wanted to take in a concubine to bear him a male heir but his wife did not approve. The boy thought for a while and said, "Uncle, do not worry. I think I can convince my aunt."

"There is nothing you can do," the uncle sadly said. Although the uncle knew his nephew was smart, he could not believe the boy could get his wife to agree to the idea. Early next morning, the boy took a tailor's ruler and started measuring the ground in front of his uncle's house. He deliberately acted in a pompous way so as to invoke his aunt's curiosity.

"What do you think you are doing?" asked the aunt. "I am surveying the property," the boy said coolly and continued what he was doing. "What? Surveying? What has our land got to do with you?" shouted his aunt. The boy stood up, cleaned his hands on his pants, and said confidently, "Aunt, I am only making preparations for myself. You and uncle are no longer young and do not have a son. If you two were to pass away, I would inherit this house. I am now surveying the house as I intend to renovate it when the time comes."

When his aunt heard this, she was furious. Saying not another word, she rushed back to her room, woke up her sleeping husband and coaxed him to take a concubine as soon as possible.

STORY 2

Near the end of the Wei era (北魏末年), around 523 AD, the soldiers in the state of Wo Ye[1] (沃野鎮) could no longer bear the torturous behaviour of their generals and staged a rebellion under the leadership of Po Liu Han Bo Ling (破六韓拔陵).

In the subsequent year, the rebellion sarmy met the Wei army at Wu Yuan or the "Five Plains". The Wei army captured a small hill while the rebellion army was trapped in the plains. Han Bo Ling knew that their position was precarious but he was aware he should understand the enemy's position before planning his next move. Therefore, he sent a spy to investigate the enemy's position from the back of the hill. The spy was to send an arrow into the sky if he came across any Wei army. Later, the spy shot two arrows into the sky — one to the left and one to the right. Han Bo Ling understood then

---

[1] *This is a place in Mongolia (內蒙五原北).*

that the Wei army had been pretending to be fighting from the top of the hill. In actual fact, it was a bait for trapping the rebellion army. Their real forces were divided into two, one on the left, the other on the right at the back of the hills.

Han Bo Ling then divided his army into three troops. Two troops were to go around the hill to launch an ambush on the two enemy troops hidden behind the hill. The last troop led by him pretended to retreat. When the Wei army saw the retreating troop, they dashed down the hill. At this moment, Han Bo Ling ordered his army to split into two groups stationed at the left and right of the path and trapped the oncoming Wei army like a fly in a pocket. In the meantime, the other two rebellion army troops had caught the Wei army by surprise. Han Bo Ling and his army won the battle.

Later in the year, the two forces met again at Bai Dao (白 道), a grassland which provided good camouflage. Han Bo Ling suspected something was amiss and looked at the grass on the two sides of the Wei army. He then realised that birds were flying above the bushes on the right side of the path. Han Bo Ling therefore divided his army into two teams with each team containing two troops of soldiers. They then attacked the Wei army from two directions like two huge pincers. As expected, the Wei troop hidden in the bushes on the right of the path was startled and the soldiers decided to run for their lives. The Wei troop on the path was surprised by the sudden change of circumstances and in the ensuing confusion, Han Bo Ling and his men won another battle.

COMMENTS & APPLICATIONS

When unsure of the enemy's situation, one should not rush into any decision. Instead, one should gather as much information about the enemy as possible and launch an attack only when certain of the enemy's position. The best way to catch a snake is to startle it by beating the bushes around it, and catching it when it appears rather than trying to ambush its nest which is often well camouflaged and difficult to locate. In Story 1, the little boy deliberately startled the snake (his aunt) to turn the situation to his uncle's advantage. In Story 2, Han Bo Ling won his battles after careful calculation of the enemy's situation.

FORCING ACTIONS INTO THE OPEN

In business as in war, it is at times necessary to "provoke" actions. The following are some examples:

1   The use of marketing and advertising gimmicks to provoke consumers into action. A marketer may use advertising themes to hasten responses to his sales: "Sale, 50% off, while stocks last!", "30% discount store-wide, 3 days only", "Special offers for the first 100 customers only". Many marketing ploys, especially those with a time-limit, often excite the consumers into making quick decisions. This is consistent with the strategy related in Story 1. By advertising sales, the marketer can determine whether the consumers are interested, and whether competitors are likely to join in. It gives the marketer a good gauge of the situation, especially during periods when sales are moving slowly.

2   Making strong opening bids at open tenders or auctions to "fish out" serious competitors and to assess other bidders' intentions. This approach is used by serious buyers at art and antique auctions in Asia.

3   Making a competitive bid to purchase another company to determine whether or not they intend to sell. Such a strategy will signal the sincerity of the offer and squeeze out other contenders. It aims to provoke the target to respond or react without alarming contenders.

4   Purchasing another company's shares to alert it of a possible takeover. The objective is twofold — to test the reaction of the company to be acquired and to determine whether there are other serious contenders. When DBS Land of Singapore bought a sizeable amount of shares in Parkway Holdings in early 1997, it was "hitting the grass to startle the snake". The intention was to determine whether it was the right moment for DBS Land to acquire a controlling stake in Parkway Holdings. Similarly, when Mr Li Ka-shing bought a 3% stake in Hong Kong Land and Jardine Matheson in August 1997, he was testing the market to see if they would try to stop him from buying into Hong Kong Land. Nine years ago, the owners resisted the takeover, and bought Li Ka-shing's shares at a substantial price premium.

"Startling the snake" into the open makes it easier to catch. Probing in the dark may prove more difficult and more dangerous.

Beware of Boomerang Effects

"Hitting the grass to startle the snake" is an offensive strategy. The person who hits the grass is in the best position to capture the snake. He must be ready and equipped with the resources, or it may backfire with boomerang effects. An example of this is how the currency crisis which began in July 1997 hit the ASEAN countries. The political leadership of Malaysia blamed George Soros and the overseas fund managers of being responsible for the attacks on the Malaysian ringgit. Unfortunately, this move drew attention to the weakness of the ringgit and the Malaysian economy. In the weeks that followed, the Malaysian ringgit fell to a historic low of 2.743 to the US dollar and 1.855 to the Singapore dollar on 11 August 1997.

By January 1998, the Malaysian ringgit fell to about 4.5 to the US dollar and almost 2.6 to the Singapore dollar. International investors decided to reevaluate the Malaysian ringgit. Overseas funds were no longer invested in Malaysia and in early August 1997 there was a fall in the Kuala Lumpur stock exchange. By the end of December, 50% of the nations' wealth was wiped out as a result of the falling stock market. To make matters worse, the central bank of Malaysia, Bank Negara, decided not to intervene as they had already incurred heavy losses propping up the value of the ringgit.

The Malaysian government failed to catch the snake it had startled after hitting the grass, and the snake began creating havoc. Hitting out at currency speculators and opportunists created more problems for the Malaysian government. Fund managers decided to withdraw investments and this caused further declines and instability to both the currency and the stock markets. Towards the end of 1997 and early 1998, the Malaysian policy-makers finally realised it was impossible to fight against the market.

When the Thai baht was floated on 2 July 1997, the intention was to boost export competitiveness of the Thai economy. Instead, the floating of the baht exposed the vulnerability of the currency and the economy. The consequences faced by Thailand far surpassed the problems encountered by the Malaysian government. The Thai baht depreciated by about 20% within a month. The damage was so substantial that on 11 August 1997, under the leadership of the International Monetary Fund (IMF), a rescue package of more than US$16 billion was announced to rescue the Thai economy.

One should therefore be very careful in hitting the grass – there may be more than one snake hidden in the grass. Unless one is ready to capture the snakes, it would be better to not hit the grass.

BEWARE OF UNINTENDED EFFECTS

The success of "hitting the grass to startle the snake" depends on how well one understands the sensitivity of the target. If the target does not respond as anticipated, the appropriate measures may not be successfully executed. Despite calls to "internationalise" the Singapore dollar, the Singapore government has repeatedly refused to do so. This is because it is very difficult to foresee the consequences. Despite complaints about the increasing strength of the Singapore dollar, the Monetary Authority of Singapore has remained firm in its policy of non-intervention. Such a tough and firm policy pays off. For example, during the currency crisis faced by several ASEAN economies in July/August 1997, the Singapore dollar was the least affected. While it depreciated against the US dollar, it appreciated against other regional currencies.

Unless there is concrete information yielding sufficient reasons, one should not startle the snake unnecessarily. Examples of not disrupting a successful formula abound. The decision by Coca-cola to replace the old coke with a new one more than ten years ago really startled the die-hard coke drinkers. Coca-cola had to reintroduce the old coke as Classic Coke to calm angry consumers.

When Mr Heng Chiang Meng, President of the Real Estate Developers Association of Singapore (REDAS) commented in August 1997 that the Singapore property market was on the verge of a collapse if nothing was done to control land sales, he was met with an unexpected response. Instead of lending their support, many developers, especially the smaller ones, were upset by his remarks. Some of his management committee members openly disagreed with him. In addition, members of the public felt strongly that downward price correction for the property market was long overdue.

Mr Heng made the same call again in mid-November 1997. This time his comments were taken seriously. The Singapore government responded swiftly announcing it would remove some of the anti-speculation measures imposed since May 1996. The circumstances in mid-November 1997 underlying the government's decision had changed. The regional currency turmoil and stock market crisis had yet to be resolved and had begun to affect the economy. The property market softened, and there were concerns that if nothing was done to prevent further decline of prices, the impact on the stock market and the banks would be significant. It became more important to protect home owners who formed 90% of the population than the small number of potential home buyers.

While Mr Heng's remarks could have incurred the wrath of potential home buyers, it was well worth it in light of the response from the government. The whole episode illustrated how difficult it is to predict the outcome once a person attempts to "hit the grass to startle the snake." Initially, Mr Heng did not get what he wanted. He was bitten by not one but many snakes! But finally, he managed to get the results he desired.

There were several reasons for the emotive outbursts against Mr Heng's remarks. Many developers had been holding on to their prices fairly well in the face of over-supply and anti-speculation measures imposed by the government. While the number of units sold had been declining since May 1996, there were signs that the volume of transactions was about to increase. Mr Heng's remarks were perceived as undermining all their previous efforts to prevent the fall.

Consumers felt that there was no reason for the big developers to call for government help when things were turning against them. Potential property buyers had been at the mercy of the developers for a number of years. They saw the property glut and the anti-government measures as signs of respite finally enabling them to buy their dream homes. Mr Heng's remarks were viewed as an attempt to enrich the big developers.

Mr Heng "hit the grass" but in this case "startled many snakes". His comments were the subject of several editorials in local newspapers, not all on his side. During a closed-door meeting on 11 August 1997, REDAS openly supported Mr Heng's position as President of the Association. This was done to counter rumours that he had offered to resign. REDAS stated that Mr Heng's comments in his letter to the Minister of National Development were not intended to be made public. Whether such efforts can appease the parties concerned can only be determined over time.

借尸还魂

BORROWING A CORPSE
TO RESURRECT A SOUL

有用者, 不可借; 不能用者, 求借.
借不能用者而用之, 匪我求童蒙, 童蒙求我.

EXPLANATION

A person that is of use may be more difficult to take advantage of (有用者, 不可借). A less useful (or weaker) person may request our assistance (不能用者, 求借). When I am able to use the weak one to my advantage, I am giving him my strength at his request (不能用者而用之, 匪我求童蒙, 童蒙求我). The phrase "童蒙" comes from *Yi Jing's* "Meng" Theory ([易经：蒙] 卦) which says that a child is weak and ignorant and needs the assistance of a teacher to become strong (喻童子弱昧, 必依附先生以强立).

HISTORICAL BACKGROUND

The phrase "Borrowing a corpse to resurrect a soul" comes from the Chinese belief that the dead can be reincarnated in another form. In the military sense, it is often used to describe a person who takes advantage of every circumstance to achieve his goal. This strategy was originally intended for offensive purposes.

The name of this strategy originated from a Chinese fairy tale described in *Yuan Qu Xuan* (元曲选：岳伯川 [铁拐李] 四) in Story 1. It has also been applied as a military strategy as in Story 2.

STORY 1

Among the well-known eight deities (八仙) in Chinese mythology, there is one called Iron-crutch Li (铁拐李). It was said that he used to be a handsome young man named Li Xuan (李玄), a daydreamer. As he was very interested in pursuing the way of the deities, the Old Deity Tai Shang (太 上 老 君) accepted him as his disciple.

One day, Li Xuan wanted to go to the Mountain of Hua (华 山) to meet the Old Deity Tai Shang. Before Li Xuan left, he told his disciple, "My spirit will be leaving my body to travel with the Old Deity. I will leave my body here and you are to guard it for seven days. If I do not return after seven days, then I have become a deity and you can cremate my body." So saying, Li Xuan sat down and meditated and his soul left his body.

His disciple sat by his body day and night without leaving it unattended for a second. When the sixth day arrived, a family member of Li Xuan's disciple came to visit him and urged him to return home as his mother was critically ill. When he heard of his mother's condition, the disciple cried out, "My mother is very sick. However, my master has not returned. If I go home now, who is to look after my master's body? But if I do not go home, my mother will not die in peace." His family member persuaded him that his mother was more important than his master. They reasoned with him that since his master had been away for six days, his organs would have decayed. It would be impossible for Li Xuan to return. So, they cremated Li Xuan's body and rushed home.

On the seventh day, Li Xuan's spirit came back but he could not find his body. His spirit could only wander around. One day, he spotted a beggar's corpse lying by the road side and remembered what his teacher told him before they parted. Resigning himself to the will of heaven, he went into the beggar's corpse. He thus became a lame beggar who had to use an iron crutch to get around.

Story 2

Qin Shi Huang (秦 始 皇) was one of the most ruthless rulers of China. During his era, the people suffered much and he was much hated. When he died, his second son, Hu Hai (胡 玄) usurped his elder brother, Fu Su's (扶 苏) position and succeeded him. Fu Su was a kind-hearted man and had often tried to persuade his father to be more magnanimous. The late Qin Shi Huang, prejudiced against him, had sent him to the borders. He was later secretly assassinated by his younger brother. However, the people did not know about his death and all of them hoped that one day Fu Su would rule. At that time, there lived a popular Chu warrior (楚国将领) named Xiang Yan (项 燕). After the fall of Chu, rumours had it that he had escaped to Jiang Huai (江 淮).

In 209 BC, two men named Chen Sheng (陈 胜) and Wu Guang (吴 广) were among nine hundred men being sent to the borders. On their way, they took shelter in an old temple from a heavy storm which lasted a few days.

At that time, there was a law stating those who had been sent to the borders must reach the destination by a certain date or they would face death by execution. Chen Shen and Wu Guang knew that they would not reach their destination before then and were very worried. Chen Sheng came up with a plan, "It is unlikely that we can leave this place alive. Why don't we stage a rebellion and try to fight our way out? Of course we need to plan our move properly. Judging from today's situation, the people have long suffered under the rule of Qin Shi Huang. If we are able to use the names of Fu Su and Xiang Yan to stage a revolution, we might be able to win the confidence of the people."

They killed the guards who were escorting them and convinced the rest of the nine hundred that that was the only way out of the situation. Chen Sheng and Wu Guang made themselves generals and fought under the names of Fu Su and Xiang Yan. The army killed notorious government officials and managed to win the trust of the commoners. Their acts provoked the sentiments of the officials who used to serve under the six nations before they were conquered by Qin Shi Huang. Eventually, the Qin Dynasty was overthrown.

COMMENTS & APPLICATIONS

This strategy advocates using other means to achieve one's purpose. It has some similarities with Strategy 3, "Kill another with a borrowed knife," (借 刀 杀 人) and Strategy 24, "Borrow a passage to attack Guo" (假 途 伐 虢). The difference is that Strategy 14 is used when one is in a desperate situation and facing danger. In these circumstances, a smart person grasps any opportunity and persuades others to help him survive. Chen Sheng brilliantly used the names of legends to stir the people's sentiments to achieve his goal. Strategy

3 is used more proactively by exploiting another party to one's advantage. Strategy 24 attempts to leverage the assistance of another party to achieve one's goals. In Strategy 24, however, the strategist would have to do the job himself.

OPERATING UNDER THE UMBRELLA OF OTHERS

A company may face severe business difficulties in marketing its products overseas without an international distribution network. It can give itself a new lease of life by manufacturing products under brand of an established company. Many Japanese companies did this in their early years of development after World War II. The Japanese manufacturers consciously and deliberately sought the help of Western manufacturers. They made and marketed countless products under Western brand names. It was only in the 1960s and 1970s that these Japanese manufacturers began to establish their own brands.

The Japanese strategy has been copied by several Asian economies in desperate economic situations. Singapore is an excellent example. When the British forces decided to pull out of the island state in the 1960s, and with the separation of Singapore from Malaysia in 1965, Singapore was in a very precarious state. It literally had to "borrow another's corpse" to survive, relentlessly persuading multinational corporations to invest in Singapore. It offered investment incentives and strived to provide a conducive business environment. These MNCs not only created much-needed jobs, they also enabled the transfer of technology and management skills. More importantly, they helped Singapore to survive by exporting the manufactured products back to the developed economies.

GOING OVERSEAS

A company faced with limited growth at home can attempt to enter foreign markets. Many Singaporean companies are doing so today. Faced with limited growth at home, and threatened by regional competitors, these companies continue to grow by investing in other countries. The Singapore government has been instrumental in the overseas drive, building industrial parks in Suzhou and Wuxi in China and Bangladore in India. To maintain high standard of living, Singapore has to depend on the prosperity of its Asian neighbours.

The strategy used by the Singapore government is not new. Many developed countries such as the United States and Japan have made heavy overseas investments for years. These investments not only help generate earnings but allow continued growth and expansion. Large corporations such as Motorola, Allied Signals, IBM and Hewlett Packard have been given a new lease of life by investing in Asia at a time when the economic growth and business opportunities in the US have slowed.

Take the case of tertiary education in the United Kingdom (UK) and Australia. The UK was an economic and political superpower at the turn of the century with many colonies around the world. In those days, the brightest and smartest children from any of the Commonwealth countries aspired to win scholarships to study at top universities in the UK. Australia enjoyed a similar status with a well-developed tertiary education system. Most of the top civil servants and bureaucrats of many former Commonwealth colonies were trained in the UK and Australia.

This reputation has changed in recent years. Due to the slowing down of their economies and severe funding cuts, many universities were forced to look for alternative sources of funding. This coincided with the demand for tertiary education in many Asian countries as a result of economic boom, giving many ailing UK and Australian universities an opportunity to use the "borrow a corpse to resurrect a soul" strategy.

Many UK and Australian universities began to export distant-learning programmes to Malaysia, Hong Kong and Singapore, as alternative sources of revenue. These universities have also increased their efforts to attract Asian students. There are currently over 30 UK and Australian universities offering a full range of courses from undergraduate to doctoral programmes.

EXTENDING PRODUCT LIFE CYCLE

Another business practice that involves the this strategy concerns the extension of a product life cycle. While it is true that most products go through the four stages of introduction, growth, maturity and decline, a marketer will attempt to extend the life cycle whenever possible. This can be done, for instance, by product improvement, product differentiation or finding new markets.

Colgate has been in existence for many years. One of its reasons for success is its ability to constantly improve the product as well as its packaging. Each time an improvement is made, the product life cycle is extended again. Over the years Colgate has introduced flavours of toothpaste, added ingredients and altered its packaging.

The search for new markets is another approach used by marketers to extend a product's life as the product's life cycle differs from country to country. For example, a product in decline in Singapore (for example, a 486 personal computer) may be at the introduction stage in countries such as China, Vietnam, Cambodia and Myanmar where there are ready markets. By exporting the "obsolete" models, the product is allowed to live again.

The demand for a product may be declining in one market, but just picking up in another. The job of the marketer is to identify such markets and to exploit the opportunities accordingly.

SELL-OUTS, MERGERS AND ACQUISITIONS

Another form of "borrowing a corpse to resurrect a soul" involves selling the company to give it a new lease of life. In business, companies which buy out other companies attract positive attention. Those who seek to sell-out are paid little attention as they are seen as losers. By selling out to a stronger and bigger company, the company may gain an extension on its lifespan. Apple's partial sell-out to Microsoft Corporation, gave it a new lease of life as Microsoft would help develop new software for them.

Mergers may also give companies a new lease of life. For example, the US$16.3 billion takeover of McDonnell Douglas by Boeing in mid-1997 has given the US aviation industry a major boost in the Chinese and other Asian markets. The American company had previously faced very stiff competition from the European conglomerate Airbus Industrie and had lost several billion dollars' worth of contracts in China to Airbus.

In the pharmaceutical industry, too, there is a trend towards mergers as a means of consolidating, and minimising competition. By joining forces, pharmaceutical companies hope to achieve economies of scale in research and development, purchasing, manufacturing and marketing. Savings generated by mergers can be as high as 25% of operating costs. To reap these savings, the American company SmithKline Beckman merged with Britain's Beecham Group Plc in 1989 to form SmithKline Beecham Plc. Similarly, Glaxo Holdings Plc took over the Wellcome Group in 1995 to form Glaxo Wellcome Plc. In February 1998, these two British rivals announced that they would merge. Had this merger been successful, it would have created a company with a market capitalisation of more than US$160 billion and annual sales of more than US$27 billion. However, negotiations were unsuccessful.

The equally competitive information technology industry is undergoing similar situations. In February 1998, Compaq announced that it would acquire Digital Equipment for US$9.6 billion. The move was aimed to broaden Compaq's product line to include Digital's high-speed Unix computers and workstations. This move also complemented Compaq's 1997 acquisition of Tandem in that it helped to strengthen Compaq's capabilities in providing IT solutions. At the same time, Digital's close association with Microsoft is an added advantage to Compaq. The acquisition will enable Compaq to compete more effectively with the other two giants — IBM and Hewlett Packard.

The acquisition of American President Line (APL) by Singapore's Neptune Orient Lines (NOL) has propelled the new company to become the world's fifth largest container ship carrier in terms of sales. The US$825 million purchase by NOL gives it stronger bargaining power in negotiating for berth rates and port facilities. It also yields good economies of scale, freight rates and reduced operation costs, helping NOL become a truly global player.

With excess capacity and falling freight rates, the shipping business has become very competitive. Companies therefore may consider merger as a way to ensure survival against intense competition.

When Renong Berhad of Malaysia sold its 32.6% stake to United Engineers (M) Berhad (UEM) for RM2.388 billion (S$1.13 billion), it was similarly seeking an extension of its lifespan. Companies may also merge for greater synergy such as the one between the Development Bank of Singapore and the Post Office Savings Bank, two of the largest banks in Singapore. When the merger is fully completed at the end of 1998, it will be the giant of the banking industry in Singapore, and will rank as the 65th largest bank in the world. The benefits generated are likely to be significant.

STRATEGY 15

调虎离山

LURING A TIGER FROM ITS LAIR IN THE MOUNTAIN

待天以困之，用人以诱之。往蹇来返。

EXPLANATION

Trap the enemy when the natural elements are to his disadvantage (待天以困之). Then create false impressions to lure him out (用人以诱之). A direct attack may prove dangerous. It is far better to lure the enemy out of his comfort and destroy him (往蹇来返). The phrase "往蹇来返" comes from *Yi Jing's* "Jian" Theory ([易经：蹇]卦：蹇者，难也，险在前也，见险而能止，知矣哉).

HISTORICAL BACKGROUND

This phrase has also been used in Chinese classics such as "Journey to the West" ([西游记]第七十六回有："...正中了我的'调虎离山'之计"). The following reflects the use of this strategy.

Towards the end of the Zhou Dynasty, Duke Zheng Wu Gong (郑武公) married his subordinate's daughter. His wife, Madam Jiang (姜氏) bore him two sons. The elder was named Wu Sheng (寤生) and the younger Duan (段). Wu Sheng was born while the mother was asleep and she hated him. Duan, the more handsome of the two, was her favourite.

Madam Jiang always tried to create discord between her husband and Wu Sheng, hoping that the ruler would change his mind and make his second son successor to his throne. But Zheng Wu Gong said, "There must be an order of seniority. The elder shall succeed. Moreover, Wu Sheng has done nothing wrong and it would be unfair to not make him the successor." Thus, he insisted that Wu Sheng should

*succeed him, and gave a small city, the city of Gong (共城),
to his second son.*

*When Zheng Wu Gong died, Wu Sheng succeeded him. He
was named Zheng Zhuang Gong (郑庄公) and became
the Duke. Madam Jiang, who was made the Grand Lady,
was very unhappy to see her favourite son given only a small
town to rule. She expressed her dissatisfaction to her elder
son, "You have succeeded your father's position but how
can you bear to see your own blood brother stuck in a small
city?" Zheng Zhuang Gong asked, " So mother, what are
your views?"*

*The mother replied, "Needless to say, you should give him a
big city such as Zhi Yi (制邑)." On hearing her reply, Zheng
Zhuang Gong responded, "But Zhi Yi is a very important
and strategic territory. My late father has ordered me not to
assign the town to anybody. Other than Zhi Yi, any place
will be fine."*

*"Then cede the City of Jing (京城) to your brother," said
the mother. Zheng Zhuang Gong's silence provoked Madam
Jiang. In her fury she said, "If you still disagree, then drive
your brother out of the country. This will be better for you."*

*"I wouldn't dare, Mother," Zheng Zhuang Gong said
apologetically, "I will carry out your wish." The next day,
Zheng Zhuang Gong announced that he would cede the City
of Jing to Duan. One of his loyal subjects, Zhai Zu (祭足),
said, "My Lord, you cannot do this. Just as there cannot be
two suns in the sky, no country can have two rulers at one
time. The City of Jing is a very important place. It is centrally
located and densely populated. Its political and military value
are comparable to that of the capital. Furthermore, Duan is
the Grand Lady's favourite son. If you allow him to rule a
big city, it might be seen that there are two rulers and the
consequences may be drastic."*

*Zheng Zhuang Gong said, "You need not say any more.
This is the Grand Lady's order." Before Duan left for his
new post, he went to the palace to bid his mother goodbye.
Madam Jiang pulled him aside and said, "Your brother has
ceded the City of Jing reluctantly. He may change his mind.
Be prepared. Once you reach the City of Jing, train your
army and be on your guard. I will help you from the palace.
My objective is to overthrow Zheng Zhuang Gong."*

When Duan took up his position, the commanders of the northern and western border territories came to congratulate him. Duan told them, "The areas under your command are part of the land ceded to me. Therefore, in future, all taxes collected from your territories must be handed to me. In addition, your armies are to come under my command!"

The two commanders were aware that Duan was the Grand Lady's favourite and that he might one day succeed the throne so they meekly submitted. From then, Duan worked hard to train his army to increase his military strength. At the same time, he expanded his influence over neighbouring territories. This was reported to Zheng Zhuang Gong at an early court meeting but he said nothing. One of his subordinates present during the meeting shouted, "Duan must be killed."

Zheng Zhuang Gong looked down and saw that it was Gong Zi Lu (公子呂), a high ranking official, who made this comment. Zheng Zhuang Gong then asked, "What are your suggestions?" Gong Zi Lu said, "It has been the tradition that those conferred land are not to hold military power. However, Duan has support both from the palace, that is, from the Grand Lady, and outside the palace from his own army which is growing stronger each day. His intention is clear — to seize your throne when the opportunity arises. Please give me permission to eliminate him now to prevent future disaster."

"But Duan has not shown any sign of rebellion!" Zheng Zhuang Gong answered. Gong Zi Lu said angrily, "He has the northern and western territories under his rule. He also collects taxes which rightfully belong to the government. Are these not signs of rebellion? How can we let him control state land?"

Zheng Zhuang Gong smiled and said, "Duan is my mother's favourite son and he is also my brother. I would rather lose a few pieces of land than hurt our relationship." Gong Zi Lu said, "I am not afraid of losing a few pieces of land, but I am worried that we may end up losing our country as well. Our people are speculating to see who will win. If we ignore him, we may have to pay for our tardiness. My Lord is gracious enough to accommodate Duan now, but Duan may not be able to accommodate my Lord in the future."

"That is enough!" Zheng Zhuang Gong retorted. "I will try to win him over!" He then adjourned the meeting and left

the court room. As Gong Zi Lu walked out, he told Zhai Zu, "The Duke cares too much about personal ties and neglects to plan for the country. I am really worried."

Zhai Zu replied, "The Duke is a capable man who doubtless, sees your point. However, he must have felt it inappropriate to disclose his true feelings before the officials in court just now. If you went to see him in private, he may have things to tell you."

Gong Zi Lu took Zhai Zu's advice and had an audience with the Duke. The Duke the reason for his visit. Gong Zi Lu said, "I came to add to what I said this morning at court. When my Lord succeeded to the throne, everybody knew that it was against the Grand Lady's wishes. She wanted Duan to be Duke. Duan is now preparing his army and it is a clear sign that he intends to seize the throne. If he gets the support of the Grand Lady and starts a revolution, I am afraid your position will be threatened." Zheng Zhuang Gong said, "I am worried that my mother will not be happy if I take drastic action."

"My Lord, if you are not decisive now, you may regret it in the future." Zheng Zhuang Gong sighed and said, "I have thought about this problem over and again. Although Duan has intentions to overthrow me, he has not blatantly rebelled. If I take steps to control him now, my mother would be displeased and others may think me ruthless. I will feign ignorance of what Duan is doing and let him have his way. When he shows clear signs of rebellion, I will have ample proof of his treacherous intent."

Gong Zi Lu began to see the Duke's plan. He said, "My Lord is indeed far-sighted. However, I am only afraid that it would be very difficult to control Duan when his power becomes too strong in future. We should think of a plan to expose him of his evil desires before he becomes uncontrollable."

"What are your plans?" asked Zheng Zhuang Gong. Gong Zi Lu replied, "My Lord, you have not been to the imperial palace to see the Emperor for a long time as you are afraid that Duan might do something drastic. Why not set a trap for Duan by pretending that you are leaving for the imperial palace to have an audience with the Emperor. This will entice him to bring his troops here. I will lead a troop to hide outside

the city of Jing so that when he and his army leave the city, we will take control of his place. My Lord, you can then lead a troop back to your palace and he will have nowhere to flee to then."

"That is an excellent idea!" said Zheng Zhuang Gong. Next morning during the court meeting, Zheng Zhuang Gong pretended to issue an order making Zhai Zu temporarily in charge of matters in the country while he went away to see the Emperor of Zhou. Sure enough, Madam Jiang thought the opportunity had come and sent a messenger to instruct Duan to raise a rebellion then.

Unknown to her, Gong Ji Lu had arranged for someone to ambush and kill the messenger while the latter was on his way to see Duan. Madam Jiang's letter was brought to Zheng Zhuang Gong, who sent his own man disguised as Jiang's messenger to Duan. Zheng Zhuang Gong's man returned with Duan's reply that the rebellion would begin on the fifth of May. Madam Jiang would raise a white flag on the city gate as a signal to the rebels.

When Zheng Zhuang Gong heard this, he said happily, "Well, all the proof is here. I wonder what Duan has got to say to that!" He then went to the palace and bid his mother farewell before proceeding with great pomp to see the Emperor. At the same time, Gong Ji Lu had his troops established outside the city of Jing, waiting for the "tiger" (Duan) to leave the "mountain" (the city of Jing).

After receiving the secret message from his mother, Duan started preparations. He sent his son, Gong Sun Hua (公孙滑) to the state of Wei (卫国) to borrow troops and then mobilised his soldiers, commanding them to protect the capital while the Duke was away. When Duan and his troops left Jing, Gong Ji Lu captured the city. They then publicly denounced Duan's evil ambition.

Duan learnt of the bad news while on his way to the capital. He panicked and ordered an immediate return to the city of Jing. However, at this time, the soldiers' morale was very low and rumours spread that Duan intended to overthrow the Duke. The truth was that Gong Ji Lu had sent some spies to infiltrate the army spreading news about Duan's real intention of going to the capital. Half of Duan's troop left him overnight. Duan was horrified when he learnt this and fled with the remaining army to Yan Yi (鄢 邑), thinking that he could garner enough followers to stage a return later.

Nevertheless, Zheng Zhuang Gong had guessed Duan's intention and captured Yan Yi before Duan did. Finally, Duan had to retreat to the city of Gong, the small city given him by his late father. Zheng Zhuang Gong and Gong Ji Lu eventually advanced with their troops on the city. Realising there was escape, and that he could no longer face his brother, Duan took his own life.

After Duan's death, Zheng Zhuang Gong asked Zhai Zhu to send his mother the secret letters she and Duan had been exchanging. When she saw the letters, she was too embarrassed to face Zheng Zhuang Gong so she quietly left the palace.

COMMENTS & APPLICATIONS

To destroy the enemy, one sometimes has to lure him from his territory and exterminate him at his weakest. "Luring a tiger from its lair in the mountains" (调 虎 离 山) is based on the understanding that one way to catch a ferocious tiger is to lure it from its hideout in the mountains into the city where it is so helpless even a dog may bully it (虎 落 平 阳 被 犬 欺). It is an offensive strategy.

CHOOSING THE SITE OF NEGOTIATION

In negotiations, it is advantageous to be on "home ground". One way to neutralise such an advantage is to lure the other party from their home ground. For example, one can invite the other party to his home ground on the pretext of allowing them to know one's business better, and even offer to pay for expenses incurred.

Being away from home, the other party will be handicapped in several ways. Firstly, it is more difficult to access information and obtain assistance. Secondly, they will need time to adjust to the unfamiliar environment in the negotiation site. Thirdly, time is against the "visitor" as he may have a plane to catch and a schedule to meet. All these disadvantages increase the pressure and stress on the visiting party, making it easier for the home party to extract more concessions and advantages.

LURING IMPORTANT FOREIGN INVESTMENTS

In the realm of international business, many countries, especially those from the less developed world, seek out foreign investments important to their economic development. For example, many Asian countries are keen to encourage world-class multinational corporations (MNCs) to set up regional headquarters and research and development (R&D) facilities in their countries.

However, to lure the "tigers" from their mountain, incentives, investment guarantees and other supporting facilities are needed. In some Asian countries, laws protecting intellectual property and rights pertaining to inventions and innovations are weak. This tends to deter MNCs which are concerned with the protection of their intellectual property, but which are able to provide high-end investments, transfer of technology and management skills. Also, MNCs working on R&D face less pressure to shift operations overseas as their highly-wired business world allows researchers and scientists to work in the comfort of home. The provision of a high quality of life and enriching lifestyle have thus become important.

To attract these value-added industries and services, some Asian governments organise high-level business trips to call on the companies directly. In Malaysia, Prime Minister Dr Mahathir has become the country's number one marketer and promoter. In 1997, he made many trips abroad to solicit business investments, especially for the multimedia supercorridor (MSC). Several big computer-related companies, including Microsoft Corporation and Intel Corporation have agreed to invest in the MSC.

Leaders of the Singapore government, including top officials of the Economic Development Board have also been hitting the road to lure MNCs to Singapore. To a certain extent, Singapore's economic success has been due to its ability to "lure the tigers from their lairs in the mountains".

ATTRACTING FOREIGN TALENTS

The Singapore government is similarly good at attracting foreign professionals to settle in Singapore. This small nation state's largest stake for survival is its human resources. Singapore put in place generous policies aimed at attracting highly qualified foreigners to work and live here. On a per capita basis, it has a high ratio of foreign talents. These talents cover a wide spectrum of industries which contribute significantly to the economic development and prosperity of Singapore. A number of politicians, top civil servants and private sector corporate leaders in Singapore today were former citizens of other countries.

In an effort to continually attract foreign professionals, the government has embarked on ambitious plans to transform Singapore into a major cultural and entertainment centre. Thus, Bugis Junction and Marina Bay will become sites for staging shows, plays and other cultural events. The government also strives to improve the attractiveness of the city state, creating more parks and improving public transport. Their latest measures include providing housing for expatriate professionals at favourable rentals.

Singapore's success in attracting foreign talents has not gone unnoticed by other nations. Dr Mahathir of Malaysia, for example, has relaxed Malaysia's policy requiring foreign investors to hire a certain quota of local workers, in his efforts to build up the MSC. Malaysia too recognises the need to rely on foreign talents in order to develop its economy faster.

In Taiwan, the government attracted many scientists and researchers working in California's Silicon Valley to return to work in their Science Park. They were lured by attractive salaries and perks. In addition, many were allowed to bring their entire research teams. Not surprisingly, the R&D activities of Taiwan have risen substantially over the past ten years. In areas such as information technology, they are able to rival the best of the West. For example, not only has Acer Computer fast become a world class player, it has acquired Texas Instrument's notebook business. Acer had the R&D capabilities to compete in the highly volatile computer industry. Its acquisition of Texas Instruments signals its intent and competence to remain a major world class producer of computers.

STRATEGY 16

欲擒故纵

RELEASING THE ENEMY TO RECAPTURE HIM

逼则反兵; 走则减势。
紧随勿迫, 累其气力, 消其斗志,
散而后擒, 兵不血刃。需, 有孚, 光。

EXPLANATION

Sometimes, it is not advisable to drive the enemy into a corner as he may retaliate (逼则反兵). The objective is not to destroy him completely as there may be good reason to keep him alive. It it better to let the enemy escape and tire himself out (走则减势) while pursuing closely behind (紧随勿迫). The enemy will soon be exhausted (累其气力) and will lose his fighting spirit (消其斗志). The best time to capture him is when he has fallen apart (散而后擒), without bloodshed (兵不血刃). This is in accordance with *Yi Jing's* "Xu" (or "need") Theory ([易经:需]卦) – once the enemy is psychologically defeated and believes that he is not able to put up a fight, the battle will be easily won (需, 有孚, 光). In war, sheer physical dominance does not ensure victory. More important is the need to win the enemy's hearts. In this way, one can secure total surrender and loyalty.

HISTORICAL BACKGROUND

This strategy originates from Lao Zi's book ([老子本义:上篇将欲夺之, 必固与之). The strategy has also been mentioned in *Tai Ping Tian Guo* ([太平天国:文书]:欲擒先纵, 欲急姑缓, 待其懈而击之, 无不胜者). The phrase "欲擒姑纵" also means "欲擒故纵" that is, to catch the enemy by deliberately (故) letting him escape, so his guard will be down. This is similar to the theory of "keeping a long fishing line to catch the big fish" (放长线, 钓大鱼).

This strategy is best illustrated by the story of how the famous Shu (蜀) adviser Zhu Ge Liang (诸葛亮) managed to subdue Meng Huo (孟获) after releasing the latter seven times.

In 225 AD, Zhu Ge Liang planned to lead 500,000 soldiers to attack the tribal states in the south-central part of China. He knew that to capture the tribal states, he would first have to win the hearts of the tribal soldiers. The leader of the southern tribes was Meng Huo, a brave and popular warrior. When he heard that Zhu Ge Liang had launched an attack, Meng Huo personally led his soldiers to meet his enemy. Zhu Ge Liang's army was led by General Wang Ping (王平). When the two armies met, Wang Ping suddenly retreated and Meng Huo gave chase. After a twenty-odd mile chase, Zhu Ge Liang's generals, Zhang Yi (张巍) and Zhang Yik (张翼) ambushed from the left and right. The southern army was badly defeated. Meng Huo tried to fight his way out but was eventually trapped between the cliffs in front and Zhu Ge Liang's men behind. He was taken alive.

When the prisoners were led to Zhu Ge Liang's camp, their chains were removed and they were given food and wine and were then released. This touched the southern people. Zhu Ge Liang then had Meng Huo brought before him and asked him, "You are now my prisoner. Do you admit defeat?" Meng Huo replied, "I was captured because I was driven to a wild mountainous terrain. Why should I submit to you?" Zhu Ge Liang replied, "Since you do not submit to me, I will release you." Meng Huo quickly replied, "If you release me, I will pull my army together. If you defeat me a second time, I will submit to your superiority."

Meng Huo mustered a new army and sent two of his chieftains who had been captured and released by Zhu Ge Liang to launch an attack againt Zhu. Unfortunately, the chieftains failed again and Meng Huo was furious, thinking that they deliberately lost the battle to show their gratitude to Zhu Ge Liang. He therefore had the two chieftains flogged. The two men were very angry and decided to betray Meng Huo. One night, they led a hundred soldiers who had been released by Zhu Ge Liang before, captured the drunken Meng Huo and sent him to Zhu Ge Liang.

When Meng Huo was brought before Zhu Ge Liang, the latter smiled, "You have said that you would submit if I took you captive again. What now?" Meng Huo argued, "My capture this time was not due to your own abilities but to the fact that my people rebelled against me. Why should I submit to you?" Zhu Ge Liang said confidently, "Since this is what you believe, I shall release you once again." Meng Huo replied, "Although I am barbaric, I know Chinese war strategies as well. If you let me go, I will regather my men and have a good fight with you. I will only submit if I lose to you in the battleground."

Zhu Ge Liang loosed him from his fetters and treated him with fine food and wine. Meng Huo was then taken round Zhu Ge Liang's tents to study the strength of the army. That night, Zhu Ge Liang personally accompanied Meng Huo to the Lu River (泸 水), where Meng Huo was allowed to rejoin his troops.

A few days later, Meng Huo's brother, Meng You (孟 优), brought a hundred men and plenty of gold and ivory to Zhu Ge Liang's tents and said to him, "My brother Meng Huo wishes to express his gratitude for your benevolence. You spared his life and so he sent me with these gifts. Moreover, he has gone back to our old home, Yin Keng Shan (银 坑 山) to gather more gifts to be presented to the ruler of Shu (蜀)."

Zhu Ge Liang knew things were not as simple as they seemed. He treated his guests with fine food and wine. Unknown to You and his men, the drinks were drugged and they fell unconscious after the dinner. Meanwhile, Meng Huo divided his men into three troops and planned to ambush Zhu Ge Liang that evening. Meng Huo thought that he would be able to capture Zhu Ge Liang alive as the latter was not prepared for him and he had his brother as a spy. But Meng Huo fell into Zhu Ge Liang's trap and he was captured for the third time.

Zhu Ge Liang smilingly said, "I have captured you yet again. Will you submit now?" Meng Huo angrily replied, "I lost this time because my brother was greedy and thus spoilt my plan. Of course, I am still not convinced of your superiority." Zhu Ge Liang said, "Well, I will have you released yet another time. Please be more careful next time." He then released them all.

A few days later, Zhu Ge Liang led his army across the Lu River and set up three large tents. When Meng Huo saw this, he led 100,000 men to meet Zhu Ge Liang's army. Zhu

Ge Liang avoided an armed confrontation, since he wanted to dampen the opposing army's appetite for battle. Instead, he secretly had his generals, Zhao Yun (赵 云) and Wei Yan (魏 延) and their men lay a trap. He then faked a hasty withdrawal, leaving behind empty camps full of supplies. Meng Huo reasoned, "Something urgent must have caused Zhu Ge Liang to break camp so suddenly. Shu is probably under attack by Sun Quan (孙 权), ruler of Wu (吴), or by Cao Pi (曹 丕), Emperor of Wei (魏). I must not miss this opportunity." He eagerly ordered his army to give chase.

Unfortunately for Meng Huo, this was yet another trap designed by Zhu Ge Liang. When Meng Huo and his army reached the other side of the bank, they realised that Zhu Ge Liang had set up fresh camps nearby. Thinking that Zhu Ge Liang would pull out a few days later, Meng Huo sent his men to ford the river. Unknown to him, Zhu Ge Liang's generals, Zhao Yun and Wei Yan had secretly surrounded the southern army. One evening, Meng Huo suddenly realised that they were being attacked by Zhu Ge Liang's army from the camps. When he tried to retreat, he met Zhao Yun. The only escape route open to him led along the edge of a dense forest. Suddenly, he saw an escorted wagon where Zhu Ge Liang sat in solitary splendour. Meng Huo immediately ordered his men to take Zhu Ge Liang prisoner. As they ran towards the wagon, Meng Huo and his men fell into a ditch dug by Zhu Ge Liang's men earlier. Meng Huo and his brother Meng You were again taken prisoners.

Zhu Ge Liang first spoke to Meng You, "Your brother is a simple fool. You should talk some sense into him. This is the fourth time I have captured him. Does he feel no shame?" Meng You blushed with disgrace and begged for clemency. Zhu Ge Liang said, "I would have killed you if I had wanted you dead. I pardon you, but you must bring your brother to his senses." He then ordered Meng You's release. The latter thanked him tearfully and went on his way.

Meng Huo was then brought before Zhu Ge Liang who said angrily, "What have you got to say now?" Meng Huo replied, "Again, I have been a victim of your strategies. I am still not convinced that I am not your match!" Zhu Ge Liang ordered Meng Huo to be beheaded. Meng Huo showed not the slightest fear but turned to Zhu Ge Liang and said, "If you let me go again, I will avenge my fourth defeat." Zhu Ge Liang laughing, ordered Meng Huo's release.

When Meng Huo finally met up with his brother, they devised a plan to defeat Zhu Ge Liang. They knew that they were no match against Zhu Ge Liang so they decided to hide in the mountains. They believed that Zhu Ge Liang and his army would leave the south after sometime since they were not used to the humid and warm temperature there. Little did they realise that Zhu Ge Liang knew their hideout from some of the southern army who had defected to the Shu army.

While Meng Huo prepared for his attack against Zhu Ge Liang, he was visited by Yang Feng (杨 锋), the chieftain of a nearby gorge, and his five sons. Meng Huo held a feast for his guests. During the dinner, Yang Feng had sword dancers perform and had his sons to serve wine to Meng Huo and Meng You. As they were about to drink, Yang Feng's two sons grabbed Meng Huo and his brother. Meng Huo exclaimed, "We are friends! Why are you doing this?" Yang Feng replied, "My brothers, my sons and nephews joined your rebellion and were captured along with you by Zhu Ge Liang. But Zhu Ge Liang released them. We are grateful to Zhu Ge Liang for his mercy, but you remain ungrateful. I want to capture you to repay Premier Zhu's generosity."

Meng Huo was again brought before Zhu Ge Liang who asked, "Are you convinced now?" Meng Huo replied, "It was not your cleverness but treachery in my own ranks that put me in your hands. Kill me if you wish but I shall not yield! However, if you set me free again, I shall return to my hometown at Yin Keng Shan and fight you there. If you are able to catch me my descendants will bow to you forever." Zhu Ge Liang let Meng Huo off the fifth time.

When Meng Huo returned to Ying Keng Shan, he sought help from his allies and launched a few attacks on the Shu army. However, they failed repeatedly and eventually Yin Keng Shan was taken over by Zhu Ge Liang and his men. Meng Huo had no choice but to ask his brother-in-law to take him, his wife and hundreds of his men to Zhu Ge Liang, pretending that the brother-in-law had taken them to surrender to the latter.

When they reached Zhu Ge Liang's camp, Zhu Ge Liang suddenly ordered that Meng Huo and his followers be searched thoroughly. As expected, they found that Meng Huo and his men had daggers with them. Zhu Ge Liang asked Meng Huo, "Well, this time I captured you from your home Yin Keng Shan. What have you to say?" Meng Huo replied, "I turned myself in this time. You did not capture me with your own skill. I shall not submit!" Zhu Ge Liang asked, "I have captured you six times and you would still not surrender. How many times do you want me to capture you before you are convinced that you are not my match?" "Seven times! If you capture me a seventh time, I shall pledge my loyalty to you and never rebel again," replied Meng Huo. Zhu Ge Liang then had them released.

After his release, Meng Huo went to the chieftain of Ma Ge gorge (马 戈 涧) for help. The chieftain lent him 30,000 men. These soldiers were clad in a kind of armour woven from vines that had been soaked in oil for six months and dried, the process being repeated several times. Thus clad, the soldiers could swim rivers without getting wet and no blade was able to penetrate their armour. The Shu army was defeated several times because of this special armour. However, when Zhu Ge Liang learnt the constitution of this armour, he ordered his men to use burning torches to set the oil-soaked armour of the soldiers on fire. Meng Huo was captured yet again.

This time, Zhu Ge Liang did not speak to Meng Huo but ordered the latter's release. Meng Huo was then taken to another tent where he and his men were served with fine food and wine. During the meal, a messenger came and said to Meng Huo, "Premier Zhu Ge Liang finds it too embarrassing to come before you again. He has commissioned me to release you. He asks you to mobilise another army against him, if you can, and try once more to defeat him." This time Meng Huo began to weep and said, "I have been captured seven times and released seven times! This has never happened in history. If I still do not appreciate the Premier's generosity, I will be so shameless!" He then took his kin and people to surrender themselves to Zhu Ge Liang.

Zhu Ge Liang's use of the strategy "Releasing the enemy to recapture him later" was greatly rewarded. He finally won the hearts and loyalty of Meng Huo and the southern people. In fact, after Meng Huo's surrender, there were no more disputes between the Shu army and the southern people.

COMMENTS & APPLICATIONS

There are several lessons to be learnt from the capture of Meng Huo by Zhu Ge Liang. In war, when the enemy is at a dead end, it may sometimes be wiser to release him and recapture him later than push him further. When driven to a dead end, the enemy may put up a deadly struggle, causing severe losses to both sides. The better strategy is to let the enemy exhaust himself and his fighting spirit before recapturing him. This advocates conserving one's energy while waiting for the moment to defeat the enemy.

EXHAUST THE RESOURCES OF THE COMPETITORS

In business, it is useful to gradually take on weaker competitors through open market competition before forcing them to surrender. A good example of this is the banking industry. If a bigger bank were to mop up the smaller banks through forced acquisitions it would appear ruthless. A better way is to allow the smaller banks to realise they can no longer compete before offering to purchase them. This was the case of the banking industry in Singapore and Malaysia. Smaller banks gradually yielded to giants such as the United Overseas Bank and the Overseas Chinese Banking Corporation.

The joint efforts by Singapore Airlines (SIA) and the Tata group to form a domestic airline in India may turn out to be a typical example of this strategy. Instead of pushing for a quick result, SIA and the Singapore government allowed domestic politics in India to gradually sort themselves out. Despite their desire for foreign investments and the obvious benefits of joint venture, this project has been stalled by vested interests of politicians since 1995. These Indian politicians will likely become exhausted, and allow joint ventures like the SIA-Tata deal to proceed. India will do well to follow in the steps of other Asian economies that have opened up to foreign investments, and have progressed as a result.

The Singapore government has been trying for a number of years to encourage small and medium-size companies, especially retailers, to consider merging or forming chain stores. This is to ensure that these stores can better compete against the larger stores, increase their productivity and enjoy economies of scale. There have been some successes, especially in the grocery business where chain stores emerged. Small retailers, however have resisted change, refusing to see the benefits of merging to form a larger chain of stores or cooperatives. These retailers include bakeries, spectacle shops, Chinese medical halls and hardware stores. It is only a matter of time before these stores will be compelled to merge and upgrade.

USE OF VARIED STRATEGIES

In the exercise of strategy, it is important to not repeat them as the enemy may recognise them, and so be prepared. Zhu Ge Liang used a variety of strategies to capture Meng Huo. He beat Meng Huo by using wits, brains and brawn to the extent that the latter had no choice but to surrender. Zhu Ge Liang's approach was similar to the sayings of Sun Zi:

> Therefore, do not repeat the tactics that won you a victory, but vary them according to the circumstances.

故其战胜不复, 而应形于无穷

In business, a company should not repeat the same strategies against its competitors if it hopes to win. For example, in advertising and promotion, new and creative themes and approaches are crucial. McDonalds deserves a mention here. It has always intrigued its customers, especially children, with a series of exciting toys or gifts, to entice children to acquire the entire collection (for example, the 101 Dalmatians and the Snoopy World Tour). McDonalds not only succeeds in increasing its sales, but makes these children its marketing agents. So successful is McDonalds in its promotional strategy that it can sell the gifts or toys instead of giving them away.

Similarly, a department store need not conduct its annual sale during a particular time. Altering its sales period would make it harder for competitors to guess the exact timing of each sale. The department store may also vary the types of items for sale and the amount of discount given. This would create more excitement for consumers, enhancing the effectiveness of the promotion.

Using varied strategies comes with several embedded advantages. Firstly, the enemy or competitor will not be able to predict the strategy and will find it difficult to develop counter strategies. Secondly, varied strategies create an element of surprise, effectively "shocking" the competitor and delaying his response. Thirdly, it becomes more difficult and exhausting for competitors to understand one's ploys. Finally, using varied strategies promotes innovation and creativity in the organisation that practises them.

WINNING THE HEART TAKES TIME

It took Zhu Ge Liang seven attempts before he finally won the heart of Meng Huo. Of course Meng Huo was an important figure in Zhu Ge Liang's overall scheme. In the context of war, it is often tempting to simply behead a "Meng Huo" if he is stubborn and unwilling to surrender. The problem, however, will not end there. A new leader will then emerge and the war may continue for much longer. As in Strategy 18, the best way to disband the bandits is by arresting their leader. Just as, when catching a snake, one must go for its head, Zhu Ge Liang went for Meng Huo.

To win the entire organisation, first win the heart of the leader. When Meng Huo surrendered, all the tribal soldiers surrendered with him. However, pride and "face" prevent a leader from giving in quickly. It takes time and effort to win his heart and confidence. Zhu Ge Liang did just that and his patience paid off handsomely.

Employee loyalty takes time and effort to build and develop too. While money and other factors are important, they are not everything. In organisations with strong union representation, it is not difficult to find "Meng Huo" characters in union leaders. Management should therefore understand the need to win the trust and confidence of the union leaders. Militant union leaders are prepared to take their followers to the streets on strikes and demonstrations. Besides direct confrontation from dissatisfied union members, poor management can also cause employees to leave. In competitive environments and tight labour markets, these possibilities will always exist.

Management of employee loyalty goes beyond providing good working conditions and high salaries; it requires winning employees' hearts. The management must be prepared to go the extra mile to make the employees feel wanted and appreciated. Every effort should be made to turn them into corporate assets rather than production units. Though some employees will leave a company for better pay, a caring management will raise the psychological and social costs for them. It is no wonder that Sun Zi commented:

> An army may suffer from flight, insubordination, collapse, ruin, disorganisation and rout. These six calamities are not attributed to natural causes. They are due to the faults of the general.

故兵有"走"者，有"弛"者，有"陷"者，有"崩"者，有"乱"者，有"北"者。凡此六者，非天之灾，将之过也。

Winning the heart also extends to persuading top-notch potential employees to join the company. High-performing executives do not actively seek alternative employment, especially when they are satisfied with their current job. For the already highly successful senior executives, the courting process may take time, demanding patience and perseverance.

STRATEGY 17

抛砖引玉

TOSSING OUT A BRICK TO GET A JADE

类以诱之，击蒙也。

EXPLANATION

Use a decoy to entice the enemy (类以诱之), get him muddled and he will fall into the trap (击[1]蒙也). This is *Yi Jing's* "Meng" (or "muddle") Theory ([易经：蒙]卦：上九，击蒙。(序卦)蒙者蒙也，物之稚也).

HISTORICAL BACKGROUND

This strategy came from the story of how two famous Tang poets, Chang Jian (常建) and Zhao Gu (赵嘏), composed their poems. Chang Jian had long heard of Zhao Gu's reputation. When he heard that Zhao Gu was coming to Su Zhou (苏州), he knew that Zhao Gu would visit the Ling Yan Temple (灵岩寺). Chang Jian therefore went to the temple and wrote two lines of poem on the wall. When Zhao Gu came and saw these he added another two. The whole poem became very well-known. As Chang Jian's sentences were not as good as those written by Zhao Gu, many people called them the "bricks" (砖) which was tossed out to attract a "jade" (玉) (Zhao Gu's sentences).

The following story illustrates the use of this strategy.

During the period of the Warring States when the seven big states were at war, chaos reigned. The state of Qin (秦国) wanted to attack the state of Wei (卫国) and allied itself with the state of Zhao (赵国) with the promise that Qin would cede the Wei city of Ye (邺城) to Zhao after the victory as a reward.

---

[1] The word "击" means to achieve success.

The Emperor of Wei panicked at the news and immediately summoned his ministers to discuss defence measures. However, nobody could come up with a plausible plan. In the end, the Emperor turned to General Mang Mao (芒 卯) for advice. The General assured the monarch that there was no cause for alarm.

Mang Mao said, "The state of Qin and the state of Zhao have never been on good terms. The main purpose of their present military alliance is to divide our state to expand their respective territories. Although the move appears threatening, each of the allies is pursuing his own goal and the coalition is not stable. In this battle, Qin is the mastermind while Zhao is an accomplice. We need only to offer the latter some benefit to instigate a break-up of the alliance."

The Emperor said, "Time is running out. How shall we go about it?" Mang Mao said, "I recommend that Your Lordship sends Zhang Yi as emissary to Zhao. He can accomplish the mission."

Zhang Yi went to Zhao and sought permission to see its ruler. He said, "From the look of things, we will not be able to hold the city of Ye much longer. The main purpose of Your Lordship joining forces with Qin to attack us is to capture that city. To avoid a war, the Emperor of Wei intends handing over to the city of Ye to Your Lordship. What does Your Lordship think of the idea?"

The Emperor of Zhao was delighted when he heard this. But he asked, "We have yet to engage in any battle. Why does the Emperor of Wei wish to give us the city of Ye now?" "The reason is quite simple," replied Zhang Yi, "Although the two states have not fought, a war would do great damage to the land and the people. The Emperor of Wei, guided by humanitarian considerations, prefers to settle the problem by peaceful means."

"What does the Emperor of Wei ask of me then?" the Emperor of Zhao asked. Zhang Yi said, "This is a peaceful settlement and not an unconditional surrender. The Emperor of Wei, when cornered, had to decide how best to solve the problem. Wei and Zhao have been allies in the past and we have enjoyed a friendly relationship. Qin and Wei have never been on good terms. Furthermore, Qin has always been a warring country and its soldiers are noted for their brutality.

Instead of losing our land to a country of barbarians, a wiser choice would be to entrust the land in the hands of our friends. Our Emperor has said that if Your Lordship is prepared to resume your friendship with our country and sever your ties with Qin, the City of Ye will be presented to Your Lordship as a token of our friendship. If Your Lordship chooses otherwise, our people have vowed to fight to protect our land. Please consider the proposal."

The Emperor of Zhao replied, "Let me have some time to ponder over your proposal and I will give you a reply tomorrow." The Emperor of Zhao summoned his minister and told him about Zhang Yi's proposal. The minister said, "Our initial intention of joining forces with Qin was to capture the City of Ye. Now we can achieve our aim without having to use our army, why not go with the proposal? When Qin captures the state of Wei, it will be much stronger than Zhao and Qin could turn against us. It would make more sense to take advantage of the present situation and help Wei. Together with Wei, we can hold Qin at bay and secure our territory."

The Emperor of Zhao accepted Wei's conditions. He immediately severed his ties with Qin and ordered the closure of the city gates so that the Qin troops could not enter. The Emperor of Qin was furious and thought the Emperor of Zhao was toying with him. He ordered his soldiers back home and cancelled the attack on Wei. From then on, Qin considered Zhao its enemy. Thinking that he would be granted his part of the bargain, the Emperor of Zhao sent an army to take over the city of Ye.

The Zhao army was met by General Mang Mao and his men at the frontier who refused to let them near the City of Ye. The general of Zhao said that he had been commanded by his Emperor to take over the City of Ye as agreed. "What nonsense is this!" cried Mang Mao, "I have been sent to protect this city. I will not hand it over!"

"But it was agreed the Emperor of Wei would cede the city to Zhao!" the Zhao general defended. "What agreement? Did the Emperor of Wei personally agree to it? Can you prove this?" The Zhao general panicked and replied, "Are you saying that the words of Zhang Yi, the emissary, do not count?"

"Emissary? Zhang Yi?" scoffed Mang Mao, "If he said so, then get the city from him! I have no orders from my Emperor to hand this city over to you. If you want the city from me, you will have to ask if my men agree! I am warning you — you had better leave this place immediately or we will attack!"

Disheartened, the Zhao general withdrew his troops and returned to Zhao. When the Emperor of Zhao heard the report, he realised he had been tricked by the Emperor of Wei. In the meantime, news had it that Qin was considering joining forces with Wei to attack Zhao. This troubled the Emperor of Zhao. After an emergency meeting with his ministers and advisers, the Emperor of Zhao voluntarily ceded five cities to Wei to persuade the latter to join forces with Zhao to prevent the attack from Qin. Thus, by pretending to give a "brick", the Emperor of Wei won a "jade" in return! Not only was the Qin-Zhao alliance broken, he gained five cities as well.

COMMENTS & APPLICATIONS

There are many ways to confuse one's enemy. One is to use a decoy. A brick is worthless when compared to a jade, although each has the constitution of stone. "Tossing out a brick in to get a jade" means to give away something of minimum value in exchange for something valuable. Zhang Yi used the city of Ye as a bait (or "brick") to break up the military alliance between Qin and Zhao, which was the "jade" the Emperor of Wei wanted. The Emperor of Wei eventually got a better bargain in the form of the five cities. This strategy can be easily used with Strategy 6 , "Making a feint to the east but hit out in the west" and Strategy 15, "Lure the tiger to leave its lair in the mountains". The application of this strategy is also similar to what Sun Zi said,

> Offer the enemy a bait to lure him;
> When he is in disorder, strike him.

利而诱之，乱而取之。

USE OF BAITS IN BUSINESS

Baits are used in business to lure big spenders. For example, casino operators would not hesitate offer free chips, food and lodging to entice big gamblers. These incentives are especially successful in Asia as people there enjoy a gamble and are easily tempted by such offers. Several Australian casinos provide luxurious limousines to shuttle their guests to and from the airport. One casino provided free chartered flights annually from Hong Kong's Kai Tak airport during the Chinese New Year period.

In the retail business, marketers often use "loss leaders" to attract customers to their stores in the hope that they will spend large sums of money on other items. Many consumers willingly become victims of these ploys. Free gifts, lucky draws and early bird specials are familiar marketing gimmicks of "tossing out a brick to get a jade". These gifts and offers may not be of significant value but are highly attractive to consumers as the marketer may have placed a high price on the gifts. This ploy is commonly used when launching new cosmetic products. Gifts with purchase are used to encourage consumers to purchase the item under promotion.

In the highly competitive hotel business, the management may offer complimentary breakfasts, daily fruit baskets and other gifts and souvenirs to attract large groups of tourists on packaged tours and conventions. The sacrifices made are "bricks" compared to the number of rooms booked. When labour is difficult to find, companies may offer perks such as transport allowances, subsidised meals, and free housing to attract workers.

INVESTMENT INCENTIVES

On the international level, an increasing number of developing countries offer incentives to attract foreign investment, especially from MNCs. Since economic development has overtaken political and ideological considerations, it is not surprising to find countries like China, Vietnam, Malaysia, and Indonesia striving to attract foreign investors.

Many Asian economies have created conducive investment climates within a short time. Their strong governments can pass laws and statutes quickly. As investment incentives are neither new nor unique, it is not difficult to copy them. China and Malaysia, for example, are known to base many of their investment incentives on those of Singapore. In a competitive environment, one economy may offer more incentives than others.

As investment incentives or climates can be easily created, MNCs should be cautious. A conducive investment climate alone is not sufficient to ensure profitability. Economic development must be supported with adequate infrastructure and physical factors such as transport system, telecommunication facilities, access to capital and financial markets and availability of skilled labour. Companies pay a costly price for overlooking these factors, as some companies in Vietnam, China and India have found.

While an attractive investment climate can be created rapidly, it takes years to build excellent infrastructural and physical facilities. In the late 1980s, in an attempt to expedite its economic development, Malaysia embarked on ambitious mega-infrastructural projects. Although desirable, these caused considerable deficits in the Malaysian trade balance as they involved substantial imports. These over-commitments contributed partially to the currency and stock market crises which began in July/August 1997. As a result, Malaysian Deputy Prime Minister and Finance Minister Anwar Ibrahim had to announce the deferment of some of these projects.

Companies should objectively evaluate the factors needed for successful overseas operations, and not be enticed by incentives alone. Developed countries such as the US and Japan, and newly developed economies such as Singapore continue to attract foreign investment despite the fact that their investment incentives are nowhere near those offered by developing economies. Their attraction to foreign investors lies in other areas, particularly their excellent and well-developed infrastructure.

In the realm of international business, it is not difficult for governments to use the strategy of "tossing out a brick to get a jade" to attract foreign investment. What they give in terms of investment incentives are nothing compared to the immense benefits obtained through economic development. It is important for the investing MNCs to decipher the value of their decisions because at the end of the day, they too want to obtain some "jade".

AUCTIONS FOR CHARITY

An interesting and noble application of the "tossing out a brick to get a jade" strategy can be found in auctions at charity functions. Auctions are becoming a popular way to raise funds. Every year, many organisations in Singapore, Hong Kong, and other Asian countries organise functions to raise money for various charitable bodies. At these auctions, the organisers display attractive items for auction to entice bidders. At a gala function for charity held by a major organisation during Christmas, imported Christmas trees and well-stocked gift hampers were auctioned for many times their original value. Occasionally, a successful bidder would return his purchase for another round of bidding.

There are several reasons why such a strategy works in raising money for charity. Firstly, the attendees are a select group of wealthy people who are able to contribute. Secondly, the event is normally attended by a distinguished guest. At the Christmas gala dinner in Singapore, the guest-of-honour is usually the President of Singapore, accompanied by the First Lady. Thirdly, in any auction, there is always a strong element of competition among bidders. As a result, the price is always pushed up. Fourthly, as the auction is conducted at an important event, there is bound to be publicity for the successful bidders. Finally, the donor does not go away empty-handed. The item that he has successfully bid for will always serve as a conversational piece.

擒 贼 擒 王

DISBAND THE BANDITS BY CAPTURING THEIR LEADER

摧其坚，夺其魁，以解其体。
龙战于野，其道穷也。

EXPLANATION

If the enemy's power-base is destroyed in an attack (摧其坚) and
its leader is captured (夺其魁), the whole organisation will break
down (以解其体). Just like a dragon from the sea wanting to
stage a war on land (龙战于野), it will face severe difficulties
(其道穷也). This is described in *Yi Jing's* "Kun" theory ([易经：
：坤]卦：象曰：龙战于野，其道穷也。)

HISTORICAL BACKGROUND

The name of this strategy is taken from a poem by Du Fu (杜甫).
The famous Tang poet once wrote in his poem *Going Out: First
Part* (前出塞):

> When using a bow, one should use a strong bow,
> When using an arrow, one should use a long arrow;
> To shoot at a person, one should first shoot his horse.
> To disband the bandits, one should first catch their leader.

挽弓当挽强，用箭当用长；
射人先射马，擒贼先擒王。

The teaching behind this poem is to nab the problem at its
roots. This is also the gist of the strategy. It is similar to another
Chinese saying, to catch a snake, one must always go for its head. If
the catcher catches hold of its body or tail, the snake can turn around
and bite him. The following story illustrates the use of this strategy.

In 757 AD, the emperor of the Tang Dynasty (唐朝), Tang Su Zhong (唐肃宗) commanded General Zhang Xun (张巡) to guard the city of Sui Yang (睢阳) from the rebels. Zhang Xun's army eventually had a fierce fight with the troops of the rebel General Yin Zi Qi (尹子奇).

General Zhang Xun's army fought bravely, and killed 5,000 enemy soldiers. The enemy camp was thrown into confusion. Nobody could locate General Yin Zi Qi. General Zhang Xun then hatched a plan to lure the rebel general from his hideout. He ordered his men to use fake arrows made of straw to shoot at the enemy. When the enemy soldiers saw this, they thought that they had defeated Zhang Xun's army and rushed to report to General Yin Zi Qi. Thus, they disclosed the location of the general. General Zhang Xun ordered his men to shoot at General Yin Zi Qi who was wounded in his left eye. Although General Yin Zi Qi managed to escape after a fierce struggle, his troop was thoroughly defeated.

COMMENTS & APPLICATIONS

A good way to destroy the enemy is to capture its leader. Without a leader the enemy troop will fall apart. In war, the commanding general plays a key role in influencing the morale and fighting spirit of his troops. Battles are lost or won depending on the strategies developed by the general. His sudden departure, either through death or capture, could cripple his troops.

This strategy complements Strategy 16 "Releasing the enemy to recapture him later". Under Strategy 16, the intention is not only to defeat the enemy, but to win their loyalty to prevent unnecessary loss of lives and resources. As the leader plays a key role in extracting a full surrender, it is therefore important to capture him first. However, the strong fighting spirit of the enemy troops may stop them disbanding, making it necessary to gradually erode their will to fight through releasing and recapturing their leader. The surrender of a charismatic and strong leader, as illustrated by Meng Huo in Strategy 16, would result in the total surrender of his army.

Strategy 18 can also complement Strategy 19 on "Pulling out the firewood from beneath the cauldron". While Strategy 18 is targeted at capturing the leader, Strategy 19 focuses on removing the leader's key lieutenants. The thrust of Strategy 19 is to remove those who are closest and most important to the leader, hence delivering severe a blow to his competitive strength. Strategies 18 and 19 bear many similarities in their application to business as both are intended to address the same root cause.

CORPORATE HEAD HUNTING

In business as in war, one way to incapacitate one's competitor is to go after its top management and/or key executives. This can be done discreetly through head-hunting firms. Departure of key executives can wreak havoc in any company. Not only are productivity and competitiveness affected, morale is also dampened. These executives may also bring along key accounts and customers from their previous firm. Their departure could seriously affect the progress of any projects they are involved in. A business leader has a determining role in ensuring the corporate health of a company. He represents the corporate values and culture shared by his subordinates. His departure therefore can have a significant impact on the company.

A good example of this is when Edmund Tie, senior partner of a large overseas property company, decided to leave. His departure generated a great deal of interest because many of his colleagues subsequently joined him to set up a rival company. Barely two years later, Edmund Tie and Company had become a major property agency.

The importance of having key executives to excel in business has motivated many companies to engage in elaborate executive searches. Luring key executives has also caught on in Asia. With the increased investments in many Asian economies, finding suitable executives to work in Vietnam, China and India has been an increasing need. American MNCs such as Allied Signals, Motorola, Dell Computers and Coca-cola have deliberately sought overseas Chinese to work in China. Many Singaporean, Malaysian, Taiwanese and Hong Kong professionals who are proficient in English and Mandarin have become convenient targets of head-hunting firms.

HEAD HUNTING FOR ACADEMICS AND RESEARCHERS

In academia, it is common to "head-hunt" professors well-established in research and with strong industrial contacts. By attracting them with appropriate salaries, incentives and perks, these professors can act as magnets to lure younger researchers to join them. In the US and Canada, such "poaching" tactics are used often. American and Canadian universities are so entrenched in recruitment that they set up search committees to find suitable candidates. In the appointment of deans of faculties such as engineering, medicine and business, the process can be even longer and more complicated.

In the realm of scientific research, no effort is spared to identify key researchers. Recognising the importance of research in the economic development of any country, many Asian economies have consciously embarked on ambitious efforts to "recapture" native scientists previously "lost" to Western countries. For example, many Taiwanese scientists have made their mark in Silicon Valley in the US. When Taiwan set up its Science Park, it went all out to "capture" these scientists by offering them immense perks to come home. Singapore did the same when it set up Science Park.

In early September 1997, Malaysian Science, Technology and Environment Minister, Datuk Law Hieng Deng, announced various incentives to attract Malaysian scientists home. These included priority in allocation of funds to open new companies and support research activities. They were also promised priority access to facilities at the Malaysian Technology Park. Other government research services were also made accessible to them on a preferential basis.

GETTING TO THE ROOT OF THE PROBLEM

To "disband the bandits by capturing their leader" is essentially to arrest a problem at its roots. For example, declining sales, high employee turnover, low morale and low productivity are symptoms of underlying problems. Management must be able to identify the root of these problems.

Declining sales could be caused by many factors such as wrong pricing, weak products, poor service, unattractive sales and compensation packages. Similarly, high employee turnover and low morale may be caused by low salaries, poor working conditions, uncooperative colleagues, difficult bosses and unrealistic goals set by management. Unless one gets to the root of the problem, it is not possible to develop an effective solution.

Unfortunately, some companies are guilty of treating problems with the wrong solutions, or of paying "lip service" to problems. These companies end up being worse-off. A good example of this can be found in Singapore's retail industry. As a result of labour shortages and increasing rentals, the costs of operation, especially labour costs, have been increasing steadily since mid 1980s. Though retailers requested that the government help reduce operation costs, there was a limit to what cost reduction could do. In an increasingly affluent and developed economy such as Singapore, rising labour and operation costs are inevitable.

The solution to the flagging retail market lies not in cost reduction, but in increasing productivity and sales. Retailers should look for ways to increase their productivity and revenue to counter the increasing costs of production. Automation, out-sourcing and mergers or alliances may be better solutions. Take, for example, the traditional confectionery/bakery in Singapore. Almost half of the shop space is devoted to baking while the other half is devoted to sales. Bakers' time as well as the baking equipment are usually under-utilised. With high operating costs in the 1990s, poor utilisation of shop space, labour and equipment can only lead to low profit margins, even losses.

In contrast, confectionery shops in Hong Kong fully understand the need to beat high rentals and labour costs. They devote the entire shop space to selling cakes and pastries and do not bake on the premises. Instead, they source their products from various professional bakeries specialising in distributing to retailers. Their products are no longer limited by the skills of their own bakers. These professional bakeries are able to enjoy economies of scale through automation and higher utilisation of equipment. They deploy their labour more efficiently, and by devoting the entire shop to sell cakes and pastries, they obtain more sales revenue per square foot of retail space.

STRATEGY 19

斧底抽薪

PULLING OUT THE FIREWOOD FROM BENEATH THE CAULDRON

不 敵 其 力, 而 消 其 勢, 兌 下 乾 上 之 象。

EXPLANATION

When faced with a strong opponent, direct confrontation may not be advisable (不 敵 其 力). It may be better to use tactics to destroy his morale (而 消 其 勢). This is in accordance with *Yi Jing's* "Lu" theory — the weak can conquer the strong ([易 经: 履] 卦 柔 履 刚 也).

HISTORICAL BACKGROUND

This strategy comes from ***Zhu Nan Zi's Book*** which says to prevent soup from boiling, the best way is to take away the fire fuelling the pot ([准 南 子: 本 经 训]: 故 以 汤 止 沸, 沸 乃 不 止, 诚 知 其 本, 则 去 火 而 已 矣.) Wei Shou of the North Dynasty (北 齐 魏 收) wrote an article (为 侯 景 叛 移 梁 朝 文) which has two sentences that run: "Pull out the firewood to prevent the water from boiling; cut the grass by destroying its roots" (抽 薪 止 沸, 剪 草 除 根). This strategy advocates eliminating the source of power. The following story tells the application of this strategy.

> *Qi Jing Gong (齐 景 公) was very upset after being humiliated by Confucius (孔 子) at Jia Gu (夹 谷). Qi Jing Gong's able minister Yan Ying had passed on and no suitable candidate could be found to replace him. Therefore, Qi Jing Gong was dismayed when he learned that Confucius was to be made an important official in charge of the state of Lu. He consulted his adviser Li Mi (黎 弥) and said, "Lu's decision to engage Confucius as its adviser poses a big threat to our stability. Our state is bound to suffer when Lu develops into a strong state. What shall we do?"*

After some thought, Li Mi said, "We should take the firewood out from beneath the cauldron and get rid of Confucius!" Qi Jing Gong asked, "How shall we go about that? Confucius is now in the good books of the Emperor of Lu!"

Li Mi told him his plan, "Has Your Lordship not heard of the saying that one will think of sex when he is fed and warmed, and one will think of robbing others when he is poor? Today, the state of Lu is enjoying peace. It is known the Emperor of Lu, Lu Ding Gong (鲁定公) is fond of women. If we present him with a bevy of beauties, he will most certainly enjoy himself with these ladies everyday and neglect Confucius. Confucius will then be angry with the Emperor and will leave the state of Lu. Your Lordship will have no fear then!"

Qi Jing Gong thought the plan was excellent and ordered Li Mi to gather 80 beauties. These beauties were specially trained in singing and dancing to prepare them for the Emperor of Lu. Once the training was completed, Qi Jing Gong ordered his men to put gold saddles on 120 fine horses. Together with the 80 beauties, the horses were sent to the state of Lu as a present for the Emperor.

A minister of the state of Lu, Ji Si (季斯), was among the first to hear the news and he immediately changed into his plain clothes and rode to the South Gate. Greeting him were the singing and dancing beauties from the state of Qi. He was totally captivated by their charm and beauty.

Ji Si was so engrossed in looking at the ladies that he had forgotten the daily meeting with the Emperor of Lu. It was only after a few summons from the Emperor that Ji Si went to see His Lordship. When the Emperor of Lu told him about the proposal from the Emperor of Qi, Ji Si immediately said, "We cannot turn down the kindness of the Emperor of Lu. It is only polite we accept his gifts!"

The Emperor of Lu had the same thought and asked Ji Si where the beauties were. Ji Si took the opportunity to be the guide and the two of them proceeded towards the South Gate. The emissary from Qi learnt about this secret mission and ordered the beauties to perform their best. The Emperor of Lu and Ji Si were completely enchanted by their heavenly beauty and were so excited that they began to dance with the girls.

Ji Si said, "Does Your Lordship want to inspect the horses?" The Emperor of Lu replied, "That is not necessary. These ladies are good enough!" When the Emperor of Lu returned to his palace that evening, he asked Ji Si to write to Qi Jing Gong, thanking him for all the wonderful gifts. The emissary was also handsomely rewarded. Ji Si was rewarded with 30 of the the beauties from Qi. From then on, the Emperor frolicked with his beauties in his palace and absented himself from his daily meetings with his subjects.

Confucius was very unhappy when he learnt of this. His student Zi Lu (子 路) said, "The Emperor of Lu has fallen into a trap and has put national affairs behind him. Teacher, let us leave this place." Confucius said, "No hurry! It is almost time for the Emperor to make his country offering (郊 祭). This is a national affair. If His Lordship has not forgotten this event, we can still stay to help out with the managing of the state. Otherwise, we will leave."

The Emperor of Lu turned up when it was time for him to make the country offering, but it was obvious to everyone present that he was not sincere. The Emperor rushed back to his palace to be with his beauties even before the ceremony was over. Confucius told Zi Lu, "Go and tell your classmates to pack their things. We will leave this place tomorrow." Confucius resigned from his post and left the state of Lu with his students.

COMMENTS & APPLICATIONS

This is the first of the six confusion strategies. When the enemy has the upper hand, instead of confronting him directly, one should scheme to deplete his resources, destroy his power and eventually conquer him. In the story, Li Mi knew that Qi could not directly confront Lu, especially with wise Confucius around. The only way was to get rid of Confucius and then destroy Lu. By removing the firewood (Confucius) from beneath the cauldron, Lu's power would be greatly diminished. This was achieved through creating confusion in the leader's judgement, through the beauties. This strategy, "Pulling out the firewood from beneath the cauldron" can easily be used with Strategy 31, "The beauty scheme".

This strategy differs from Strategy 15, "Lure the tiger to leave its lair in the mountain" in that the latter is targeted at the leader himself. It also differs from Strategy 18, "Disband the bandits by capturing their leader" as Strategy 18 involves capturing the leader. In contrast, Strategy 19 concerns removing either the leader's right-hand man or his crucial supports. It is tantamout to "Killing two vultures with a single arrow".

Strategies 18 and 19 complement each other. As applied to business, these strategies are similar as both aim to remove underlying causes of problems. They could be used effectively with several other strategies such as Strategy 5, "Looting a house on fire" when the leader and assistants are removed; with Strategy 6, "Making a feint to the east but hit out in the west" as a way to distract the target before striking.

REMOVING KEY CORPORATE LIEUTENANTS

An effective way to incapacitate a corporate leader is to remove his able "lieutenants", as Li Mi did to the Emperor of Lu. This is particularly useful when direct confrontation/competition is not advisable. There are a number of ways in which such a strategy can be played out. The first and most direct way is to lure these capable "lieutenants" away with better salaries, incentives and working conditions.

The second way to remove key executives is to sow discord between them and the CEO or with the organisation. Some companies have resorted to these low-down tactics. For example, they may spread rumours that the CEO's leadership styles and business practices are stifling the growth and careers of his subordinates. Alternatively, the company could be painted as one with a bleak future not worth working for. When rumours are heard often enough, they gain credibility.

The battle for talents between the private and public sector in many Asian and other countries is a good illustration of this strategy. While public sector organisations, such as the civil service, provide job security, private sector firms have often painted them as being bureaucratic and poor payers. Many young and mid-career civil servants, especially talented ones, opt to leave for the private sector whenever the opportunity arises.

Among Asian countries, Singapore is probably the most successful in attracting and retaining the best talents in the civil service. It does so by offering attractive scholarships and sending candidates to be trained at the world's best universities. These candidates are bonded to serve various government bodies for five to six years. To attract them to stay on, the Singapore government offers competitive salaries and attractive career paths to high potential candidates. Over the years, Singapore has attracted some of the brightest talents to the civil service, the army and the police.

Other public sector organisations have experienced mixed results. One example is the hospital service. Since the 1980s, a greater number of younger and talented government doctors have resigned to join private hospitals or to set up their own practices. This was largely due to the unsatisfactory terms and working conditions of government hospitals. The higher salaries offered in the private sector were an added incentive. A combination of push and pull factors therefore caused the doctors to leave in increasing numbers. In a concerted effort to improve the medical service, the government embarked on an ambitious plan to restructure all government hospitals. The plan included improving the existing terms of service, renovating existing buildings, constructing new buildings, and upgrading facilities and equipment.

As Singaporeans become more affluent, the demand for high quality health care is likely to increase. As a growing regional medical centre, Singapore also attracts wealthy patients from neighbouring countries. With growing demand for private health care, restructured government hospitals need to continue upgrading services and facilities to compete effectively. More importantly, they have to develop better packages to retain the better and younger doctors, surgeons and nurses who are their key personnel.

MAJOR ACCOUNTS AND ANCHOR TENANTS

In agency businesses such as trading houses, some products account for a large percentage of corporate sales. For example, according to the Pareto principle, 80% of a company's total sales could be accounted for by 20% of its customers. Under such circumstances, the loss of agency rights on these profitable products can damage the company. Competitive firms will often try to wrestle the agency rights of these products away from the incumbent.

Many companies such as law firms and advertising agencies have key accounts which fuel their profitability and sales. The loss of such accounts would significantly affect competitiveness. Therefore these key accounts are often hotly contested. The best executives, including senior management, are assigned to look after these accounts to ensure they are given the best attention, and to prevent them from being poached by competitors.

In the retail business, owners of shopping centres court large departmental stores or supermarket chains as anchor tenants. By themselves these operators would be unable to attract customers. Anchor tenants are like the firewood that fuel the cauldron. They help lure smaller stores to the shopping centre and contribute significantly to the landlord's rental revenue. It is therefore common to find new shopping centres going "all out" to lure existing and successful anchor tenants from established shopping centres.

Owners of new office buildings also strive to entice key anchor tenants from rival buildings. These tenants lend prestige to the building, helping to attract other tenants and increasing rental yields. The landlord may at times offer preferential terms to anchor tenants.

AVOID HEAD-ON COMPETITION

A related application of this strategy is the avoidance of direct confrontation when faced with a much stronger competitor. Often it is not possible to take on the larger competitor head-on in advertising and promotion. Take the case of the small retail store versus a large departmental chain in a large shopping centre. Instead of competing head-on, the small retail store normally rides on the promotional campaigns of the larger store. When the large department store has a sale, the smaller store marks down its prices a few dollars below those of identical items in the larger store. They use low cost, in-store promotional stickers and banners to attract customers. The larger store has paid the cost of advertising while the smaller one "steals the firewood".

How should a smaller company avoid competing head-on against a larger one? To begin with, the small company should avoid going after the same markets. Instead, it should try to find its own niche by proactively seeking out markets, products, product features or other areas ignored by the large company. By avoiding the giant, and by concentrating on areas ignored by it, the smaller company will eventually develop its own strengths.

This was how Dell Computer managed to create such a huge impact on its larger competitors such as Compaq, Hewlett Packard and IBM. Instead of following the industry practice of distributing the computers through agents and retailers, Dell Computer decided to sell direct to the consumer, allowing its customers to order directly by telephone or through the Internet. More significantly, Dell allows customers to indicate their specification and then manufactures the computers accordingly. Dell sells highly customised computers in the most direct way, cutting distribution costs and shortening delivery time – benefits of high value to customers. Concurrently, it pursues a policy of sourcing the cheapest components. Take its notebook for example. The carrying case, battery, and disk-drive are made in China, many computer parts are made in Taiwan, the Intel chip comes from the US, and the units are assembled in Malaysia.

Dell Computer "pulled the firewood from beneath the cauldron" of the larger players in the industry. The conventional agents and distributors were the "firewood". By removing the "firewood" and going direct to the customers, Dell Computer not only created a new and different way of marketing computers, but a more effective and profitable one. Dell Computer did not produce a new or better computer. It assembled the various parts of the computer quicker than others. The innovation was not in the product, but in the way the computer was re-packaged and sold.

混水摸鱼

CATCHING A FISH IN
TROUBLED WATER

乘其阴乱，利其弱而无主。
随，以向晦入宴息。

EXPLANATION

The literal meaning of the strategy is to take advantage of the
"troubled" or muddy situation in which the fish is unable to see
clearly and has restricted movement. In such circumstances, catching
the fish by hand may be good enough. If the water is clear, putting
one's hand in would frighten the fish away. Conversely, the muddy
situation also provides opportunities for more than one predator
to exploit the situation without being detected. This strategy is
similar to the Chinese saying, "Throwing a rock down a well after
the enemy has fallen in" (落井下石). When the enemy is in the
well, his movements are restricted, thus it is easy to destroy him.

In warfare, when the enemy is in a state of confusion
(乘其阴乱), one should take advantage and gain control when he
is weak and without proper direction (利其弱而无主). The best
way to control the enemy is to let nature take its course (随), as all
men have to eat and rest (以向晦入宴息).

HISTORICAL BACKGROUND

This strategy comes from the *Tales of the Three Kingdoms* (三国志：
蜀志先主传) which describes how Liu Bei (刘备) expanded his
kingdom using the strategy. Liu Bei had Zhu Ge Liang (诸葛亮) to
thank for his ability to capture the state of Jing (荆州) and the state
of Yi (益州). This eventually enabled him to share ancient China
with the Kingdoms of Wu (吴) and Wei (魏).

STORY 1

The State of Jing was in a geographically advantageous position and many leaders at that time had been eyeing this piece of land. The ruler of Jing was Liu Biao (刘 表). Liu Biao was a man with many weaknesses. He trusted no one and was always indecisive. He did not form alliances with any of the leaders who were vying for power at that time. In contrast, the State of Yi was wealthy with food and granaries. Its ruler was Liu Zhang (刘 璋), who was a weak and useless man. The people of Yi had long wanted to replace him with a more capable ruler.

Zhu Ge Liang first teamed up with Sun Quan (孙 权), another powerful warlord, to defeat Cao Cao (曹 操). This eventually led to the famous war at Chi Bi (赤 壁) where Cao Cao was badly defeated. After the victory, Zhu Ge Liang managed to capture the State of Jing and used it as a base. He then waited until there was internal confusion in Liu Zhang's administration to take the State of Yi as well. In both instances, Zhu Ge Liang was able to utilise the opportunity where the enemy was in a state of confusion to his (or Liu Bei's) advantage.

The strategy works in two different circumstances — where there is already a state of confusion and where there is yet to be one. In the first situation, one need only take the opportunity to "catch the fish". In the second, one may need to create confusion before advantages can be gained. This is more difficult to do. The story of how Cao Cao won the battle at Guan Du (官 渡) illustrates the latter.

STORY 2

When Cao Cao was fighting at Guan Du (官 渡 之 战) his army ran out of supplies. He therefore ordered his men to go to the warehouses at Wu Chao (乌 巢), belonging to the Yuan (袁) army, to steal supplies. Cao Cao's men managed to get some Yuan army uniforms and those at the front line were asked to dress like the Yuan army and carry the Yuan flag. The whole team then went to the warehouses at night. Whenever they met the Yuan army, Cao Cao's men would claim they were the reinforcements sent by the main base back home. When they reached the warehouses at Wu Chao, the men suddenly set fire to some of the camps and there

*was instant confusion. The Yuan army could not distinguish
their own men from the enemy and Cao Cao managed to
take control of the situation and gained control at the Battle
of Guan Du.*

COMMENTS & APPLICATIONS

Confusion provides exploitable opportunities to the enemy. Cao
Cao and Zhu Ge Liang both capitalised on chaotic situations to
gain the upper hand. "Catching a fish in troubled water" implies
that as long as one is opportunistic, gains can be made, depending
on how one exploits a situation.

This strategy can be used in conjunction with Strategy 12,
"Stealing a goat along the way" and Strategy 6, "Looting a house
on fire", in that it is often possible to benefit from situations where
the enemy is totally confused. The strategy can also be used with
Strategy 13, "Hitting the grass to startle the snake" if the enemy
can be startled into confusion. Where the leader of the enemy relies
heavily on a handful of capable "right-hand men", this strategy
can be used with Strategy 19, "Pulling out the firewood from the
cauldron". When the leader is temporarily stunned by the loss of
capable "lieutenants" that is the opportunity to exploit the ensuing
confusion.

AVOIDING CONFUSION

From a defensive perspective, "Catching a fish in troubled water"
implies that to avoid being exploited, one has to ensure there is no
confusion within one's organisation. As the great military strategist
Sun Zi said,

> A confused army provides victory for the enemy.

是谓乱军引胜

A company should ensure it does not create confusion within
its rank-and-file. The following are some things that can cause
confusion:

1   Unclear policies and procedures
2   Poor communication channels
3   Weak feedback mechanisms
4   Contradictory messages and signals
5   Rewards not commensurate with performance

6   Not delivering promises to employees and consumers
7   Loss of top or key executives

When not properly addressed, confusion causes frustration and can lead to morale problems. When employees begin to fight one another, they provide opportunities for exploitation by competitors. They may begin to poach employees and approach the company's customers. The company's performance can be severely affected. In an extreme case, the confused company may even become the target of a take-over bid.

To avoid confusion, a company should stay united and focused, providing an impetus for the rank-and-file to scale greater heights, stronger teamwork and team-building. With an effective leader, a company can be pointed in a purposeful direction and few competitors will be able to derail it. Confusion can lead to employees becoming directionless. Instead of operating as a team, selfish behaviour may emerge. When employees are only concerned about themselves, the decline of the company is in sight.

Companies today are prepared to invest in training and development. Courses on team building and teamwork have become increasingly popular. Some courses include outdoor activities and boot camps. These outdoor activities are designed to improve teamwork, and many of them resemble military training. Concepts on effective communication (an important area in building corporate unity) are also built into such exercises. As competition increases among Asian companies, and as the demand for talented professionals increases in the next 10 to 20 years, more Asian companies are likely to invest in training programmes to help build corporate unity and loyalty.

EXPLOITING CHAOTIC SITUATIONS

In a confusing business or market situation, a proactive and optimistic company will seek to exploit opportunities, while reactive and pessimistic companies will lament the dangers. In an economic recession, for example, not every business is set for doom. Pawnshops are likely to boom in a recession, while essential products like rice, salt and toilet paper are unlikely to be threatened by a recession. When the domestic market is in a recession, overseas markets may be booming. Companies prepared to venture abroad are unlikely to lose out. While the domestic economy in Japan hardly grew between 1996 to 1997, companies that exported their products to high growth economies like China continued to enjoy healthy profits.

Tertiary education in Australia and the UK faced a similar situation in the 1980s and 1990s. With severe cuts in funding from the government, many of the more entrepreneurial universities sought to export their degree programmes to Asian countries where there was a demand for paper qualification. Some Australian and British universities set up distance learning programmes in economies like Singapore and Hong Kong. As Singapore and Hong Kong are free market economies, these overseas universities were able to operate freely in the 1980s. Following their success, many less reputable institutions began to follow suit, expanding into other Asian countries such as Malaysia, Indonesia, and China. Today, the tertiary education provided by overseas institutions in these Asia economies resembles a very muddy situation in which the questionable operator is able to exploit the vulnerable consumers who are hungry for paper qualifications. Many of these overseas universities teamed up with small local companies which did not provide the facilities needed for the proper training of tertiary students. This muddy or troubled water has to be cleared before more innocent "fishes" are sacrificed to some of these greedy operators.

"Catching a fish in troubled water" can also be illustrated by two corporate moves by the Lippo Group of Indonesia and Singapore's Keppel Group. The main target of the Lippo Group was the Prime Savings Bank of the Philippines. Prime Savings Bank experienced huge loan losses due to poor management. After heavy cash withdrawals in April 1997, the bank almost collapsed. Despite having a network of 51 branches, it was in serious trouble, and this provided an opportunity for the Lippo Group to acquire a controlling stake in the bank.

A Filipino bank related to the Prime Savings Bank was in similar trouble a month earlier. The Monte de Piedad and Savings Bank had been facing serious management problems for over two years. It suffered from bad credit policies and screening criteria, causing massive loan losses. Many of its borrowers could not be traced. Under normal circumstances, it would be impossible to buy into another foreign bank as the industry was highly regulated by the local government. However, in troubled waters, as in the cases of Prime and Monte de Piedad, the Lippo and Keppel Groups were viewed as white knights who saved the damsels in distress.

ASIAN CURRENCY AND STOCK CRISES IN 1997

The Asian currency and stock crises which occurred during the third quarter of 1997 were classic examples of how international speculators attempt to exploit a chaotic situation. The speed and ruthlessness with which several Asian currencies and stock markets were attacked amazed the public. Within weeks, billions of dollars were wiped out by these speculators. Many sold short, aggravating the crises by pushing both the currencies and stock markets down. While the affected Asian governments paid a high price to defend their currencies and stock markets, many speculators benefited from their woes.

Prime Minister of Malaysia criticised and warned foreign fund and currency managers. But this did not prevent the Malaysian ringgit from dropping further. Concurrently, the Malaysian stock market took a severe beating. Compared to the beginning of 1997, it lost about 50% in terms of market capitalization.

There are useful lessons to be learned from the currency and stock market crises in Asia. Firstly, when there is money to be made, do not be surprised that investors may turn into speculators. Their changing roles fuel the problem even more. Secondly, when the stakes are high, moral standards may be compromised. When gains and losses are high, greed and selfish behaviour may emerge, and national interests compromised for the sake of making more money. Thirdly, in times of chaos, the number of opportunists and exploiters increases, and their behaviour becomes more ruthless. Fourthly, large sums of money can still be made when the markets are down. Fifthly, it is important not to overreact in chaotic situations as this may cause more confusion.

These crises taught some Asian economies to be prudent in their economic expansion and growth. While it is not possible to fuel economic growth without causing severe imbalances in trade and huge current account deficits, development has to be matched by increasing exports to finance the imports. They cannot be achieved by borrowing short-term funds to finance long-term projects. The economy should be managed in a way which does not make it vulnerable to external exploitation.

STRATEGY 21

金 蝉 脱 壳

MAKING AN UNNOTICED ESCAPE LIKE A GOLDEN CICADA SHEDDING ITS SKIN

存其形, 完其势; 友不疑, 敌不动.
巽而止, 蛊.

EXPLANATION

By preserving the original formation of an army (存其形) and the strength of its force (完其势), one will not arouse the suspicion of the allies (友不疑). And the enemy will not be roused to action (敌不动). However, in actual fact, one is secretly diverting his main strength to attack the enemy from another direction. This is in accordance with *Yi Jing's* "Gu" (or "Confusion") Theory ([易经: 蛊] 卦).

HISTORICAL BACKGROUND

The phrase "金蝉脱壳" has been repeatedly used in some Chinese classics like *Yuan Qu Xuan* (元曲选) and *Journey to the West* (西游记). For instance, in *Yuan Qu Xuan*, Bang Lao scolded his friend for being negligent and letting the captives run away like a golden cicada shedding its skin: [元曲选:朱砂担] 第一折云: "(邦老照科云) 兄弟, 与你一搭儿买卖呀, 他们倒做个 金蝉脱壳计去了也, 打你这弟子孩儿, 你怎么放了 他去."

Journey to the West tells a story of Monkey and Piggy pursuing a "tiger". When the tiger stopped by a cliff, Monkey hit it hard with his rod. However, the "tiger" seemed hard as a rock, and it hurt Monkey's arm hitting it. Then Piggy, using his rake, peeled off the tiger skin that had been thrown over a rock. Monkey exclaimed that the tiger had escaped using the strategy of "Making an unnoticed escape like a golden cicada shedding its skin".

[西游记] 第二十回云: "却说那行者、八戒, 赶那虎(指黄风大王的前路先锋)下山坡, 只见那虎跑倒了, 塌伏在崖前. 行者举棒, 尽力一打, 转震得自己手疼. 八戒复筑了一钯, 亦将钯齿迸起. 原来是一张虎皮, 盖着一块卧虎石. 行者大惊道: '不好了! 不好了! 中了他计也!" 八戒道: '中他甚计?' 行者道: 这个叫做 '金蝉脱壳计': 他将虎皮盖在此, 他却走了."

The following story illustrates how this strategy was used.

In the second year of the West Han (西汉二年) era, Xiang Yu (项羽) led his troop to attack Liu Bang (刘邦) and the latter was cornered into the city called Xing Yang (荥阳). Although Liu Bang's man Chen Ping (陈平) managed, through trickery, to divert Xiang Yu's adviser Fan Zeng (范增) away, Xiang Yu and his troops still surrounded Xing Yang. The Han soldiers became worried when their food supply diminished as the days went by.

At this time, the Han General Ji Xin (纪信) told Liu Bang, "The situation looks desperate. I am willing to be Your Lordship's substitute to trick Xiang Yu into believing that I am Liu Bang. Please take the opportunity to escape, my Lord." Liu Bang adopted the suggestion. That night, he ordered the release of a bevy of women and two thousand armoured soldiers from the East Gate of Xing Yang. Ji Xin sat in the Lord's carriage with the flag of Liu Bang planted on the left of the carriage.

Ji Xin lied to the enemy soldiers that the Emperor of Han was surrendering as the city was running out of food. The Chu soldiers were overjoyed at this news. Liu Bang took the opportunity to escape with ten soldiers from the West Gate. When the Lord's carriage drove near, Xiang Yu realised that it was Ji Xin who was sitting in the carriage. Xiang Yu asked eagerly, "Where is Liu Bang?" Ji Xin replied, "The Han King has taken this opportunity to escape." On hearing this, Xiang Yu exclaimed, "What? Escaped?" He knew that he had been tricked by Ji Xin and ordered that Ji Xin be burnt to death.

COMMENTS & APPLICATIONS

When things look unchanged on the surface, the enemy may not suspect internal changes, and this facilitates the secret execution of major plans. This is the rationale behind Strategy 21. When a cicada metamorphosises, it sheds its old skin on the branch of a tree. This abandoned "shell" looks deceptively real. When faced with defeat, an enemy may use this strategy to escape unnoticed (for example, by covering up its retreat by not breaking camp), and thus be like the cicada that has shed its skin.

This strategy is designed not only as a means of escape. It can be used by the retreating army as a cover-up for a counter-attack when the enemy is unprepared. This strategy involves deception, just as the old skin of the cicada creates an illusion of the real cicada. Thus, this strategy is similar to what the great Chinese military strategist, Sun Zi, said:

> Therefore, when capable, feign incapability;
> When active, feign inactiveness.
> When near to the objective, feign that you are far away;
> When far away, make it appear that you are near.

故能而示之不能， 用而示之不用，
近而示之远， 远而示之近。

Strategy 21 can be used with Strategy 7, "Creating something out of nothing" in that the enemy can be deceived or distracted by a mere illusion, the decoy of the "empty shell".

Hence, this strategy can easily be used with Strategy 8, "Secret escape through Chen Cang" and Strategy 6, "Making a feint to the east but hit out in the west". When the enemy is completely deceived by the cicada's "empty shell," other strategies like Strategy 12, "Stealing a goat along the way" and Strategy 5, "Looting a house on fire" can be applied.

CONTINGENCY PLANNING

A direct application of Strategy 21, "Making an unnoticed escape like a golden cicada shedding its skin", is the use of contingency planning. A company cannot rely on only one course of action. To ensure success, it needs alternative courses of action, should the main plan fail. Alternative courses of action can also be a means of escape, and when used appropriately, may result in victory. It is like what Sun Zi called the "zheng" (正) and "qi" (奇) forces which operate like interlocking rings, with no beginning and end. In application, one force acts as the striking force, while the other acts as the decoy or deceptive force. However, the enemy will find it hard to determine which force is real.

A very interesting example to illustrate the use of this strategy in the modern corporate boardroom has to be Coca-Cola's introduction of New Coke in the 1980s (*covered in greater detail in Strategy 8, "Escape through Chen Cang"*). Coca-Cola, in an attempt to arrest its loss of market share to Pepsi, introduced the New Coke. The market's adverse reactions, however, forced Coke to reintroduce the original coke formula as the "Classic". To the dismay of competitors, and the delight of customers, Classic Coke returned within a matter of months. This could only have happened if Coca-Cola had a contingency plan on the stand-by. Shedding its old skin (old Coke), Coca-Cola re-emerged stronger, with a new "golden cicada" (the Classic Coke). To top it off, they successfully launched a new brand (New Coke), and more than recaptured all its previous lost market share.

WITHDRAWAL OF EXPATRIATE PROFESSIONALS

This strategy should not be interpreted as a means to practice deliberate deception in business. Rather, it is intended to provide an escape without arousing the attention or suspicion of those around. In this way, one can exit quietly while conserving and accumulating resources for deployment elsewhere. It is also an attempt to create competitive advantages, which need not result in loss or disadvantage to others, as it is possible and important to strive to create win-win situations.

Many American and Western multinational corporations often practise this strategy of "making an unnoticed escape like a golden cicada shedding its skin" in their personnel policies. When an American MNC first invests overseas, it will usually staff local operations with expatriate professionals to signal its commitment. It will gradually replace these expatriate employees with other expatriates (gradually shedding the cicada's skin without being noticed)! Finally, it will reduce the number of expatriate employees, replacing them with locals. Phasing out employees this way allows the MNCs to redeploy these valued employees elsewhere to start new overseas ventures.

The policy of replacing expatriate staff with locals is not necessarily a reflection of the lack of commitment on the part of these MNCs. On the contrary, giving the locals responsibilities allows them to accumulate tremendous amounts of exposure and experience. This is a concrete way to transfer management skills, expertise and know-how.

Their willingness to groom locals to take over top positions in running companies have caused American MNCs to be well-received by many Asian countries. In fact, American companies are generally well-known for their willingness to impart management skills and technological know-how to the less developed countries. Singapore, for one, benefited tremendously from the presence of MNCs in the early years of her economic development in the 1960s and 1970s. Today, Singapore continues to rely on MNCs for investment in high technology areas such as wafer fabrication plants and computer disk drives. In the process, many Singaporeans have become CEOs of the subsidiaries of these MNCs, including many overseas factories and plants. In contrast, Japanese companies tend to be more conservative in such areas. As foreign investors come under increasing scrutiny, the Japanese may have to change their stance in due course.

DIVESTING/REDUCING INVESTMENT & EQUITY

Strategy 21 can also be applied in situations where one may try to reduce his stake or investment without arousing the suspicion of others. For example, when a foreign investor senses that things are not going as well as expected, he can invite local participation by divesting some of his equity to them. Alternatively, he could sell his entire stake to local investors. To not cause alarm, he may volunteer to stay with the company in an advisory capacity. By staying on, he creates the impression that he has not abandoned the company. In reality, he already has no stake (and thus, no risk) in the company. Should the situation turn adverse, he can walk away, scar-free!

In the operation of hotel properties, international management chains have been using this strategy of "making an unnoticed escape like a golden cicada shedding its skin" for years. Typically, these management chains will opt for a percentage of sales revenues as its fees. They do not take any equity stake. This approach is particularly useful in managing hotels in countries where there are high political risks and other problems, such as currency exchange. When situation sours, these operators can simply catch the next flight out of the country. They lose nothing, as they have invested nothing in the first place. What is left behind would be the empty shell of the hotel building, including its prominently displayed name!

This clever practice of international hotel chain operators has been actively copied in many other services like legal and accounting practices, management consulting and hospital management. Many internationally established firms use commissioning or franchises to operate overseas to reduce exposure to risks. However, in recent years, many local governments and investors have demanded that these international service providers should take up some equity stake as well. This is particularly so in the hotel business. Some property owners now insist that the operators take an equity position before engaging their services. In some instances, they have also requested that local personnel be trained to ensure that there is transfer of technology and management know-how, an especially important move if equity options are not available. These measures are taken to ensure the golden cicada does not leave an empty shell behind.

Taking a Company to Public Listing

Interestingly, one of the most creative applications of the strategy "Making an unnoticed escape like a golden cicada shedding its skin" is the ability to take a privately owned company into public listing. In the process, the owners can easily reap many times their original investment, yet without losing control of their company so long as they retain controlling interest.

Typically, owners start off modestly, gradually building the business till sales and earnings are large enough to attract public investors. This is when public listing becomes a possibility. Through the market mechanism, the owners, with the help of investment (merchant) banks, would capitalise their business, and then float a substantial portion of their shares for public subscription.

By going for public listing, many owners become instant millionaires. This was the case for the Ngiam brothers when they listed their company, IPC, in Singapore. Similarly, the Koh brothers became multi-millionaires when they listed their construction company (of the same name) on the Singapore Stock Exchange in 1997. In Singapore, the effects are not very dramatic owing to the small market size. In the US, the most noticeable examples include Bill Gates of Microsoft and Michael Dell of Dell Computers. These gentlemen became multi-billionaires after listing their companies publicly.

Many good reasons support the decision to take a company to public listing. As mentioned above, it is the best way to realise returns on one's hard work, without forgoing control of the company. Typically, the payback is enormous. By bringing in public funds, the owners pass the risks of further expansion into the hands of shareholders while they, the owners, continue at the helm. With increased capital from new shareholders, the company can expand more rapidly. In addition, it allows the company to bring in professionals to help run the company and to carry out research and development (R&D). While Bill Gates and Michael Dell were personally involved in R&D when they first started, they are now no longer required to perform such functions. Instead, they now function as chief executive officers (CEOs).

Bringing in professional expertise is key to ensuring continued success. Original owners can gradually phase themselves out in the running of the company they have created, either opting to hold some shares, or to sell their stakes. This was what Steve Jobs did when he sold Apple Computers to Microsoft in August 1997. Similarly, original owners and descendants of companies gone public like IBM, Hewlett Packard, General Electric, General Motors and Motorola are basking today in their immense wealth. Indeed, they have succeeded like the golden cicada that has shed its skin!

STRATEGY 22

关门捉贼

SHUTTING THE DOORS TO CATCH THE THIEF

小敌困之。剥，不利有攸往。

EXPLANATION

The best way to destroy a weak enemy is to first have him surrounded (小敌困之). As Sun Zi said, "When outnumbering the enemy ten to one, surround him" (十则围之). According to *Yi Jing*'s "Bo" Theory ([易经：剥] 卦), it is not advisable to pursue a weak but agile enemy (剥，不利有攸往[2]). This will only exhaust one's strength, and make one vulnerable to the enemy's ambush.

In the same way, when catching a thief, one should shut off all routes of escape. If one gives chase without sealing the exits, the thief, seeing the possibility of escape, will put up a strong struggle. However, once the exits are sealed, the thief loses his fighting spirit, making his capture easier.

HISTORICAL BACKGROUND

The strategy uses the word "thief" (or "thieves") to refer to small groups of enemies which may not be very powerful but are able to launch sudden ambushes. The characteristics of these enemies are: they are agile and mobile, and can appear in the least expected moments and places; and though small, they have enormous potential to cause destruction.

As described in the book by famed ancient Chinese politician Wu Qi (吴起) in *Wu Zi* (吴子), if an escapee is not afraid of death, his strength can frighten ten thousand people (一人投命(拼命)，足惧万夫). Therefore, an enemy with a chance to escape, can still put up a fierce and debilitating struggle, no matter how weak or small he seems. The best way to defeat this

---

[1] "剥" *refers to a very dispersed and weak enemy.*

[2] "攸往" *means to chase after.*

enemy is to cut off all routes of escape. Sun Zi, the great military strategist, also held a similar view when he advocated, "Do not press an enemy in a desperate situation" (穷 寇 勿 迫). The following story illustrates this strategy.

> *Near the end of the Tang Dynasty (唐 朝), the political situation was very bad and the people suffered under the poor leadership of the Tang emperors. Therefore, many peasants and commoners decided to stage a revolution. In 875 AD, when Tang Xi Zong (唐 僖 宗) was the emperor, a man named Huang Chao (黄 巢) led a group of commoners and took over the control of the palace at Chang An (长 安). However, Emperor Tang and his men managed to escape to Cheng Du (成 都) and prepared to launch a retaliation.*
>
> *In 881AD, Huang Chao sent General Shang Rang (尚 让) to ambush the city of Feng Xiang (凤 翔). However, General Shang Rang underestimated the potential of the Tang army and was badly defeated. The Tang army pursued the enemy and General Shang Rang rushed back to Chang An to inform Huang Chao of their precarious situation. Huang Chao discussed with his advisers and decided to adopt the strategy of "Shutting the door to catch the thief". Huang Chao suddenly announced that they should vacate Chang An so the whole army retreated to the hills nearby. When the Tang army fought their way into Chang An, they were surprised to discover not one of Huang Chao's men. They then decided to enjoy themselves and started looting the place and raping the women in the city. That night, Huang Chao's men led by General Meng Kai (孟 楷) suddenly returned and sealed off all the escape routes. They then launched an ambush on the Tang army. The Tang army, caught by surprise, were trapped and destroyed. Thus Huang Chao recaptured Chang An.*

COMMENTS & APPLICATIONS

This strategy is very effective when the enemies are few and weak, and without strong leadership, making them easy prey. It differs from Strategy 16 "Releasing the enemy to recapture him later" in that in Strategy 16, the enemies are not weak, are not necessary trapped, and have a strong leader who must be tackled first. Given their strengths and strong leadership, these enemies are unlikely to surrender easily, so a head-on confrontation will cause heavy casualties. A more pragmatic approach is to win the "heart" of the leader. Strategy 16 is offensive in nature and is used by an attacker who, though possessing advantages of time and resources, is unwilling to risk resources unnecessarily.

In contrast, Strategy 22 "Closing the doors to catch the thief" involves a weak but agile enemy that has no strong leader and where the destruction of the enemy can be done in the quickest and most efficient way. This is because when all the escape routes are shut, the enemy's agility would be of little use. On the other hand, when there are some escape routes, an agile enemy can exploit them very quickly. Interestingly, when all escape routes are shut, agility may turn into confusion (just imagine how a group of moneys would behave under such a situation)! This would be the opportunity to destroy the enemy as illustrated in the above story on how Huang Chao managed to recapture Chang An. It would result in a situation where the strategy "Throwing a rock down when the enemy is in the well" could be easily applied. Similarly, Strategy 20, "Catching a fish in troubled water" can also be used when the enemy is denied any escape route. In fact, if there is no hurry to move in for the "kill", one can also use Strategy 4, "Conserving energy while the enemy tires himself out" with Strategy 22.

HANDLING WEAKER PRODUCTS AND BRANDS

As applied to business, this strategy advocates that when the competitor's product or brand is weak, a head-on promotional or price war is not necessary. Instead, one can "choke" the competitor's brand by surrounding it with one's stronger brands and products. This has been the repeated strategy of well-established products and brands entering markets in less developed countries. Instead of competing head-on on price, these brands often play up their strengths through intensive advertising and promotion, with heavy emphasis on quality, styling, packaging, design and point-of-sales. Through this, they captured substantial market shares.

Good examples can be found in the case of China. Many Western brands have begun to dominate the Chinese market in consumer products like beer, soft drinks and clothing, though these products are sold at price premiums. Shampoos by Proctor & Gamble are pegged at more than double the price of local products, but still sell like hot cakes in China.

The overwhelming success of imported products caused Chinese manufacturers to appeal to the government to urge consumers to support local brands. However, more than patriotism is required to turn the tide. This is because many Chinese manufacturers are weak and lack the financial resources and management expertise to fight these "giants". To counter the onslaught of foreign brands, Chinese manufacturers must make conscious efforts to improve the quality of their products, design and packaging. More importantly, they must improve their mastery of marketing, especially advertising and promotion, brand development and image-building.

Foreign products and brands have themselves become victims of stronger players. For example, in consumer electronics and durables like television sets, cameras, refrigerators, sound systems, video-cassette recorders and video cameras, Japanese manufacturers have established a strong presence internationally. Manufacturers of other countries have gradually been eliminated. The few surviving brands are constantly surrounded by stronger Japanese brands, locked in with no escape route.

EXPLOITING THE ADVANTAGES OF SIZE

Another application of this strategy in business is to exploit the advantage of size. Take the example of the retail gasoline industry in Singapore. Gasoline is a homogeneous product. Despite the existence of several brands in the market, few consumers are brand-conscious. Consumers hardly drive around shopping for their favourite brand of gasoline. Rather, gasoline is purchased out of convenience. When the gas tank is low, the consumer finds the most convenient gas station for a top-up. *Convenience* dictates his purchasing habit.

In Singapore, Shell is the largest operator in the retail gasoline industry. It controls over 40% of total market share while other operators – Esso, British Petroleum (BP), Caltex and Mobil – have about 11% to 17% each. As convenience influences purchasing behaviour, market coverage, as determined by the number of gas stations, is critical. Shell has the largest distribution network in Singapore. It has more than double the number of outlets of each of its competitors. It is no wonder that Shell is number one! Given the high cost of property and land in Singapore, it has not been easy for competitors to increase the number of their outlets.

Given Shell's enviable position, it has seldom initiated any price or promotional wars in the retail gasoline industry. Instead, it has chosen to compete by surrounding its competitors with an extensive distribution network. More often than not, smaller competitors would start a promotional war to steal some market share. Shell only retaliates, and often in a big way, when it senses the possibility of losing a significant market share. It will literally "out-gun" its competitors to teach them a lesson before leading the industry back to normalcy.

In Singapore's retail gasoline industry, while the other operators are small compared to Shell, they are nonetheless big players and subsidiaries of large, world-class corporations. Thus, they exercise their agility in the local market by using "hit and run" strategies. However, the same cannot to be said about the local grocery and retail shops. Over the past few years, many of these small retailers in Asian countries have been overwhelmed by large international departmental stores, supermarkets and chain stores with the financial muscle and management expertise to dominate. Being global players, they also enjoy tremendous economies of scale. Their ability to expand quickly through chain stores (for example, 7-Eleven) or franchising (fast-food chains) pose greater threats to the local operators.

This gives grist to the mill for resentment among local retailers against bigger operators. Unlike the international players, they neither have the expertise nor financial resources to expand their businesses, let alone venture overseas. The resentment was so intense in Indonesia that riots broke out 1997 where the locals were incited to even set fire to some of these large supermarkets and departmental stores. Their reactions caused concern, and large operators have begun to review their expansion plans.

ZERO-SUM OUTCOME

One of the greatest setbacks of this strategy that it is premised on a zero-sum outcome. In war, this may be inevitable, but in business, it is likely to encounter severe backlash or resistance. Businesses should seek win-win outcomes to be accepted by the business community.

While it may be difficult to ensure a win-win outcome for competitors, a company should attempt to procure winning outcomes for consumers and related parties. This cushions backlash from direct and indirect competitors. *Timing of entry* into a market also helps a company achieve a win-win situation. For example, when a market is fast-expanding, there is enough room for everyone, including new players. However, if the market is stagnant or in decline, any gain by one party has to come at the expense of another. If the gaining party happens to be a large and new foreign player, it may become the target for criticism and resentment.

As a result of the 1997 currency and stock market crises, many Asian companies, with shares trading at historical lows, or which are severely in debt, have become vulnerable to foreign takeovers and buyouts. This is aggravated when they are asked to open their economies to foreign participation as a condition for assistance from the International Monetary Fund. While many large foreign companies will be tempted to apply the "Shutting the doors to catch the thief" strategy to acquire significant stakes in Asian companies, these companies should progress with caution to avoid backlash. In particular, they should be sensitive to the sentiments among the Asians in crises.

In applying this strategy of "Shutting the doors to catch the thief", one must be fully aware that consequences may extend beyond the direct effects on the target(s) concerned. The strategist must balance all these factors. It pays to invest in data gathering and business intelligence so as to understand the market and the theatre of operation better. Finally, it still pays to seek win-win outcomes.

远交近敌

BEFRIEND THE FAR AND
ATTACK THE NEAR

形禁势格，利从近取；害以远隔。
"上火下泽"。

EXPLANATION

Sometimes, because of geographical constraints (形禁势格), it is more beneficial to attack a nearby enemy (利从近取) than to attack another far away (害以远隔). If the situation permits, form a temporary alliance with a distant enemy to destroy the enemy nearby. *Yi Jing's* "Kui" Theory ([易经：睽]卦) uses this analogy: though flames burn upward and water flows downward, one can still forge an alliance between them despite their different aims (上火下泽，睽。君子以同而异).

HISTORICAL BACKGROUND

This strategy comes from the story of how the Emperor of Qin conquered the neighbouring states and eventually, his "allies". The story is recorded in the *Book of the Warring States* ([战国策：秦策三]).

> *During the time of the Warring States, the Emperor of the state of Qin (秦国), Emperor Zhao Xiang (昭襄王), wanted to attack the faraway Qi State (齐国) in order to expand his own kingdom.*
>
> *At that time, every nation planned to conquer the others in hopes of expanding its kingdom. Qin was situated at the border and was the largest and most powerful state of all. Its power was so much feared that the other warring states kept an alliance just as a defence against Qin. While it was difficult for any state to attack Qin, it was equally difficult for Qin to attack the faraway states. So, Qin adviser Fan Sui*

(范 雎) proposed the "Befriend the far and attack the near" strategy as a way to break the deadlock.

To have the army attack a faraway state would create problems, two of which was transportation and food. The long journey would exhaust the men and animals alike. They needed a strategy to capture the states nearest to Qin. This would allow swift movement of troops and reinforcements, and would deter other states from assisting for fear of reprisal. More importantly, being farther away, they would have a false sense of security, thinking that their distance keeps them safe from attacks. So, Qin sent out strong signals to the faraway states, luring them into believing that Qin would not be hostile to them. This effectively broke the defence alliances between the states.

Adopting Fan Sui's strategy, the Emperor of Qin first destroyed neighbouring states like Han, Wei and Zhao. Having expanded his territory, he gradually took down the states which were farther away like Chu (楚), Yan (燕), Dai (代) and Qi (齐). Thus, by going after the easiest and most accessible targets first, the Emperor of Qin was able to build his empire.

COMMENTS & APPLICATIONS

When under attack, form alliances with neighbours so as to defeat or deter the enemy. However, when launching an attack, the strategy advocates attacking neighbouring states for geographical advantages, while befriending states farther away, to exert pressure on neighbouring states.

This strategy has some applications in today's complex international relations. It is sometimes easier to enter into a partnership with a faraway state than with one nearby. A country will always be more guarded with a nearby state as policies enacted by them may have vast impact.

A current example of this strategy in politics is Israel. It is situated in a precarious region, surrounded by hostile neighbours. Its history since formation has been fraught with countless wars with Arabic neighbours. With its very small population of a few million Jews, it has survived hostilities from neighbours many times more populous. One reason for Israel's survival is its strong allies in distant places, in particular, the United States, who has remained a strong supporter through the years. Together with some other nations in the West, the US provides a delicate balance in the Middle-East.

Israel is not the only country that relies on befriending faraway states to buffer its political situation. Smaller and weaker nations, especially those from the developing world, use this strategy frequently. In fact, their reliance on faraway but stronger countries extend beyond that of political support. Often these faraway nations (especially the United States) provide other assistance such as economic aid. In the 1997 drought in North Korea, assistance came from even farther away – help offered on purely humanitarian grounds, with no political strings attached.

Though this strategy appears illogical at first look, it can be lethal. The shrewd strategist can combine it with other strategies such as: Strategy 27, "Pretending to be insane but remain smart", or "Pretending to be a pig to prey on the tiger", and Strategy 1, "Deceiving the heaven to cross the sea", and Strategy 6, "Making a feint to the east but hitting out in the west".

STRATEGIC ALLIANCES WITH DISTANT PARTNERS

Using strategic alliances to "Befriend the far and attack the near" is popular in the airline industry. A good example is the strategic alliance between Delta Airlines, Singapore Airlines (SIA) and SwissAir, formed in the 1980s – the Global Excellence Alliance. With it, the airlines enlarged their market share and passenger traffic by catering to markets in Asia, Europe and America. This could not have been achieved if the alliance had been between regional airlines or neighbouring countries. Each member of this alliance was thus enabled to compete more effectively within its region.

Interestingly, after eight years of partnership, SIA found the Global Excellence Alliance unproductive and decided to leave it on 24 November 1997. On the same day, SIA forged a new alliance with Germany's Lufthansa Airlines which included code sharing and other tie-ups. This new strategic alliance with Lufthansa is very significant in that it paved the way for SIA to join the Star Alliance. Consisting of five of the world's biggest airlines — United Airlines of the US, Thai Airways International, Air Canada, Germany's Lufthansa, and the Scandinavian SAS Airline — the Star Alliance was formed in May 1997 to give member airlines competitive advantages against similar alliances in Europe, Asia, and North America. Brazil's Varig subsequently became its sixth member. With this cooperative partnership, price competition lessened and cost savings increased. If SIA joins the alliance it will have air routes spanning the globe.

British Airways (BA) established a strategic alliance with Qantas Airlines in 1995 where BA owned 25% of Qantas. This alliance provided, among other things, interchangeability of tickets, flexibility in passenger routing and code-sharing on the UK-Australia route. Effectively, the alliance allowed both airlines to capture a larger share in their markets.

The success of the BA-Qantas alliance and the lucrativeness of the kangaroo route prompted SIA to forge a new alliance with Ansett (the other major Australian airline) and Air New Zealand on 20 June 1997. The alliance, one of the largest in the Asia-Pacific, involved an established network of 223 aircrafts covering over 200 cities in 47 countries. The tie-up was a boon to Ansett which had been putting up a hard fight against Qantas. The alliance allowed Ansett to feed its passengers to Europe and America through Singapore, boosting competitiveness and profitability with greater economies of scale in marketing, promotion, information systems and purchasing. Ansett also enjoyed better bargaining power in negotiating with airplane suppliers, and an increased inflow of international traffic. Clearly, the commercial alliance with SIA and Air New Zealand is a strategy to "Befriend the far and attack the near".

Similar alliances can be found in the shipping industry, for example Global Alliance and Grand Alliance. In car manufacturing, Kia Motors Corporation (the second largest South Korea car maker) announced in February 1997 its ambitious globalisation drive through alliances with foreign partners in 23 countries, despite its severe financial difficulties. The alliances was meant to enable Kia compete more effectively in its overseas markets in Asia, Europe, America and Latin America. In the telecommunications industry, the most effective way for any new player to take on the large local incumbent is to team up with strong distant partners.

Wherever these alliances are formed, the objective remains the same — to team up with a foreign partner to compete more effectively against local and regional competitors.

INTERNATIONAL TRADE AND INVESTMENT

It is usually easier to attack nearby markets than those further away. In international trade and investment, companies find it easier to conduct business in neighbouring states than in faraway countries as they are more familiar with the culture, market conditions and social and political climate. The proximity allows better control and management as well.

Many American companies, in the early years of growth, were content to "attack" the Canadian and Mexican markets. The farthest they would venture was Western Europe and Latin America. But when these nearby states stagnated, increasing numbers of American companies ventured further. This came in the 1980s, a period which also saw the tremendous growth opportunities in Asia.

Their initial efforts were directed towards Eastern Europe. However, the chaotic political and economic conditions in there did not allow them to profit much. So, they switched their attention to Asia. However, given a choice, it is always easier to "attack" markets that are closer to home. Had the American and European continents continued to experience vibrant and sustainable economic growth, they may not have invested as aggressively in Asia as they are currently doing.

Singapore illustrates a different angle to this strategy. Recognising that the local economy would not provide sufficient impetus for growth, the government urged local companies to invest abroad and to internationalise their operations. When the call was made in the 1980s, Singapore companies began to "attack" the United States and European markets, thinking that they were large and lucrative. Unfortunately, these were distant markets of which Singaporean companies had little knowledge.

Not only did cultural and social differences present a challenge, these advanced economies had highly competitive world-class business players and products. Now no longer able to supply low-cost labour-intensive items, Singaporean companies faced tough competition from low-cost competitors like Malaysia, Thailand and China, and at the high end of the market from the United States, Europe and Japan. Sandwiched in this tight spot, Singapore companies did not fare well. The distance and time differences also made management, communication and control difficult.

As a result of early failures, the Singapore government quickly shifted its "battle cry" from internationalisation to regionalisation, with the focus on Asia, especially on neighbouring countries. In addition, many Singapore companies also learned to team up with companies in the developed world (typically not from the region, hence resembling "befriending the far") that can provide technological or other kinds of support.

The advantages of focusing on the region are many. Firstly, many Asian markets are in the same time zone. Closer proximity means less travelling time and hence, better control. Secondly, Asian economies like China, Indonesia, Vietnam, and India, after opening up to the world, have experienced high economic growth. Hence, it makes better sense to concentrate on these growing markets than to direct long-distance efforts on the matured markets of Europe and America. These latter economies were stagnating in the 1980s and their growth rates in the 1990s were lower than most Asian economies.

Thirdly, the social and cultural contexts in Asian markets are more familiar to multi-cultural Singapore. Fourthly, with a strong distant partner, the strength and credibility of the company are enhanced. Finally and most significantly, export and business opportunities for Singaporean companies abound. With Singapore's economic success, it has become a model these Asian economies aspire to emulate. Singapore's strong branding in these newly developed Asian economies enable Singaporean companies to enjoy relative superiority in their offerings of products, services or investments.

Singapore companies have experienced considerable success in their regionalisation efforts. Besides being the largest investor and trade partner with Malaysia, Singapore is now a major investor in Asian economies like China, Vietnam, Indonesia, Myanmar and Cambodia.

Indeed, there are sound reasons for dealing with the more familiar than to tackle the unfamiliar and unknown, where the risks are higher and the returns unpredictable. The conventional wisdom of "high risk, high return" does not necessarily hold true.

Franchising and Licensing

Franchising and licensing have become important business arrangements in doing business in many developing economies. Other than fast food chains, there are many other Western chains that have made tremendous inroads in the Asia market through franchising and licensing. Their businesses cover a wide spectrum of products and services. Good examples include Hard Rock Cafe (restaurant), Delifrance (pastry), Haagen Daaz (ice-cream) and Starbucks (coffee).

In a franchising arrangement, the local operator (franchisee) secures the right to use the franchisor's name and market the products with assistance form the latter. Typically, the franchisee puts up most of the capital as well as pay a franchising fee. As the franchisor has an international or global reputation and is able to provide expert marketing and consulting services. Such a business arrangement allows the franchisee to secure a large domestic market share very quickly. In fact, more often than not, the arrival of these franchises pose severe threats to the local competitors. One only needs to witness the significant inroads made by these international franchising chains to realise the market impact made by them in economies like Singapore, China, Hong Kong and Taiwan.

In a franchising arrangement, the franchisee can also hold the rights to market the franchisor's products to other markets around his own country. Thus, by "befriending the far" (teaming up with a strong franchisor) the franchisee is able to "attack the near" (domestic and regional markets).

Licensing operates on a similar principle, although it occurs mainly in manufacturing. The local company normally has the necessary production capabilities, including quality control standards and procedures. Unfortunately, it lacks the marketing skills, the established distribution networks and the power of a world class brand to pull in consumer demand. Thus, a local company would typically seek out an established foreign partner. It would then manufacture and market its products under the well-known brand name of the foreign partner. The product is usually sold to markets around the region, and may include the domestic market of the local manufacturer.

Like franchising, licensing covers a wide range of products such as sportswear and equipment (such as Yonex, Reebok, Adidas and Nike), shirts and men's apparel (such as Arrow, Manhattan, Valentino and Christian Dior) and furniture (such as Ikea). By "befriending the far" the local manufacturer is able to quickly "attack the near", that is, the domestic and regional markets.

STRATEGY 24

假途伐虢

BORROW A PASSAGE TO ATTACK GUO

两大之间，敌胁以从，我假以势。
困，有言不信。

EXPLANATION

A smaller state situated between the enemy and oneself (两大之间) should be given immediate support if the enemy threatens to control it (敌胁以从). In this way, one will earn the trust of the smaller state and may eventually exert one's influence over the latter (我假以势). Mere words without action (有言不信) will not win the trust of a small force in a precarious situation (困).

HISTORICAL BACKGROUND

This strategy comes from the *Left Story* (左传) regarding how Jin (晋国) destroyed two nations, Yu (虞) and Guo (虢) under the pretenxt of borrowing the road through Yu to destroy Guo.

During the Spring and Autumn period, there were two small neighbouring kingdoms, Yu and Guo. Both bordered on the much larger and more powerful kingdom of Jin. Jin had an ambition to colonise the neighbouring states to expand its territory and a Jin official, Xun Xi (荀息) devised the perfect plan.

The king of Jin, Jin Xian Gong (晋献公), threw a lavish banquet for the ruler of Yu and enticed him with treasures — a fine stallion, a priceless jade and a beautiful woman — into giving Jin troops a passage through Yu to attack Guo.

The adviser from Yu, Gong Zi Qi (宫子奇) warned his Emperor against taking the offer. Gong said that the relationship between Yu and Guo was akin to the lips and teeth, that is, if the lips (Guo) were gone, the teeth (Yu) would freeze (辅 车 相 依, 唇 亡 齿 寒). If Guo fell into Jin's hand, Yu would be captured soon after. The Emperor of Yu did not heed his adviser and agreed to Xian Gongs request. So, Guo was captured by a surprise attack from Jin. On their return to the kingdom of Jin through Yu, the Jin troop launched a surprise attack on the kingdom of Yu. Yu fell easily into the hands of Jin.

COMMENTS & APPLICATIONS

A smaller state sandwiched between the enemy and oneself deserves support especially if it has a decisive influence on the outcome of the battle. By helping it when it is in trouble, one can gain its support. It would be to one's detriment to allow the smaller state to be captured or utilised by the enemy. Helping the smaller state would earn its gratitude, and even a possible alliance. This is akin to acquiring the smaller state! Similarly, two smaller states under attack by a bigger state should not play against each other as that may lead to their eventual destruction. This is the rationale behind Strategy 24.

This strategy has some similarities with Strategy 3 "Kill another with a borrowed knife" and Strategy 14, "Borrowing a corpse to resurrect a soul". There are some subtle differences, however. "Kill another with a borrowed knife" is used in a proactive manner. The strategist *exploits another party* and uses him to accomplish his goals. By "Shifting the blame to someone else", he uses the other party as "hatchet man" or the "fall guy". In Strategy 14, the strategist is in a *desperate position*, and has to make a life or death decision. The *personal stakes* are very high.

In contrast, Strategy 24, "Borrow a passage to attack Gu" he *leverages the assistance* of another party (or parties) to achieve goals. Unlike Strategy 3 which involves the use of a "hatchet man", the strategist has to accomplish the goal himself. At the same time, he may also destroy those who have assisted him. Thus, he will "Kill two vultures with a single arrow" (一 箭 双 雕).

MARKETING UNDER OTHER COMPANIES' BRANDS

One of the best illustrations of the use of this strategy in business is how the Japanese manufacturers penetrated world markets by borrowing "passages" from their Western counterparts (*also explained in Strategy 3 "Kill with a borrowed knife"*). When Japan industrialised after World War II, its products were relatively unknown. To establish a foothold, and to understand distribution channels, Japanese manufacturers sold their products under European and American brand names. Japanese manufacturers thus "borrowed a passage" to access world markets.

Having gained the necessary experience, Japanese manufacturers developed their brand names in the 1950s and 1960s. By the 1970s, Japanese products and brands had become symbols of high quality, comparable to that of their Western competitors. By the 1980s, Japanese manufacturers began to dominate in many products, and in some instances, literally eliminated their competitors. Few analysts would have expected the extent of their success in the early days when they first borrowed "access routes" from their unwary competitors.

Japan started from a position of weakness. After World War II, its economy was at its worst and the country was in ruins. It was never perceived as an economic threat and was not taken seriously. In fact, under the Marshall Plan, the US played a key role in restoring and rebuilding Japan's economy. Because they did ignored this fast-emerging potential threat, these competitors paid a high price.

To a large extent, the Japanese strategy had been copied by the Koreans. By studying the Japanese, the Koreans were able to shorten their learning experience to build global brands. While the Japanese took about 50 years, the Koreans took less than 30 years to build up global brands like Hyundai, Goldstar, Samsung, and Ssangyong.

The successes of the Japanese and Koreans suggest that it is worthwhile to begin humbly by "borrowing passages" from the stronger established competitors. The caveat is, having secured the passage, these companies must quickly build their strength, and cannot continue to rely on "borrowed passages". This is one lesson that newly opened economies like China, Indonesia, and Vietnam must learn as these countries welcome their European, Japanese, and American partners "blindly" and are too contented marketing products under foreign brands. Little effort has been made to develop their own national brands.

BACKWARD/FORWARD INTEGRATION AND PIGGYBACKING

The Hour Glass is one company that has adopted this strategy to pave its growth into the 21st century. A watch retailer listed on the

Singapore Stock Exchange, it started from humble beginnings. As of July 1997, it had 15 watch boutiques in Singapore, Australia, Hong Kong, Indonesia, Malaysia and Thailand, with plans for expansion in Vietnam, China and India. Its strong reputation as an upmarket watch retailer was supported by its exclusive wholesale agency for brands like Brequet, Hublot, Bertolucci, Burberrys and Revue Thommen.

However, a retailer is still a retailer, regardless of the number of outlets it has. In an effort to be a bigger player in the industry, The Hour Glass decided to pursue a *backward integration* strategy by getting into watch manufacturing. To do it with minimal risks, the company "borrowed a passage" to achieve its objective. In 1994, it bought a 51% stake in Daniel Roth for S$2.6 million. Having successfully secured a passage, it went on to buy another "path" into the manufacturing business when it bought a 66% stake in Gerald Genta and its distribution arm in Monte Carlo in 1996 for S$11.6 million. With these investments, The Hour Glass managed to combine its international marketing and advertising skills with strong manufacturing that included in-house design expertise.

Both Daniel Roth and Gerald Genta are well-known Swiss brands. They excelled traditionally in making top quality watches, but paid little attention to advertising and promotion. They also lacked the capital for expansion. With the injection of funds from The Hour Glass and its established networks in Asia, the two brands had a new lease of life. For The Hour Glass, this was the perfect way to enter manufacturing. Thus, by borrowing "passages" literally from one another, the alliance resulted in a *"win-win"* business marriage.

Of course, the backward integration practised by The Hour Glass is a creative way of expanding a business by "borrowing passages" from others. Instead of starting from scratch, the company chose to *integrate backward or forward,* benefit from existing expertise, and thus leapfrog ahead.

When it is not possible to pursue a strategy of forward or backward integration, other alternatives can be explored. For example, one can piggyback on established distribution houses to distribute products. In Japan, trading houses provide this function very effectively. Small manufacturers who do not have a marketing arm rely on companies like Proctor and Gamble to provide a passage for them to the various markets of the world.

Similarly, many cottage industries in the developing countries rely on similar distribution channels. Handicraft and hand-made products, for example, are sold through middlemen who purchase these products from village homes. In Turkey, many beautifully hand-woven silk and wool carpets like the *Hereke* (a well-known brand name) are sourced in this way. Without the middlemen who provide the passages, these wonderfully made pieces of art may never be available to the outside world.

DIVERSIFYING THROUGH ACQUISITIONS

Another application of the strategy of "Borrowing a passage to attack Guo" is in business *diversification* through acquisition, a quick way to expand the business. Building a new business takes time and effort. Expertise has to be developed gradually. If a new business grows too slowly, economies of scale will not be enjoyed. Yet, diversification is necessary to spread business risks over a wider portfolio of products and services. Besides providing opportunities to tide over business cycles, diversification allows a company entrance into other fast-growing businesses. Companies with large cash reserves may find diversification through acquisition an attractive option. Companies with limited cash may need diversification to allow them to get into new businesses and new markets quickly.

A good illustration is IPC's acquisition of Hagenuk in September 1997. IPC, a computer manufacturer based in Singapore, had been trying very hard to look for new business opportunities to balance its highly competitive and volatile computer business. Its profits had been in decline since 1996. The opportunity came when it managed to up its stake in Hagenuk Telecom GmbH, a German company manufacturing wireless telecom systems, from 37.5% to 75%. With the initial investment of S$67.5 million, IPC plans to acquire Hagenuk Telecom as a 100% subsidiary. This purchase allowed IPC to diversify into the telecommunications business, a sunrise industry expected to grow in Asia over the next 10 to 20 years. With Hagenuk's connection, IPC set up a joint venture in China in September 1997 to produce wireless technology products for the China market.

Another company employing this tactic was Keppel Corporation. Years ago, Keppel Corporation (previously Keppel Shipyard) embarked on a similar strategy to diversify, acquiring financial institutions and insurance companies. Today, Keppel Corporation is a well-diversified company with a wide spectrum of products, services and operations in many countries. Sembawang

Corporation (previously Sembawang Shipyard) did the same. Its highly diversified businesses today includes telecommunications.

In response to the call by the Singapore government for companies to go international and to ensure competitiveness against MNCs, Singaporean companies are likely to diversify through acquisition. For Singapore to have home-grown MNCs, it has to "borrow a passage to attack Guo". Sembawang Corporation, for example, has secured a deal to buy a 51% controlling stake in Delifrance Asia on 2 October 1997 for a cool S$165.8 million. Delifrance Asia is a French-owned cafe chain listed on the Singapore Stock Exchange with 154 outlets in the region (as of October 1997). However, when approved, it would cost the company over S$325 million to take over Delifrance Asia completely. This acquisition gave Sembawang Corporation its long-awaited chance to diversify into the food business with a well-established household brand.

With plunging value of stocks and market capitalsation in Malaysia, Indonesia and Thailand, many opportunities can be exploited in these cash-strapped companies. The more enterprising and cash-rich Singapore companies can explore the possibility of acquiring these companies to diversify and expand into the region. While there are inherent risks, the returns are likely to be worth the effort. Given the sound economic fundamentals of these countries, there is reason to believe that a turnaround is in sight. A lost opportunity may not be recovered.

LISTING COMPANIES ON FOREIGN STOCK EXCHANGE

In the arena of finance, companies also use the "borrow a passage to attack Guo" strategy. When a company finds it difficult to raise capital from the local market, it will seek to get listed on a foreign stock exchange. Because of high economic growth in China, many Chinese businesses have listed their companies in Hong Kong and Singapore. The Hong Kong Stock Exchange (HKSE), in particular, is a hot favourite for the companies from China. By having their companies publicly listed on the HKSE, these Chinese companies find it easier to raise funds for expansion. Overseas listing also give these companies better exposure to international investors. A very good example is the case of Creative Technologies. Although the company had its origin in Singapore, it decided to seek listing in the United States. As a result, Creative Technologies is not only able to raise substantial capital in the United States, but is able to market its products to the largest market in the world. If it had chosen to remain in Singapore, it may not be able to achieve its current status as a global company.

An increasing number of Indonesian companies are listing their companies on the Singapore Stock Exchange (SES). As of July 1997, the largest Indonesian company to be listed on the SES (Asia Food & Properties) had a capitalisation of US$2.9 billion. This was followed by the food group, QAF, with US$2 billion capitalisation. Unlike companies from China, Indonesian firms tend to *inject their global assets* into already listed vehicles in the SES. For example, as of July 1997, the Salim Group (owned largely by Liem Sioe Liong) owned 70% of QAF, and 56% of UIC, a commercial property company that controls Singapore Land. The Sinar Mas Group (owned largely by Eka Tjipta Widjaja and family) owned 98% of Amcol Holdings and 100% of Asia Food & Properties. The family of Putera Sampoerna owned 66% of Transmarco, and the Riady's family controlled 80% of the food group Auric Pacific.

By taking over existing listed vehicles on the SES, these Indonesian companies are actually borrowing a passage to inject their global assets into Singapore. This is a strategic move by these Indonesian conglomerates to hedge their financial and capital risks in a "safe" economy like Singapore. Through these listed companies, the Indonesian conglomerates were also able to generate alternative sources of funds and to raise capital in Singapore dollars, an important move, considering the weakening Indonesian rupiah.

Like China, Indonesia does not have a well-developed stock market and shares are not widely traded. In using such a strategy, these Indonesian corporate movers are able to gain access to some of the most developed capital markets (besides Singapore, some of the Indonesian companies have also gained access to the stock exchanges of the United States) in the shortest possible time. By taking over existing publicly listed companies, they are also using Strategy 30 "The guest takes over as host". Between 1992 to 1996, a total of 13 companies listed on the SES were taken over by Indonesian business groups.

偷 梁 换 柱

REPLACE SUPERIOR BEAMS AND PILLARS WITH INFERIOR ONES

频更其阵, 抽其劲旅, 待其自败, 而后乘之。
曳其轮也。

EXPLANATION

Find a chance to change the enemy's battle array frequently (频更其阵), and take away its main source of power (抽其劲旅). Wait till it is unable to cope with the situation (待其自败) before attacking it (而后乘之). This is in accordance with *Yi Jing's* "Ji Ji" Theory ([易：既济]) that if one is able to take control of the big wheels of a truck, he will also be taking control of the direction where the truck goes (九二, 曳其轮, 贞吉).

Pillars and beams are important structures in a building. The quality of the pillars and beams determine the stability of the building. The arrangement of an army troop has parallel significance. A troop is divided into four wings: north, south, east and west. The foremost and the last rows will face each other and they are called "Tian Heng" (天衡) or "Sky Balance". "Tian Heng" are the main beams of the troop. The row branching from the centre to the two sides is known as the "Di Zhou" (地轴) or "Axle of the Earth" and these form the pillars of the troop. This is supposedly the best arrangement for both defence and attack. Therefore, a smart general would usually place his best men in the "Tian Heng" and "Di Zhou" positions. If the people in these two positions are replaced with soldiers of inferior quality, the troop is weakened and may lose the battle.

HISTORICAL BACKGROUND

This strategy advocates using trickery to replace something real (strong) with something false (weak). It works in the same way as

"Steal the dragon and replace it with the phoenix" (偷龙转凤) and "Use the false to pass off as the real thing" (以假乱真). In the Chinese classics ***The Dream of the Red Chamber***, how Jia Bo Yu (贾宝玉) married Xue Bo Chai (薛宝钗) thinking that he was marrying Lin Dai Yu (林黛玉) is an illustration of this strategy.

第九十七回写道: 一丫头见李纨说: 大奶奶! 只怕林姑娘不好了! 那里都哭呢."偏偏凤姐想出一条 "偷梁换柱"之计为宝玉完婚, 林姑娘竟这样小小年纪就作了北邙乡女(葬身异乡)!

The following story describes the usage of this strategy.

Before Emperor Qin Shi Huang (秦始皇) died while on a hunting trip, he knew he was not to live for long and wrote a will to his eldest son Fu Su (扶苏), asking Fu Su to ascend his throne after his death. The emperor sealed the letter and left it with official Zhao Gao (赵高). Zhao Gao, however, did not send the letter to Fu Su.

Prime Minister Li Si (李斯) was afraid that news of the emperor's death would lead to civil war among the lords and so refused to release the information to the public. The emperor's body was left in the carriage. They continued delivering food to the carriage daily, and the officials continued to conduct daily meetings with "the emperor" outside the carriage until his body was safely transported to the capital Xian Yang (咸阳). When news of the emperor's death was finally released, the most pertinent issue at hand was the succession of the throne.

It turned out that Zhao Gao was once the personal tutor of Hu Hai (胡亥), the youngest son of the Emperor Qin Shi Huang and he was a favourite with the prince. He knew that if Hu Hai were to succeed the throne, he would be given vast power. Therefore, instead of giving the will of Qin Shi Huang to Fu Su, Zhao Gao told Hu Hai, "When the Emperor died, he left a will to his eldest son appointing the latter to the throne. He did not mention how the kingdom should be divided among his children. Therefore, when your brother succeeds the throne and you are left with no land to rule, what would happen to you?"

Hu Hai replied, "It is only right that my late father the Emperor elected the eldest son to be his successor. My duty as a younger brother is to follow." Zhao Gao rebutted, "This statement is incorrect. Now, the power is in our and Li Si's hands. Why don't we change the will?"

"It's illogical that the youngest instead of the eldest should be elected as successor to the throne. It is also unfilial to not obey the Emperor's will. This will anger the people and may cause unrest," Hu Hai replied with great unease.

Zhao Gao kept nudging Hu Hai till he finally agreed to Zhao Gao's plan.

Zhao Gao with Li Si, conspired against Fu Su, forged another will and had the rightful successor sentenced to death.

COMMENTS & APPLICATIONS

This is the first of the six deception strategies. Though often condemned, deception strategies are commonly used in war. The primary aim of doing so is to create advantages against the enemy. But in applying these strategies in business, one must be very careful to not engage in unethical or illegal acts. A company may still create advantages for itself through legal means. This is where creativity and innovative thinking are required.

Among the six categories of strategies, deception strategies provide the most potential and possibilities in terms of applications and combinations with other strategies.

SHORT-CHANGING THE CONSUMER

In the business world, there are no shortage of cases where unscrupulous businessmen or companies cheat unwary consumers. Examples can be found in the construction and renovation business. It is very easy for contractors to promise and even show their customers superior products such as tiles, marbles and cement, and replace them with inferior ones. The consumer is often not able to detect differences in quality. Moreover, materials like cement, pipes, beams and electrical systems are not visible from the outside. The brands of products such as paints, electrical wires and pipes are also indistinguishable once they are used.

Unethical practices by contractors have caused buildings to collapse or become fire hazards. During the construction boom, standards tended to be compromised when regulators did not exercise close surveillance and monitoring. We often hear of buildings catching fire as a result of poor workmanship and materials. In the more extreme cases, entire buildings collapse, the result of unscrupulous contractors who "replaced superior beams and pillars with inferior ones".

To prevent these unethical practices and to protect the consumer, strict building codes and practices have been developed. Some governments, like Singapore's, insist that contractors provide a period of warranty, during which all defects detected would be repaired.

Other examples of malpractice can often be found in businesses such as motor repair and custom tailoring. For example, in Thailand, unwary tourists are tempted by very cheap and efficient custom tailors offering tailor-made business suits within 24 hours. Unfortunately, unscrupulous tailors may substitute inferior materials (for example, in the paddings and linings) for the quality ones they used to lure the tourists. The severe defects are only discovered after the suit is sent for dry cleaning. By then, the tourist would be thousands of miles away.

Diners in Asia too complain about the suspect quality of sharksfin, abalone, mushrooms, birdsnest, and other exotic but expensive dishes. Some restaurants display enticing pictures which look nothing like the actual dishes they serve!

Burden of Proof on the Consumers

One way unscrupulous businesses get away with their trickery is because the *burden of proof* lies with the consumer. The consumer is usually handicapped by his lack of expert knowledge, and usually ends up at the losing end. Even if the consumer suspects he has been cheated, it takes too much time, effort and money to take the culprit to court, and all that for an uncertain outcome.

Take the case of packaged tours commonly advertised in the newspapers and tour brochures. The operator may "promise" a lot of attractions to lure customers. The operator may state in writing that the tour includes all meals, accommodation at deluxe hotels, admission to places of attractions, baggage handling, and so on. However, these written statements are fraught with problems and their interpretations can be very deceptive.

To begin with, the quantity, quality and variety of "all meals provided" are not stated. Thus, tour members can be served insufficient or poor quality food at each meal. Secondly, "deluxe hotels" do not indicate quality, nor do they necessarily include attached bathrooms with hot water! Thirdly, admission to most places of attractions could exclude places where admission charges are high. The tour could bring members to places with no admission charges. Finally, while baggages are handled, tips may be required.

Most annoyingly, tour operators always include an escape clause in their printed materials which absolves them from all responsibility. Typically, they will use phrases like "subject to availability" or "places of visit, accommodation... may be substituted". This makes it almost impossible to fault them even if they deliberately "replace superior beams and pillars with inferior ones". Many are keen for regulations to be put in place as malpractices tarnish the image of a country and its tourist industry.

PIRATED GOODS

Pirated goods is another area where "Replacing superior beams and pillars with inferior ones" has been used very conspicuously. Without doubt, producers of fakes should face tough penalties for flagrantly violating copyright and trademark laws, and for robbing producers of genuine products of billions of dollars of lost sales and profits. The existence of a market for fakes testify to the existence of customers willing to pay for these products.

Interestingly, some of the biggest culprits that violate copyright laws are not found among Asian countries — the region commonly associated with piracy. In fact, Italy which used to be well-known for its brands, has now become the most well-organised producer of pirated goods. Like Russia, Italy now appears regularly on the "blacklist" of intellectual property right violations of many countries. Pirating branded goods has become a huge industry in Italy. In early 1997, the Italian law enforcers conducted massive raids in the cities of Milan, Florence and Tuscany. Confiscated products covered a wide range of established brands like Chanel, Dior and Gucci.

Fakes made in Italy, especially for leather goods, so closely approximate the genuine articles that they are passed off as the real products and sold to countries like Japan, the United States, Switzerland and Canada. Few customers, including original manufacturers, are able to tell the difference! Today, Italy and Russia have begun to rival the traditional producers of fakes in economies like Thailand, China, Hong Kong, Malaysia and Taiwan. The range of products has also expanded drastically to books, computer software, video tapes, video compact discs (VCDs), digital video discs (DVDs) and cassettes. As of 1997, it is estimated that the market for fakes is worth over US$7 billion a year, and growing.

At times the consumer may be aware that he is not buying the genuine product, but he still persists in doing so. This is particularly true for pirated products like CD-ROMs, computer software, cassettes, VCDs and DVDs. For their extremely low prices, these are very attractive despite their quality. Pirating of computer software is rampant because they are easily copied, and detection is difficult.

Manufacturers of original products have found that the best way to combat piracy is to go to the source instead of pursuing the individual consumers. These manufacturers engaged private investigators and obtained court injunctions to raid the producers and distributors of pirated goods. They also took extensive advertisements to warn and educate consumers against purchasing pirated goods. Their efforts have met with some success. However, so long as the original products are sold at high prices, there will always be unethical businessmen willing to take the risks of "replacing superior beams and pillars with inferior ones". This will continue to be so as long as there is demand for the pirated products.

MAKING CONSUMERS AWARE OF REPLACEMENTS

On the positive side, if consumers are made aware of replacements, the use of this strategy may bring in more sales for the creative businessmen. A good example is the sale of Japanese cars to China in the late 1970s and 1980s when China had just opened up for trade. Many organisations in China did not have large financial resources to purchase luxury cars and limousines then. To cater to the limited budgets of their Chinese clients, Japanese manufacturers like Toyota re-engineered and reconditioned used cars and sold them as "new" ones. For a period of time, it appeared that the Japanese automobile makers were going to dominate the Chinese market they captured a sizeable share of the Chinese corporate market.

The European and American car makers were unwilling to do what the Japanese did. To them, it was unethical to conduct any "backward" engineering or innovation. The result — they lost out in China in the early years. Fortunately for them, the Chinese economy has since grown substantially. Luxury European and American limousines like Volvo, Mercedes, BMW, Cadillacs and Rolls Royce have now become affordable. These products have become status symbols owing to their uncompromising adherence to high quality.

In *parallel importing*, companies have exploited this strategy to their advantage. Parallel imports are products made by the same manufacturer, but brought in from other countries, and may come without warranties or guarantees. As MNCs have factories and plants in many countries, parallel importers source the same products from countries that offer them at the best prices. For example, Mercedes and BMW have plants in several countries. So it is possible to bring in these luxury cars from countries other than Germany, such as South Africa. Some parallel importers of cars in Singapore used this approach to offer cars at substantially lower prices.

Besides cars, parallel imports have extended to many other branded goods such as clothing and shoes. In most instances, consumers are made aware that the products that they buy cannot be equated to those bought directly from the authorised dealers or agents.

An increasing awareness that consumers should be educated about their rights as well as responsibilities have caused governments, especially those in Asia, to encourage the setting up of Consumers' Associations. In countries like Singapore, the Consumers' Association has become an important mechanism by which consumers can seek redress. The Consumers' Association also serves to alert consumers against companies known to engage in questionable practices. Singapore's Consumers' Association occasionally publishes the names of blacklisted companies.

In the final analysis, the consumer must exercise caution in making purchases so as not to be easily duped.

STRATEGY 26

指桑骂槐

POINTING AT THE MULBERRY
BUT SCOLDING THE LOCUST TREE

大凌小者，警以诱之。
刚中而应，行险而顺。

EXPLANATION

A stronger force can use warning or admonishment to control a lesser force (大凌小者，警以诱之). A proper display of power will receive support and the use of a decisive method will demand reverence, as described in *Yi Jing's* "Shi" Theory ([易：师]：刚中而应，行险而顺。以此毒(治)天下，而民从(拥护)之). It is not necessary to destroy the smaller force when one is very strong. Teaching it a lesson by issuing a warning would suffice.

This strategy is similar to the Chinese saying, "Kill the chicken to scare the monkeys" (杀鸡警猴). Monkeys are intelligent animals, known to be afraid of blood. So monkey trainers will slaughter a chicken in front of the monkeys to frighten them into obedience. As a military strategy, it is usually used to enforce adherence to military rules, as seen in this story.

HISTORICAL BACKGROUND

Sun Zi once brought his set of war strategies to meet the Emperor of Wu state, He Lu (阖 闾). Emperor He Lu was pleased with Sun Zi's war strategies and asked him for a demonstration. He challenged Sun Zi to apply his strategies to train his imperial concubines. Sun Zi agreed to the Emperor's challenge, provided he was given full authority to carry out his orders. Emperor He Lu agreed and summoned his harem of 180 beauties to pose as soldiers. Sun Zi divided the ladies into two troops and appointed the Emperor's two favourite concubines the leaders of the troops. He then taught them the strategies of war.

The next day, Sun Zi gathered the ladies in the field and

invited Emperor He Lu to view the display. Sun Zi instructed them, "At the first sounding of the drum, both troops are to get in line. At the next, the troop on the left is to march to the right and the troop on the right is to march to the left. At the third, both troops are to fight against each other and will stop only when you hear the sound of the gongs." To signal his seriousness, Sun Zi ordered executioners to be present.

When Sun Zi gave the signal, the ladies burst into laughter, and none followed his instructions. Sun Zi said seriously, "You have not understood what I have been telling you. As this is the first time that orders are not carried out, the fault lies with me, and I shall bear the responsibility."

Sun Zi then explained the movements to the ladies all over again. However, when he started sounding the drums, the ladies again tittered. Sun Zi said, "I have repeatedly explained my commands to you and you should have understood them. However, you have not acted according to orders. This is the fault of the two leaders." Sun Zi then ordered the immediate execution of Emperor He Lu's two favourite concubines.

The Emperor of Wu was shocked and asked the execution be stopped. He Lu said, "I am certain of your capability now. These two are my favourite concubines and I will be miserable without them." However, Sun Zi replied, "According to your wish, I have made them leaders of the troops. They have committed a major crime by not adhering to the commands given to them as leaders. If they were to be pardoned, nobody would obey your commands in future." Sun Zi rejected the Emperor's pleas and ordered the two concubines to be beheaded. As Emperor He Lu had delegated full authority to Sun Zi, he could not do anything to save his concubines.

The rest of the maidens were all shocked at the executions. Sun Zi reappointed another two concubines as leaders. He went on to give the instructions again. When he sounded the drums this time, everyone in the troops performed exactly as they were told. Sun Zi reported to the Emperor that everything was in order now and invited the Emperor to view the newly-trained soldiers. The Emperor, although saddened at the death of his two favourite concubines, was very impressed with Sun Zi and made the latter the chief commander of his army.

COMMENTS & APPLICATIONS

Although there are many similarities between the mulberry and locust trees, the two are different. Pointing at the mulberry and scolding the locust tree means to correct someone indirectly by punishing another. This strategy advocates indirect confrontation with subordinates to make them conform to the rules.

By executing Emperor He Lu's favourite concubines, Sun Zi frightened the rest of the imperial ladies into compliance. This allowed him to carry out the seemingly impossible task of training these ladies. Sometimes it is necessary to take severe action on a few culprits to send a strong signal to the rest about the consequence of disobedience. When the punishment is severe, it stuns others into compliance.

Strategy 26 can be used effectively with other strategies such as Strategy 7, "Creating something out of nothing" creating a "mountain out of a molehill." It can also be used with Strategy 17, "Tossing out a brick to get a jade" when the sacrifice involved is small. When the rest of the target is in a state of shock (like the other concubines in the story), the strategist can also apply Strategy 20, "Catching a fish in troubled water" or Strategy 22, "Shutting the doors to catch the thief".

SEVERE PUNISHMENTS ON OFFENDERS

On the political front, the clampdown on the dissidents at Tiananmen on 4 June 1989 is a good illustration of this strategy. The tough action taken by the Chinese government might appal foreigners. However, from a macro and strategic perspective, the Chinese government would rather sacrifice a few hundred Chinese than to lose an entire nation of 1.2 billion people. The actions sent a strong warning to potential dissidents. This clampdown was done to "kill the chicken to scare the monkeys".

Despite severe criticisms of the Tiananmen episode, China's growing political and economic stability after 1989 show that the Chinese government had acted in the interest of the country. After 4 June 1989, no other massive protest or demonstration has erupted. Instead, the Chinese are now busy contributing to the impressive economic development of their country. Foreign investments have increased even more significantly in recent years. As of 1997, China alone accounted for more than 50% of foreign investments in Asia.

In the area of law enforcement, the Singapore Government is probably well-known for the use of this strategy. Severe punishment is meted out to law-breakers to deter potential culprits. Drug trafficking, kidnapping and armed robberies resulting in deaths incur the death sentence. Other offences like littering, traffic violations and spitting in public are punished too. Besides being fined, litter bugs are made to clean public places amidst publicity. One illustration to show the effectiveness and demonstrative effects of such a strategy involves a wealthy remisier who abused his Area Licence Scheme label (ALS) which permits entry into restricted traffic zones during peak hours. The law requires that an ALS may only be used for one vehicle. This man owned three vehicles — a Volvo, a Rolls-Royce and a Mercedes-Benz. Though he purchased an ALS for his Rolls, he used it on his Mercedes to gain entry into restricted zones. When he was caught red-handed by the Land Transport Authority of Singapore, he was fined S$800 and jailed for two weeks on 11 July 1997! Although the penalties were subsequently reduced, the severity of the initial punishment left a tremendous impression on many Singaporeans. Ironically, each ALS label costs only S$60, a sum he should have easily been able to afford. The severe punishment imposed and the publicity (featured on the front page of the local English daily — *The Straits Times*) scared the "monkeys" and deterred potential culprits!

Singapore's law enforcement system has been harshly criticised by other countries. However, Singapore has one of the lowest crime rates in the world. This record is particularly notable considering that it is a city state with a high density population, 20% of whom are foreign workers. Many other Asian countries, having found a tough stance against law offenders more successful, have also done the same.

As a Warning to Others

This strategy can easily be applied in many business situations. A senior executive with over 20 years service in a Malaysian conglomerate decided, for personal reasons, to resign, giving a short notice, to join another company. The boss, a prominent business tycoon, felt an acute loss of face, especially since he felt he had treated this senior executive very well. Therefore, he tried to make the departure of this executive very difficult. He issued legal letters to the executive hinting about certain corporate practices this executive did not adhere to. The issues involved were minor, and the whole episode resembled the saying of using a sledge hammer to kill a fly. The intention of the boss was not to pick on this senior executive alone, but to use this situation to signal to other employees that they too might face similar consequences if they decide not to tow the line.

What this Malaysian tycoon did is not unusual. A company may sack a difficult employee as a warning to the rest. Instead of sacking the employee for poor job performance, the company may choose to issue a letter of warning or reduce the employee's benefits such as a cut in monthly salary, elimination of bonus, reduction or forfeiture of leave.

In business competition, a larger competitor may use this strategy on its smaller but trickier competitors. Good examples can be found in the retail gasoline industry. Often, in order to gain market share, one of the smaller players would initiate a price or promotional war, which can be quite costly to all the players. The longer the war persists, the higher costs would escalate. To restore order, the leader often has to teach the violators a lesson. This is normally done in one of or a combination of the following two actions:

1   Offer greater discounts than the smaller players, and pledging to offer further discounts should the rest try to out-do it.
2   Offer more generous and attractive promotional items and gifts.

Such actions usually cause severe hardship to smaller players. The retail gasoline industry tends to be homogeneous and oligopolistic, and economies of scale always favour larger players. The smaller players are easily squeezed out of profits, with some even going into the red.

Having taught the smaller players an expensive lesson, the leader can then lead the industry back to normal price levels by announcing a future date in which prices would be adjusted upwards. In almost all instances, the smaller players would join the move for an upward price revision.

In Singapore, when the smaller retail gasoline operators like British Petroleum (BP), Caltex, Mobil and Esso tried to grab bigger market shares through various promotional or price reduction gimmicks, they would provoke an intense business war among themselves. However, if they provoked the largest operator, Shell, they often ended up the losers. This is because Shell has over 40% of the retail gasoline market share in Singapore. One of these four smaller operators found out just how difficult it was to take Shell on when it once offered a car (costing US$100,000) as a top prize for a draw. Shell countered with a luxury apartment easily six to eight times the car's value!

In an industry where the product is homogeneous and oligopolistic, the smaller players will benefit from using non-price tactics to improve their market positions. These may include improving the services at the point of sale and providing auxiliary service (such as a mini-supermarket at the gas station, selling telephone cards, parking coupons and stamps). If gifts or other promotional methods are used, they should be done discreetly and be restricted at the local level. They could try using the "hit and run" strategy and limited promotions to selected stores or districts, making it harder for the bigger players to respond effectively.

BEING IN A POSITION OF STRENGTH

To use the "pointing at the mulberry but scolding the locust tree" strategy, one must be in a position of strength for the threats to be taken seriously. As an illustration, when SIA entered into a strategic alliance with Ansett Airlines of Australia and Air New Zealand in June 1997, Qantas Airways (the other major Australian airlines) threatened to respond aggressively and take a hostile posture should SIA enter into an equity deal with Ansett. These threats fell on deaf ears however, as SIA was an acknowledged world-class airlines in its own right.

Even a country may not use "strong arm" tactic when the chips are not stacked in its favour. For example, in the currency crisis started in 1997, the Malaysian Prime Minister initially spoke harshly against those "responsible" for raiding the Malaysian ringgit. To some extent, Dr Mahathir was trying to use the "pointing at the mulberry but scolding the locust" strategy. His stern warning was calculated at scaring away the "monkeys". Unfortunately, the chips were not in the favour of Malaysia, and they could not contend against market forces, especially since the real opponents could not be identified.

For this strategy to work, the economy must have *strong and sound macroeconomic policies*, and a *resilient financial system* to act as strong defences. In addition, the system must be able to provide *timely and reliable information for market reactions*. There must also be *consistent and transparent* policies so that investors will gain confidence in the country. Finally, the government must be open to *constructive criticisms and market feedback*.

At the time when the Malaysian ringgit was attacked, few of the above factors were in Malaysia's favour. It had over-built, especially on mega projects. It had over-committed itself and as a nation, it was highly geared and had severe current account deficits. Its financial institutions had over-extended credit and were in no position to withstand strong assaults by foreign speculators. Information was incomplete, giving the impression that the country could still live on borrowed money and extended credit. Government policies were also inconsistent, giving wrong signals to investors and the public. The Malaysian government was criticised by some foreign analysts for its frequently changing policies. In the midst of the crisis, some of its announcements (such as the curb on currency trading) caused foreign investors to lose more confidence. Finally, the government did not heed the repeated warnings by analysts to slow down its economic growth, especially on expenditure on mega projects.

Fortunately, the Malaysian government began to take concrete actions to address some fundamental issues affecting its economy. In his 1997 budget, Malaysian Finance Minister, Mr Anwar Ibrahim, announced numerous policies to put the Malaysian economy back on track. The Malaysian government also demonstrated its readiness to take painful and pragmatic approaches to solve its problems by reviewing policies, cutting expenditure and making a concerted national effort at belt-tightening. The determination of the Malaysian government to resolve its economic difficulties was best illustrated by the fact that as of early 1998, it did not have to turn to the International Monetary Fund (IMF) for assistance.

Like Malaysia, Thailand, Indonesia and the Philippines were hit hard by economic trouble. They, too, had experienced similar problems of over-expansion and over-leveraging. However, their political leaders refrained from criticising foreign investors and currency speculators. choosing instead to face the music squarely. Their political leaders did not even try to use the "pointing at the mulberry but scolding the locust tree" strategy as a "scare tactic" against foreign investors, realising that they were not operating from positions of strength.

假痴不颠

PRETENDING TO BE INSANE BUT REMAINING SMART

宁伪作不知不为，不伪作假知妄为；
静不露机，云雷屯也。

EXPLANATION

It is better for one to pretend that he knows nothing and take no action (宁伪作不知不为) rather than to pretend that he knows everything and rush into a situation hastily (不伪作假知妄为). One should prepare his forces in the dark and not let others know of his secret (静不露机) and wait for an opportunity to strike, just as lightning and thunder wait to strike in winter (云雷屯之). The phrase "云雷屯之" comes from *Yi Jing's* "Tun" Theory ([易：屯] 卦：云雷屯，君子以经论). When one faces a strong opposition, it is better to keep a low profile, and pretend to be stupid so the enemy will not be alerted. Meanwhile, one can secretly prepare for the vital strike to eliminate the enemy.

To use this strategy, one has to perfect the art of deception because it takes discipline to feign weakness when one is really strong. It requires self-imposed humility, something which few can muster. Yet when one is able to achieve such a skill, he is able even to "Pretend to be a pig to prey on the tiger" (扮猪吃虎).

HISTORICAL BACKGROUND

Many ancient warriors used this strategy to achieve their aims. The story of how Si Ma Yi (司马懿) killed Cao Shuang (曹爽) as described in "Han Jin Chun Qiu" (汉晋春秋) is one illustration of this strategy.

> *During the era of the Three Kingdoms (三国时), before the King of Wei (魏) died, he told his loyal subject Si Ma Yi to take care of his young son, crown prince Cao Fang (曹芳),*

who was eight years old then, so the latter could be the next emperor. Si Ma Yi agreed and together with another General Cao Shuang, they assisted the young emperor in ruling the kingdom. Initially, Cao Shuang held Si Ma Yi in reverence. However Cao Shuang's adviser warned him to not allow Si Ma Yi too much military power for fear of an attack. Cao Shuang realised the implication and schemed to remove Si Ma Yi from his position of influence.

Eventually, Cao Shuang won Si Ma Yi's men over to his camp. Si Ma Yi feigned illness and refused to go out of his camp despite the defection of his men. Cao Shuang sent an emissary to test Si Ma Yi, but the latter pretended that he was near death. When the emissary left, Si Ma Yi told his sons and subordinates of the feud between himself and Cao Shuang. He wanted Cao Shuang killed so he could regain his military power. Not long after, Cao Shuang left town on a hunting trip. Si Ma Yi then reorganised his men, killed Cao Shuang and regained his power.

COMMENTS & APPLICATIONS

In some situations, it is better to retain a low profile so as to not attract unwanted attention. The Chinese saying "The smart appears to be silly" (大 智 若 愚) means that people who are smart usually do not give themselves high visibility to protect themselves.

Strategy 27 is similar to Strategy 6, "Making a feint to the east but hitting out in the west" and Strategy 10, "A dagger sheathed in a smile". Strategy 6 is based on diversion, so it is similar to Strategy 27. The main intention of Strategy 10 is to win the trust of the opponent before delivering the fatal strike. The smile is used to "deceive" the opponent into lowering his defences. Strategy 27, however, does not have a negative connotation. It is generally used to describe extremely bright persons whose outward appearances or lifestyles may deceive others as to their true selves. These three strategies complement each other and can be used interchangeably. They can also be used with other strategies, depending on the objectives of the strategist.

BUSINESS TYCOONS AND TOP EXECUTIVES

Many successful Chinese business tycoons apply this strategy very well. Despite their immense wealth, they typically keep a low profile and avoid publicity. For example, while their names may sound familiar, one is rarely acquainted with the faces of Chinese tycoons like Wee Cho Yaw, Kwek Leng Beng, Ng Teng Fong and Ong Beng Seng of Singapore; Khoo Kay Peng and Robert Kuok of Malaysia; Li Ka-shing of Hong Kong; Lien Sioe Liong, Mokthar Riady and Ciputra of Indonesia. They avoid publicity and do not like their photographs taken for media purposes.

Japanese tycoons adopt a similar posture. Other than Mr Morita of Sony Corporation, one seldom finds much publicity about the personalities and private lifestyles of top Japanese executives. Despite the great success of their corporations, these tycoons rarely appear in international magazines and papers. If they should appear in public, they may not be recognised.

In contrast, many American CEOs thrive on publicity. Their photographs appear regularly in the news, television and magazines like Fortune, Newsweek and Time. They rarely shunt interviews and engineer events to publicise themselves, including writing books and articles. Even their private lives come under media scrutiny — Bill Gates' wedding generated much media hype. This would never be tolerated by most Chinese and Japanese businessmen.

While there is nothing wrong with creating publicity especially where publicity and media interest may generate a higher profile for a company and its products, the price one has to pay is the loss of privacy and an increase in vulnerability. The enquiring media, having found a person very approachable, will keep coming back for more. The more one is probed, the more is known. It then becomes very difficult to withhold information. This is when one becomes vulnerable. At times, even top corporate secrets like new products, research and development, acquisition and expansion plans can be unintentionally leaked out through pressure from the media.

SELF-ENFORCED HUMILITY

In the context of an organisation, it is also useful to not disclose one's cards, especially about one's ambitions and intentions. For example, a very talented and ambitious executive should be cautious about announcing his desire to succeed his boss or to become the CEO. If he does not have broad-minded bosses and colleagues, he might find himself out of a job in no time, or be out manoeuvred in corporate politics. Like in the game of poker, it is wise to conceal some cards. Better still to behave humbly and act "stupid" at times to not provoke competitors.

In business competition, Japanese businessmen are known for "pretending to be insane but remaining smart". They appear humble and rarely offer their opinions, always projecting the impression that they have much to learn from their competitors. While most are aware of Japanese successes in consumer products and electronics, few realise that nine of the top ten banks in the world today are Japanese! They have also begun to excel in high fashion and medical equipment — areas which are not traditional their strengths.

Despite Japan's slow economic growth and banking crisis in the mid 1990s, many Japanese companies have been quietly taking concrete steps to improve international competitiveness. Among other measures, Japanese companies have begun shifting their investments and factories to Asia — the mega market of the 21st century. From putting in a modest 12% of foreign direct investment (FDI) in Asia in the 1980s, Japan had upped its FDI stakes in Asia to 35% by the 1990s. In addition to taking advantage of the lower production costs in Asia, this move allowed Japanese companies to "disguise" their exports into the States under the labels "Made in China", "Made in Malaysia" and "Made in Thailand".

It would be a grave mistake for the Western countries to write-off Japan because of its economic and banking woes in the mid 1990s. Instead, they should be vigilant and learn from history. Each time Japan was faced with severe economic challenges in the 1970s and 1980s, it came out stronger and meaner with better ways of doing things. Concepts like quality control, just-in-time system, and lean production system were products of past economic crises. During these times, the Japanese kept a low profile, giving the impression that their economy and companies were in the doldrums. They would not crow about their achievements or progress. In this way, they avoid attracting the attention of competitors, and might even lower their defences. This gives them more breathing space and time to respond with better strategies. Their subsequent actions will then catch their competitors by surprise, making it easier to overrun them.

FAKERY AND ILLUSIONS

"Pretending to be insane but remaining smart" is a deception strategy. In war, it is designed to create advantages through using fakery and illusions. In the words of Sun Zi:

Therefore, when capable, feign incapability; when active, feign inactivity. When near to the objective, feign that you are far away; when far away, make it appear that you are near.

故能而示之不能,用而示之不用,近而示之远,远而示之近.

Illusions confuse the enemy from learning one's real intentions, making one unpredictable in the enemy's eyes and hence, affect his assessment. Each time you engage the enemy, he has to reassess you all over again. In this way, he has to commit more time and resources as each round of engagement is like a new battle (*see also Strategy 16, "Releasing the enemy to recapture him later"*).

In the case of faking (as in what Si Ma Yi did) the defences of the enemy are lowered because of the pretence of incapability, vulnerability, humility and weakness. Thus, when the enemy is arrogant and least prepared, that is the best time to strike. This is illustrated by the Sun Zi's advice:

> In the beginning of battle, be as shy as a young maiden to entice the enemy to lower his defences. When the battle progresses, be as swift as a hare to catch the enemy unprepared.

是故始如处女, 敌人开户后如脱兔, 敌不及拒.

By pretending to be vulnerable like a helpless young maiden, you will not appear to be a threat to the enemy. This gives you the opportunity and time to assess the enemy, gather and organise your troops and resources and to plan your strategy and line of attack. When you launch the attack, be like the hare — alert, quiet, swift and sudden — and the enemy will be caught off-guard. As in the story, Cao Shuang never expected a "dying" Si Ma Yi to strike so swiftly and suddenly.

Fakery and illusions can also be used to create surprise when engaging the enemy. The sudden change from incapability to capability, from weaknesses to strength, from vulnerability to aggression will stun the enemy for a while. As Sun Zi aptly puts it, the enemy would never expect that a demure young maiden can strike with the swiftness of a hare.

In a similar way, the meek Japanese must not be taken lightly. Historically, Japan has been regarded as the weak maiden. Even as late as the early 1970s, she was seen as a nation with little economic potential — only a young, demure, and vulnerable maiden who should be rescued. However, in the 1970s, the Japanese lady grew up quite suddenly and began to demonstrate a big appetite. She moved swiftly, quietly and unnoticeably for a long while, carving out large market shares in the world market before she was finally noticed. By then, the impact was so momentous that it was quite impossible to dislodge her. Suddenly, the demure and helpless maiden was transformed into a sumo wrestler!

Thus, despite the problems faced by failures of financial institutions in 1997, the Japanese have built up substantial "reserves" to wear out the storm. They should therefore not be taken lightly. If their track records are anything to go by, they will emerge from their slump stronger than before.

上屋抽梯
REMOVE THE LADDER AFTER THE ENEMY ASCENDS TO THE ROOF

假之以便，唆之使前，
断其援应，陷之死地。
遇毒，位不当也。

EXPLANATION

Pretend to expose one's weakness (假之以便) to lure the enemy into one's trap (唆之使前). When the enemy is within one's control, cut off its supply routes (断其援应) and eventually destroy him (陷之死地). This strategy warns against taking a small advantage when one can go for the kill, as that may result in one's destruction, as in *Yi Jing's* "Shi Ke" Theory [易：噬嗑]: 遇毒, 位不当也. The key to this strategy is the "ladder" (梯). This ladder acts as the bait to arouse the curiosity of the enemy. Once the enemy is up on the roof, the ladder is removed, trapping the enemy.

HISTORICAL BACKGROUND

This strategy originates from the "Story Of the Three Kingdoms" (三国志：蜀书：诸葛亮传).

STORY 1

Towards the end of the Han Dynasty (后汉末), around 210 AD, Liu Bei (刘备) went to seek help from a man called Liu Biao (刘表) in the state of Jing (荆州). Liu Biao had two sons, Liu Qi (刘琦) and Liu Zong (刘综), borne to him by two wives. Liu Zong, the younger son, was borne by the second wife Cai (蔡). Under her influence, Liu Biao favoured Liu Zong. Liu Qi thus felt very oppressed. When Liu Bei and his adviser Zhu Ge Liang (诸葛亮) came to visit Liu Biao, Liu Qi sought Zhu Ge Liang's advice for the latter was a brilliant strategist. Zhu Ge Liang refused him several times. Finally, one day, Liu Qi lured Zhu Ge Liang up the roof and asked his men to remove the ladder. Liu Qi then said to Zhu Ge Liang, "Well, now we are neither in the heavens nor on the ground. I will honour whatever advice you give." Zhu Ge Liang saw his sincerity, so he told him to imitate the example of Prince Zhong Er (重耳) of Jin and leave his home temporarily in case his stepmother and brother plot to harm him after his father's death. Liu Qi took the hint and eventually requested his father to send him far away from home.

STORY 2

The following story, also adapted from the *Story of the Three Kingdoms* (三国志：蜀书：诸葛亮传、李严传), tells of how Zhu Ge Liang managed to trap a majority of Si Ma Yi's soldiers using this strategy.

In 223 AD, after Liu Bei's death, Zhu Ge Liang helped Liu Chan (刘禅) become the emperor of Shu (蜀) ruling over the states in east central of China. Zhu Ge Liang always had the ambition of helping the emperor to gain control of the whole China and to restore the Han Dynasty (汉朝). At that time, the states in the northern region of China were under the rule of Cao Cao (曹操). A total of six wars were fought between the Shu army and the Wei (魏) army from 227 till 234 AD. The following happened in the fifth war between the two armies (around 231 AD).

Zhu Ge Liang met with the famous general Si Ma Yi at the mountain of Qi (祁山). During a fierce battle, Si Ma Yi lost three thousand men. However, Zhu Ge Liang's army also suffered casualties and urgently needed food and supplies from home. The general in charge of the transportation, Li Yan (李严), was a timid person and he was afraid that the food and supplies might be lost on their way because of the persistent rain. He therefore faked a command from the emperor Liu Chan and summoned Zhu Ge Liang back to Cheng Du (成都).

When Zhu Ge Liang got the news, he was afraid that something bad might have happened back home, so he reluctantly planned to return. However, he knew that if he were to return at this moment, Si Ma Yi and his men would give chase. Therefore, he had to come up with a plan to defeat the Wei army on their way back so that they could have a safe retreat. As Si Ma Yi was a cautious person, Zhu knew his plan must have an advantage that could bait him. He therefore came up with the strategy "Remove the ladder after the enemy ascends to the roof".

Si Ma Yi was all prepared for another attack from Zhu Ge Liang when he received news that the Shu army was pulling out from their camps. He found that hard to believe as the Shu army had been winning so far. Though his advisers asked him to give chase, Si Ma Yi was cautious. He led his men to Zhu Ge Liang's camp sites and found them abandoned. When Si Ma Yi saw that Zhu Ge Liang had really retreated, he planned to launch an attack on the Shu army with another general, Zhang He (张 合). Zhang He was to lead a troop of ten thousand men while Si Ma Yi would lead the next thirty thousand close behind. They figured that with so many men giving chase, Zhu Ge Liang would not be able to employ any strategy against them. Nevertheless, Si Ma Yi warned Zhang He not to under estimate Zhu Ge Liang as the latter was well-known for his use of strategies.

Zhang He was a brave warrior who had followed Cao Cao through many battles. He and his army finally caught up with the Shu general Wei Yan (魏 延) and his army. In the ensuing fight, Wei Yan feigned defeat and retreated. Zhang He gave chase. Suddenly, Wei Yan disappeared round a corner. Fearing a trap, Zhang He stopped to investigate, but was puzzled to find no trace of the army. Just then, another Shu general Wang Ping (王 平) launched a surprise attack. When Zhang He saw Si Ma Yi and his army not far away, he thought that reinforcements were near, so he fought bravely against Wang Ping. Wang Ping again feigned defeat and retreated into the woods. Zhang He gave chase.

As before, Wei Yan and Wang Ping would fight a few rounds and then retreat deeper into the woods, discarding their armour as they went. Zhang He was thus led in the chase till they came to a valley.

Zhang He, anxious to destroy the Shu army, and thinking that reinforcements were close behind, entered the valley. The pathways were very narrow and blocked with armour discarded by the retreating Shu army. Zhang He's army cleared the way as they pushed deeper into the valley. Then suddenly, thousands of arrows volleyed down from the cliffs. Zhang He then realised that he had been tricked. He immediately ordered a retreat but it was too late. The outlet had been blocked by the Shu army with huge rocks. Zhang He was eventually killed and his army destroyed. When Si Ma Yi came with reinforcements, all they saw were bodies. Fearing that Zhu Ge Liang might launch another ambush, Si Ma Yi could only retreat with his army.

Comments & Applications

The phrase "Remove the ladder after the enemy ascends to the roof" has two different meanings. The first means to put oneself in a position where there is no turning back, forcing a final and powerful response from the enemy. This is akin to a Chinese proverb, "Destroy the cauldrons and sink the boats" (破 釜 沉 舟). This was what Liu Qi did to force a response from Zhu Ge Liang in the first story. The second is to lure the enemy into a position where it cannot turn back, cut off its supplies and eventually destroy it. This is the meaning more frequently ascribed to this strategy, and is illustrated in the second story.

To use this strategy, there must first be an appropriate "ladder" to lure the enemy up the roof. The bait must be conspicuous enough to be noticed. Setting up this "ladder" is the key. With an enemy who is anxious to win, one must first pretend to be weak. This was exactly what Zhu Ge Liang did to Zhang He. With one "victory" after another, Zhang He became arrogant and forgot that he was drawing further away from reinforcements. When he was trapped in the valley, the escape was sealed, and he perished.

How attractive the "ladder" is depends on the enemy. If the enemy is simple, a simple trap may do the trick. Zhang He was not exactly a simple enemy. He was one of the bravest warriors of his time. Thus, Zhu Ge Liang had to design a more complicated scheme to lure Zhang He deeper into his trap before executing the final blow. This was necessary because Zhang He's commander, Si Ma Yi, was also a well-known strategist.

Strategy 28 can be used with strategies such as Strategy 1, "Deceiving the heavens to cross the sea", Strategy 10, "A dagger sheathed in a smile", Strategy 15, "Luring the tiger from its lair in the mountains" and Strategy 21, "Making an unnoticed escape like a golden cicada shedding its skin". Once the opponent has been tricked other strategies can be applied. These may include Strategy 20, "Catching a fish in trouble water" and Strategy 22, "Shutting the doors to catch the thief.

CREATING ADVANTAGES FOR ONESELF

This is one of the six deception strategies. In applying this strategy to business, one must be careful to not violate legal and ethical codes, or one will suffer legal penalties and be condemned by society at large.

While outright attempts to cheat cannot be condoned, efforts to create advantages for oneself without violating ethical or legal codes are acceptable business practices. However, in business, the line between creativity and deception can be a very thin one. When creativity ends and deception begins is very debatable and subjective. Advertising, for instance, is known as a creative discipline. But it can be equally deceptive. The following advertising messages are some illustrations of what companies have used (authors' comments in brackets):

1   "Sale, while stocks last". (In reality, there could be plenty of stock)

2   "Sales period extended due to overwhelming response". (This is contradictory. If sales are good, why extend it? It should read more like, "Due to poor response, please come and support us"!)

3   "Consumer demand is overwhelming, so we are giving further discounts!" (Another contradictory statement. If demand has really been good, prices should be increased instead. The statement should be, "We are cutting prices to attract more customers" or "We have made a mistake in pricing, so we are now adjusting our prices downwards".)

Despite such misleading (or creative?) statements, consumers flock to sales with little hesitation. More often than not, they overspend on more items than they will ever need. Sales gimmicks and slogans are indeed enticing "ladders"!

In the home renovation business, the smart contractor entices the consumer with an attractive basic package, which costs a fairly substantial sum of money. Having lured his customer with the basic package, the contractor then invites him to add other features to the renovation. The typical justification used is, "Since you are already going to spend so much money, this additional sum will not make much difference. And it will cost more if you decide to do it later." With this kind of persuasion, the consumer may end up spending more than twice his original budget before he realises it!

This strategy can also be applied in the sale of high ticket items with accessories. For example, vendors of personal computers (PCs) are fond of advertising a model with attractive features and price. However, in the same advertisement, he will cleverly include the possibility of upgrading the processing chip, the RAM, or the hard disk, and so on. Thinking that he has already gotten a bargain on the advertised model, the consumer often opts for some upgrading.

INCREMENTAL TRAPPING

Interestingly, one can find this strategy of "Removing the ladder after the enemy ascends to the roof" being applied in the retail business, such as the sale of Scribe handmade leather shoes from Bally, a well-known Swiss brand. In the UK, a pair of Bally shoes retails for about £375 (about US$630) as of 1997, still cheaper than in most Asian cities. As such, it is quite common to find many affluent Asian male tourists wanting to purchase a pair or two when in the UK. Knowing the purchasing power of these Asian tourists, the shrewd salesperson will begin by reinforcing his sales pitch with the unique features of the shoes to stir the ego of potential customers. Once the sale is done, he will try to sell the customer other shoe accessories like socks, shoe polish, and perhaps even a second pair of less expensive shoes for casual wear. Having spent a large sum of money on just one pair of shoes, the other expenses appear small by comparison. Thus the consumer is "trapped" into spending more without realising it.

The casinos are well-known for this too. In the early 1990s, and especially during Chinese New Year, Melbourne's Crown casino chartered a Boeing 767 to transport the big-time gamblers from Hong Kong's Kai Tak airport. Crown Casino would pay for everything — flights, hotel accommodation, meals, tickets to shows and golf games. From a public relations angle, the Crown argued that the complete free package was designed to reward its top 1% high rollers from Asia (an attractive "ladder" indeed). In reality, these high rollers would probably roll away more of their wealth in sunny Victoria during one of these annual incentive trips.

Recently, in October 1997, the Consumer Association of Singapore had to resort to blacklisting four timeshare companies

— St Honorine World Leisure, East West Gold Club, Premier Holidays and Holiday Marketing International — for using high pressure and emotional tactics to lure consumers into buying timesharing resorts and properties. Typically, these companies would inform the potential customers that they have won free trips or holidays. All they need to do is report to the company's premises to claim the prizes. However, on arrival, these supposed prize winners find that they have to sit through a long sales presentation, lasting a few hours, on various timesharing resorts. Before long, the weaker ones find that they have become the victims of emotional sales tactics that pressure them into signing sales contracts.

This tactic uses the free trip as a "ladder". Once the victim has ascended to the roof, the ladder is removed. When the buyers of the timesharing resorts subsequently tried to claim their free trips, various reasons were given to deny them of the opportunity. This caused much unhappiness and resentment, and resulted in many complaints against the companies. Unfortunately, it was difficult to prove that these "victims" were duped by emotional selling pressure as they signed the contracts willingly.

While it would appear that the consumers in such cases might end up as losers, these companies do not emerge the winners either as they have been blacklisted. The negative publicity generated not only affected the four companies concerned, but also created a bad image for the entire timesharing industry. It will take a while for consumers to regain confidence in purchasing timesharing properties.

STRATEGY 29

树 上 开 花

DECK THE TREE WITH FLOWERS

借局布势，力小势大。
鸿渐于陆，其羽可用为仪也。

EXPLANATION

Borrow a setting to boost one's image (借局布势). Although one may be on the weak side, one's battle array can appear strong (力小势大). This is similar to the saying in *Yi Jing's* "Jian" Theory that the flock of wild geese flying across the sky appears to be invincible because of the thick feathers on their wings ([易：渐]：上九，鸿渐于陆，其羽可用为仪). This story illustrates how the strategy came about.

HISTORICAL BACKGROUND

In 420 AD, Emperor Song Wu Di, Liu Yu (宋武帝刘裕) started his Song (宋) empire in the southern part of China. Nineteen years later, Emperor Bei Wei Tai Wu Di (北魏太武帝) took control of the northern part of China. From then, these empires polarised.

Song Wu Di died after two years as emperor, and was succeeded by his son Song Wen Di (宋文帝). In the subsequent years, the soldiers from Bei Wei launched a number of attacks on the Song empire. Song Wen Di dispatched his able general Tan Dao Ji (檀道济) to defend the empire.

Once, the Bei Wei soldiers attacked the town of Ji Nan (济南) and in 20 days, over 30 battles were fought between the two armies. The Song army won the battles and pursued their enemy all the way to the city of Li (历城). Tan Dao Ji then became overconfident, and did not keep up his defences. The

Bei Wei army took the opportunity to ambush their enemies. Most of the Song army's food supplies were destroyed by fire.

As they were running low on food, Tan Dao Ji decided to retreat to the city of Li. At that time, a defector from the Song army reported the condition of the Song army to their enemy. The Bei Wei army therefore decided to launch a fierce battle to annihilate the Song army. When the Song army saw that they were surrounded by the enemy, many were very worried and a few ran away. Tan Dao Ji told his men not to worry.

That night, the Song camps were fully lit and Tan Dao Ji personally led a few men to their warehouses to count their food supplies. They started measuring their stock and even counted out aloud. Someone peeped into the warehouses and saw numerous sacks full of beautiful white grains. This news went to the ears of the generals leading the Bei Wei army. They were told that the Song army had lots of supplies and if they were to fight against the Song army, they would definitely lose the battle. Then the Bei Wei generals assumed they had been misinformed so they could be trapped, and ordered the defector beheaded.

Little did the Bei Wei army realise they had been tricked by Tan Dao Ji. Tan Dao Ji was not measuring rice in the warehouses. He had ordered his men to fill the rice sacks with white sand topped with a layer of rice. The next day, he ordered his men to gear up in armour while he himself wore plain clothes. He then rode a huge carriage and paraded on the street. The Bei Wei army had been defeated by Tan Dao Ji several times. Thus when they saw the confident Tan Dao Ji, they did not dare to launch an attack on the Song army as they were afraid that Tan Dao Ji had other tricks up his sleeves. Tan Dao Ji therefore used the strategy "Deck the trees with flowers" to escape from a very precarious situation.

COMMENTS & APPLICATIONS

Typically, a tree rarely bears flowers. However, if one decorates it well with fake flowers, someone may be taken in. The idea behind this strategy is to use materials or methods to enhance one's position and to deter the enemy. In a situation which is not advantageous to oneself, or when one is waiting for the right moment, a proper use of this strategy will bring one through a crisis.

Strategy 29 can be used with Strategy 1, "Deceiving the heavens to cross the sea". It can also be used with Strategy 7, "Creating something out of nothing" and Strategy 14, "Borrowing a corpse to resurrect a soul". Like the other deception strategies, Strategy 29 can be combined with the other strategies. On its own, any deceptive strategy is only intended as a short-term scheme. It cannot be used as a permanent ploy.

THE ART OF PACKAGING AND BRANDING

One good illustration of how this strategy can be applied is in product packaging. Packaging has been raised to a fine art among the Japanese. A simple box of candy in a Japanese departmental store in Tokyo or Osaka can be couched in amazingly detailed and extensive packaging. To eat the candy, one has to remove several layers of wrappings! The product itself is quite ordinary, but the packaging makes it look spectacular and expensive. Indeed the form has overtaken the substance!

The Japanese art of "deceptive" packaging to project a favourable image is used extensively in many products, including Japanese cuisine. The preparation and presentation that go into serving *sushi, teppanyaki, kaiseki and sashimi* make them look very artistic and elaborate. Their expensive look justifies the high prices charged for them. In reality, the amount of food served may not be substantial. The cost is not derived from the food but from the packaging. So elaborate is this quest for perfecting the art of food preparation that it requires five years of training to be a qualified *sushi* chef!

Similarly, the price paid for dining at a fine restaurant is not confined to the food alone. Much of the cost can be attributed to the decoration and furnishings of the restaurant. These frills, including the services provided by the waiters and waitresses, give a very up-market image and ambience, and the resulting high prices.

The cosmetic industry, too, favours elaborate packaging. Perfume bottles, for one, are clearly distinguishable by their intricate designs and styling. Exquisite materials such as crystal and gold trimmings are commonly used. It is no exaggeration to say that the packaging often costs more than the perfume. In the marketing of exquisite liquor, a similar strategy is used. Louis XIII, a well-known "XO", is sold in a crystal bottle with gold trimmings. The price? A hefty US$1500!

It is a pity that many developing economies in Asia have yet to master the art of packaging. Consequently, their products have not been able to command high prices. Take the example of clothing. Despite the delicate and elaborate details of a batik shirt from Malaysia or Indonesia, it has not been able to match the prices of foreign-made shirts. Though quality of materials used may be similar, the difference in value can be astronomical. For example, a shirt made by many Asian companies may cost no more than US$10 while a Valentino could cost over US$100! While brands do play a big part in augmenting the value of a product, Asian shirt manufacturers like batik makers, do better if they can pay more attention to packaging.

It is interesting to study why shirts like Valentino, Dior and Varsace cost so much when compared to less established brands. No doubt their materials may be better and their designs more appealing. But, one main difference lies in the packaging and marketing of these brands. They rely on creative advertising, exclusive sales outlets or upmarket department stores, distinctive displays of products, the use of expensive-looking packaging materials, and clever descriptions of the product (such as "double mercerised cotton" and "double thread golden needle stitching"). They also use supermodels and celebrities to market their brands. Their attempts to "deck the tree with flowers" really work well!

Packaging and branding are ways to increase the value of the products. Very often, the price premiums enjoyed are remarkable. These are areas Asian companies should pay attention to. As Asian consumers become more affluent, they are likely to go after the frills. One only need to look at the markets in Hong Kong and Singapore to appreciate Asian affluence. The time has now come for Asian marketers to "deck the tree with flowers".

In the car manufacturing business, the Japanese companies were known to use this strategy to their advantage in the 1960s and 1970s when they first entered the world market. Recognising that they could not compete head-on against the better quality American and European models, the Japanese car makers had to find their marketing niches. They found that the American automobile makers tended to sell the car as a base model then make the consumer pay for all the extra accessories like radial-ply tyres, air-conditioners and radio-cassette players. Ultimately, the price of the car might cost up to 30% more. Exploiting this weakness of the American car makers, the Japanese car was sold as a "fully-loaded" model with all accessories included, and more, all at one price. By "decking the tree with flowers", the Japanese car appeared to be great value for money. It was thus no surprise that Japanese cars made significant inroads into the US car market. Today, all the American and European car makers have adopted the Japanese strategy.

The Japanese are well-known for the art of packaging products to augment their value. One only has to witness the attention to details in the packaging of a can of Kirin beer or Japanese fruits to understand how the Japanese have perfected packaging into an art. These are merely low-ticket items. With high-ticket items, they go into greater details. In fact, the sophistication (and to some extent, obsession) that goes into making the Japanese product look better can be quite mind-boggling.

PACKAGING OF SERVICES

In the service area, there are also many areas in which this strategy has been applied. For example, many banks have developed priority and private banking services for their high-end customers. Essentially, the service is the same. However, they "dress" it up with many frills, and in the process, levy a higher charge. Some exclusive golf and social clubs operate on the same principle. In Asia, where many customers are quite status conscious, these clubs would offer a range of services exclusive to members. Members are then prepared to pay high entrance fees and monthly subscription charges. To signify their status and exclusivity, these clubs even provide distinctive car park labels, name-tags (for golf bags) and membership cards (at times doubling as credit cards) for their members. Despite paying high monthly subscription fees, many members do not patronise their clubs frequently. Small wonder then that club operators in Asia are doing a roaring business as they can afford to offer more memberships without overtaxing facilities.

In an attempt to retain its frequent flyers, Singapore Airlines (SIA) introduced a whole range of services to "pamper' their priority passengers. As of 1998, the perks for the Priority Passenger Service (PPS) Club members include:

1   Extra baggage allowance
2   Priority baggage handling
3   Special check-in counters
4   Guaranteed seat and priority wait-list
5   Automatic reconfirmation of return flight

6   Extended use of Silver Kris lounges and other contracted/alliance lounges around the world

7   Worldwide emergency assistance service

8   Emergency medical insurance scheme

9   Travel accident insurance cover

10   Discounted rates at selected hotels

11   Discounts on Avis car rentals in numerous countries

12   Dining privileges at selected restaurants

13   Further discounts on duty-free shopping outlets and in-flight sales

14   Shopping privileges and discounts at selected stores and mail order catalogues

15   Reduced application fee for Executive Telecard and waiver of annual subscription fee for the Singapore Telecom's International Calling Card

16   Special priority magazine

17   Free annual subscription to a magazine of the passenger's choice

18   Special gift for those who re-qualify as a priority passenger

19   Eligibility and bonus mileage for Frequent Flyer Programme.

To boost loyalty among its PPS Club members, SIA introduced the Solitaire PPS Club membership in 1995 for those who have:

1   Accumulated a minimum of 250 flight sectors or 800,000 km and

2   Completed an uninterrupted period of at least 5 years as a PPS member.

Solitaire PPS Club members are given additional privileges:

1   A supplementary card for the spouse with the same benefits.

2   Enjoyment of SIA First Class lounge at all times, regardless of class of travel and airlines.

3   First class check-in counter for member and accompanying family members regardless of class of travel.

4   Double the normal baggage allowance.

5   Solitaire check-in counter in Singapore.

To top it off, a life membership was also introduced to Solitaire PPS Club members who have accumulated at least 3 million kilometres or 1000 flight sectors with SIA. From a basic air travel service, SIA has been able to "deck the tree with flowers" and make services to its PPS Club members appear very exclusive and prestigious. Each of the "perks" offered is not particularly attractive by itself, nor would many of the services be used at any one time. However, when bundled as a package, the whole concept is very attractive. It is no wonder SIA has been voted the best airline in the world for many years in a row. Such an achievement would not be possible without the quest for continual innovation, and the strong support from loyal customers.

PRIVATE RESIDENTIAL PROPERTIES

Improving the offerings or benefits of the product is indeed an art in which the marketer has demonstrated his ability "to deck the tree with flowers". The residential property market in Singapore is a good example. Over the last ten years, as a result of intense competition as well as the effects of the 1985 and 1986 economic recession, companies that survived have become very bold and creative in marketing residential properties. No longer do they market properties as homes (the core benefit). Instead, they have included many other features of the tangible and augmented levels in their marketing strategies (*see Figure 1*).

At the tangible level, some property developers have concentrated on improving the quality of their products. For example, in the 1970s and 1980s, properties built by Far East Organisation (FEO) were known to be of poor quality. However, since the start of the 1990s, FEO has embarked on a systematic programme to improve the quality of their properties. No effort

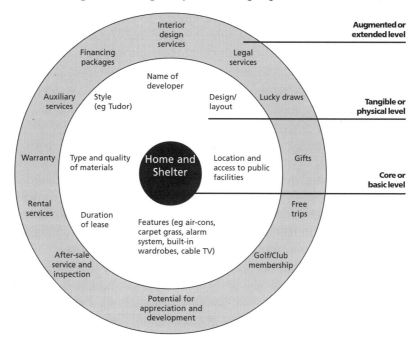

Figure 1 Three product levels of a residential property

has been spared as they continue to pay special attention to the quality of materials used, the features offered, the design and style of the buildings, the layout of the homes, and so on. The result is that they have become the first developer in Singapore to achieve ISO 9002 certification in project management in 1994.

One of FEO's condominium projects, Dover Parkview, launched in January 1996, is certainly ahead with its many state-of-the-art features: magnetic card control lockset systems, audio-video intercoms, wall-mounted hair dryers, designer wardrobes, hotel-style electronic safes, gold-chrome finished sanitary fittings, video-on-demand, and cable television services, amongst others. On top of these features are other attractions: a choice location near major tertiary institutions and premium secondary schools, junior colleges and shopping areas, private air-conditioned bus services to the nearby MRT station, lush tropical landscaping, and a multitude of facilities which include a club house, four tennis courts, a large swimming pool with underwater music, a children's pool, a splash pool, timber sunning deck, sauna rooms, jacuzzi, family furo bath, outdoor keep-fit station, jogging track, gymnasium, barbeque pits, and ample parking lots.

The developer of Dover Parkview also boasts of its Proteq 8X computerized security and home automation system that provides security by monitoring the various entrances and rooms in the house. What's more, the system enables the owner to control lighting and air-conditioning from wherever he is, via a telephone. Dover Parkview was marketed as more than a home with its futuristic and intelligent features.

Another Singaporean company, Ban Hin Leong, has traditionally enjoyed a strong reputation as a high quality property developer. Sensing the need to build up its market presence, it embarked on an ambitious marketing and advertising programme (beginning in the 1990s) to promote a common brand name for all its residential properties - Springleaf Homes. By 1996, it had achieved some success in establishing this brand name. The promotion of a brand name for residential properties is not unique to Singapore. In Malaysia, Sunrise Berhad has established a very strong brand name for its condominiums in the state of Selangor.

Property developers have thrown in many other features to provide a more attractive package to potential buyers. Features like free valuation, free or low legal fees, 100% financing, extended repayment schemes, interior design services, warranty, lucky draws, free gifts, free seminars, rental and resale services have been utilized by the innovative property developers.

A good example of an innovative developer that has exploited all the three product levels is Sunrise Berhad of Malaysia. Besides having a strong brand name, Sunrise is known for its attention to detail in the construction of its condominiums. Besides its choice locations, attention to design, style, features, and the quality of materials used also set them apart. More importantly, while the property is under construction, Sunrise keeps its customers posted on the progress of the project. It also sends interesting and favourable news clippings and articles pertaining to property trends and prices — to assure buyers that they have made the right decision.

As the construction of the property is about to be completed, Sunrise offers, through one of it subsidiaries or associated companies, interior design packages and other related services. It even offers after-sales services such as organizing free seminars, talks, parties and other social gatherings for its buyers! Indeed, many of the features shown in Figure 1 are offered by Sunrise Berhad. It comes as no surprise that Sunrise Berhad is fast emerging as the leader in condominium development in Malaysia.

Among the various product benefits offered by Sunrise, the unique pricing strategy adopted for one of its condominiums, Kiara Palma, deserves special mention. Kiara Palma was launched in January 1992, at a time when the trend of condominium prices was unpredictable. The market was then filled with rumours of an impending glut of condominiums and a fear of falling prices was prevalent among property analysts and potential buyers. To counter these fears, Sunrise came up with its "recession-proof" scheme to express its confidence that its properties would never depreciate in value. It did this by "guaranteeing" its properties against impending recessions or fall in prices. The scheme worked as follows — Sunrise would reimburse the buyer, over a 36-month period, 10% of the original purchase price of the condominium unit bought upon handing over possession of the property. This benefit was only applicable to the first buyer and lapses if the property was sold any time before or after possession.

The creatively designed recession-proof scheme (at the an augmented level of the product) effectively locked the buyer to his purchase for a period of five years as it takes about two years for the condominium to be built, and three years for the rebate to be completed. Empirically speaking, the probability of a property depreciating over a five year period is very low. In fact, few property slumps last that long. Moreover, in the event that the price of the property declines, the buyer will be unlikely to sell as he has a 10% price cushion.

There is more to Sunrise's recession-proof scheme when one analyses it carefully. Firstly, it eliminates speculators as few would be prepared to hold the property for five years. The 10% rebate over the 36-month period is effectively a price discount which can only be gained by holding on to the property. The price would have to rise higher than the 10% for the seller to benefit as he would lose the rebate the moment he sells the property. As the new buyer cannot gain from the scheme, he is likely to push down the price anyway. Secondly, Sunrise is effectively borrowing "in advance" from the buyer on an interest-free basis. This is a creative way of borrowing from the buyers to finance the whole project. Thirdly, Sunrise is guaranteed the collection of its monthly maintenance and management fees, and sinking fund contributions for the first three years upon handing over possession of the properties to the owners. This is because such payments can be automatically deducted from the monthly rebate. In fact, this was exactly what they did when the property was handed over to the buyers in late 1994! Finally, Sunrise is almost certain to have a large pool of long term investors from among its owners — an important factor for increasing the future value of the property.

STRATEGY 30

反客为主

THE GUEST TAKES OVER AS HOST

乘隙插足, 扼其主机, 渐之进也。

EXPLANATION

Try to put a foot in when there is a crack (乘隙插足) and eventually, control the brain of the enemy (扼其主机). This involves a logical sequence and is in accordance with *Yi Jing's* "Jian" Theory ([易:渐] 卦:渐之进也 ..... 进得位, 往有功也).

HISTORICAL BACKGROUND

The meaning of this strategy is that if the host does not know how to take care of his guest, the host will, in the end, be taken care of by the guest. It signifies a person in a passive position changing into an active position. In a military sense, it means a weak army becoming strong and taking initiative instead of being controlled by the circumstances.

> *During the period of the Warring States, many states were looking for capable people to fill the posts of advisers to the kings. Su Qin (苏秦) was born in Luo Yang (洛阳) and was once a student of the famous Gui Gu Zi (鬼谷子). To persuade the states to adopt his political plans, he went to Qin (秦), Zhao (赵) and later met up with the envoys of Yan (燕). Eventually, he was appointed the chief ministers of six states. Therefore, from a guest, Su Qin became a host. Another example is seen in the episode of how Gou Jian (勾践) elevated himself from a slave to a guest of Fu Chai (夫差) to finally defeat the latter (see Strategies 5 and 31).*

COMMENTS & APPLICATIONS

This strategy advises one to make the best use of opportunity to get the upper hand. To switch from the position of a guest to that of the host is a difficult move, involving several steps and detailed planning.

Firstly, for a person to become the host, he must be noticed and be invited as a guest. Secondly, as a guest, he must ensure that he does not antagonise the host so as not to arouse the host's suspicion. Thirdly, there must be a "crack" or exploitable opportunity. Fourthly, he must put his foot into this crack (or hold this opportunity). Fifthly, he must exploit this opportunity to expand influence and control. Sixthly, he must wrestle for full control and overpower the host. Finally, having become the host, he should quickly consolidate his power to ensure that he cannot be deposed. In using this strategy, one must patiently wait for the opportunity.

CAMBODIA CRISIS IN JULY 1997

"The guest takes over as host" is a strategy commonly exhibited in politics. Often, a political party in government may invite some prominent or influential personalities to join the party in order to shore up its power. These personalities however, may gradually build their own influence and power base and may seek to depose the party leader.

The political crisis in Cambodia as of mid July 1997 is an example of how this strategy was used. After barely four years of sharing power with Prince Norodom Ranariddah as co-Prime Minister, Hun Sen decided to seize power for himself. Thus, after two days of fighting, the Hun Sen forces ousted the First Prime Minister, Prince Norodom Ranariddah in early 1997. Hun Sen's actions were condemned by the United States and frowned upon by many other countries. The Security Council of the United Nation also called for an end to the violence. Meanwhile, ASEAN (Association of Southeast Asian Nations) decided to delay the entry of Cambodia as a member state. As of late 1997, no conclusive ending to the violence appeared to be in sight. Hun Sen, however, had made some compromises, including an announcement that he would call for an election by 23 May 1998.

Here, it is important to understand the history behind the conflicts. Cambodia was invaded by Vietnam in 1978. Then, the Vietnamese ousted the Khmer Rouge which was led by the reviled Pol Pot. After seizing power, the Vietnamese installed Hun Sen as

Head of the Cambodia government which was effectively controlled by Hanoi. Thus, Hun Sen was an "invited guest". After the withdrawal of Vietnamese occupying forces from Cambodia in 1989, turmoil broke out again. Subsequently, the United Nations (UN) stepped in to restore order. The 1991 Paris Accord provided for a huge peace keeping operation until a UN-sponsored election in 1993. Hun Sen was invited to be part of a coalition government.

Since forming the coalition government, Hun Sen gradually extended his influence. Sensing that the opportunity was ripe, Hun Sen decided to "take over as host". Indeed, the political climate in Southeast Asia in the 1990s is very different from the 1970s and early 1980s. With the end of the Cold War, the collapse of the Soviet Union, and the increased interest in economic development by China and Vietnam, external parties are unlikely to exert much pressure on Hun Sen's actions. More importantly, the United States, while condemning the violence, is unlikely to take firmer action, given their other priorities and the reduced importance the US has placed in this region. In fact, the rather delayed and weak response by the UN Security Council (which came only about a week later) was an indicator that Hun Sen might just get away with becoming the host!

FOOT-IN-THE-DOOR APPROACH

In the business area, the use of this strategy can be easily illustrated. It is quite common for any company to invite/allow a new shareholder (who could be of another company) as a means to increase its financial strength and influence. When the new shareholder holds a substantial number of shares, he may be given one or more board seats. The problem begins when the new shareholder has his own personal agenda. Over time, he can garner more shares from the open market or even buy from other minority shareholders on a block deal basis. Once he has gathered enough shares, he can mount a complete takeover of the company. Thus, when Singapore's DBS Land bought over the shareholdings of one of the major shareholders of Parkway Holdings (another company listed on the Singapore Stock Exchange involved in health care business) in May/June 1997, rumours were rife that DBS Land's final intention was to take control over the running of the health care business from Parkway Holdings. The purchase of a substantial shareholding (which already won it a couple of board seats) was but the first step in the whole process of "The guest takes over as host". It is like the foot-in-the-door approach.

In Asia, many newly developing countries are reluctant to allow foreign companies to own 100% of their investments. Joint ventures are preferred in China and Vietnam. Foreign investors have to strategise to benefit from the immense economic growth and business opportunities in the Asian countries. Instead of insisting on 100% ownership, foreign investors should explore the joint-venture mode, even if they have to accept less than 50% shareholding. Over time, they can try to win the confidence of the local partners. If possible, they can even buy over their stakes.

It is important that in using this strategy, one should wait patiently for the opportunity to present itself. Chinese investors from Hong Kong, Taiwan, Indonesia and Singapore have demonstrated greater superiority in this, in their ventures in China. Typically, they would get themselves "invited" by pledging to build roads, schools, libraries and hospitals in the province/city they intend to invest in. They would invest in these projects without returns. They may also hand out generous donations for various community projects. In doing so, they make themselves very much welcomed by Chinese authorities and local communities. They have become important guests. Their investment perspective is long term, and they operate on the premise of "how much am I prepared to lose".

The overseas Chinese approach is in sharp contrast to many American and Western companies which are more interested in their return-on-investment (ROI) and bottom-line (profits). These force the American and Western investors to become more short-sighted and mercenary in their approach. In addition, they want as much control as possible from day one, that is, they want to play host right away. Not surprisingly, they encountered difficulties and reported much frustration in their dealings with China.

Overseas Chinese, on the other hand, scored with the Chinese. Amazingly, even their small and medium-size companies adapted well to the difficult business conditions in China. For the Western countries, their successes, thus far, have been confined to very large corporations like Coca-Cola, McDonalds, Motorola, Allied Signals, Hewlett-Packard and Johnson & Johnson. To be more successful, companies from the Western world must learn how to use this strategy of "The guest takes over as host".

INVOLVING LABOUR IN MANAGEMENT

Interestingly, the July 1997 move by Singapore Airlines (SIA) to invite Mr Lim Boon Heng onto the Board of Directors is an example of how the host has actually invited the "guest" to become a co-host as well. As of July 1997, Mr Lim was a cabinet minister and the secretary-general of the National Trade Union Congress (NTUC) of Singapore. By inviting the union chief onto its Board of Directors, SIA was openly acknowledging the need to actively involve labour in its management.

The conventional stance in management-labour relations has always been confrontational. This is particularly true of Western companies. For example, at a time when British Airways had been doing very well, and was ranked as one of the most efficient and competitive airlines in the world, its cabin crew went on a strike in early July 1997. Although the strike lasted only a few days, the after-effects lingered on as the crew continued on go-slow actions, such as reporting sick. It resulted in the loss of millions of pounds in profits for British Airways.

Sensing intense competition ahead, and that the "host-guest" relationship between labour and management must not persist, SIA took the unusual approach of inviting labour participation into management. This could not have come at a better time. After 50 years of operation, SIA had become too bottom-line conscious. Many of its over 15,000 employees from five unions felt strongly that SIA had lost its "human touch" towards the rank-and-file. To compete effectively into the 21st century, workers must actively participate in contributing towards the company. Having the union on board therefore made tremendous sense.

With the financial crisis that started in July 1997, the participation and involvement of the union in key decision-making become even more critical for SIA. In fact, several Asian airlines such as Cathay Pacific Airways, Malaysian Airline System, Thai Airways International, Garuda Indonesia, Sempati Air, Korean Air Lines and Asiana Airlines were badly hit by the currency turmoil. Some resorted to slashing airfares and delaying delivery of new aircrafts. Other airlines (for example, Qantas Airways and British Airways) that operated routes into and out of Asia from countries not affected by the currency crisis had also begun to feel the effects of declining air traffic. Thus, competition among airlines in the Asian region is likely to intensify for the remaining years of this century.

Having the union boss on the board of management would definitely give SIA the extra leverage needed to meet the challenges ahead. Other than representing the welfare and interests of employees, the union boss can help to reflect the views of the management to the workers in a better perspective. This will help to facilitate change and implement difficult policies essential for moving SIA forward and riding the "turbulent storms" in the financial crisis. Thus, in this case, by inviting the "guest" to become a "co-host", both management and employees of SIA stand to benefit. In addition, being the national airlines of Singapore, and a big contributor to the economy, Singapore also stands to gain. It is a win-win-win formula.

When Chrysler Corporation of the United States was faced with threats of bankruptcy and union unrest in the late 1970s and early 1980s, it took a similar step. Lee Iacocca, the Chief Executive Officer and Chairman invited the boss of the auto-workers' union to sit on the Board of Directors, and to be involved in the management of Chrysler. As it turned out, with the strong support of the union, Lee Iacocca successfully turned the company around and made a name for himself. Thus, when applied in a positive way and with some modifications, the strategy of "The guest takes over as host" can be effectively used in business.

PROFIT-SHARING AND STOCK OWNERSHIP SCHEMES

Management and union have traditionally adopted contradictory goals and objectives. They tend to view each other with suspicion and often engage in confrontations. This is particularly true in countries such as Britain and the US where management and union typically lock-horns aggressively in negotiation of collective agreements. To achieve their objectives and strengthen their bargaining power, union workers resort to down tools, work-to-rule and other industrial actions during the negotiation process. Strikes are also common when the union workers are not happy with the terms and conditions offered by management. Management too resort to threatening tactics, including the sacking order. Without doubt, negotiating the collective agreement is always a very tense and expensive exercise. Workers' strikes can cost severe loss of wages and revenues. An extended strike may cause financial setbacks that will take months to fully recover from. Striking is definitely a lose-lose situation.

In an effort to win the support of the workers, some enlightened companies have begun to offer profit-sharing and stock-ownership schemes to employees. These schemes are designed to involve the rank-and-file in the management of the company and to allow them to contribute more directly to the bottom-line. When employees own shares in the company, they will work harder so that the price of the share will rise further. In fact, they can see the direct effects of their hard work. One recent and significant case has to be that of Dell Computer. Many of its employees have been made millionaires as a result of several stock splits over a period of 10 years! Similarly, when the employees are able to have a share in the profits of the company, they will be more willing to engage in measures that help to improve productivity and efficiency. Afterall, when the company makes greater profits, they stand to gain.

Interestingly, profit-sharing and stock-ownership schemes can be likened to the strategy of "The guest takes over as host" because the worker (the guest) is now very much the host in that he has a direct stake in the company. As such, he is likely to take an active interest in the welfare and progress of the company. This is a creative way to change the roles of management and union from the conventional confrontational stance to a cooperative posture likely to create win-win outcomes.

STRATEGY 31
美人计
BEAUTY SCHEME

兵强者，攻其将；将智者，伐其情。
将弱兵颓，其势自萎。
利用御寇，顺相保也。

EXPLANATION

With regards to an enemy with strong troops (兵强者), one should aim to control its general (攻其将). Against an intelligent enemy general (将智者), one should plot to dampen his morale (伐其情). Once the general's fighting spirit is quenched, the army will be weakened (将弱兵颓，其势自萎). Therefore, one should try to hit the enemy at its weaknesses while conserving one's energy (利用御寇，顺相保也). This is in accordance with *Yi Jing's* "Jian" Theory ([易经:渐]).

The beauty scheme is precisely targeted at the weakness of the general. This is because most men (and generals are no exception) have a great passion and weakness for beautiful and charming women. Once charmed, his judgement will be impaired as he would be ruled by his heart and nto his head. He then becomes vulnerable to exploitation.

HISTORICAL BACKGROUND

This strategy is taken from **Han Fei Zi** about how Jin Xian Gong (晋献公) took down the states of Yu (虞) and Guo (虢) by presenting to the ruler of Yu a piece of priceless jade and a beautiful woman (*see Strategy 24*).

韩非子:内储说下:晋献公伐虞、虢，乃遗之屈产之乘，垂棘之璧、女乐二八，以荣其意而乱其政

One illustration of this strategy is the story of how the King of Yue (越王) avenged his shame (*see also Strategy 5*).

STORY 1

During the Spring and Autumn Period (春秋时期), the States of Wu (吴国) and Yue (越国) were constantly at war. First, Wu lost to Yue and then Wu got the better of Yue. During this time, the King of Yue, Gou Jian (勾践) slept on a bed made of twigs and tasted the gall-bladder of a pig to remind himself of the shame and humiliation he received from the King of Wu, Fu Chai (夫差).

At that time, Gou Jian had a capable subject named Fan Li (范蠡). As Fu Chai was constantly protected by bodyguards, Fan Li decided the best way to get near him was to present him with a beautiful woman. After a long search, he finally found Xi Shi (西施) who was washing yarn by the river when he met her.

Xi Shi was only eight years old then but she was already a raving beauty. Fan Li paid a large amount of money to her parents and brought Xi Shi back to his place. He engaged teachers to teach her poetry, painting, dancing and court etiquette. When Xi Shi was sixteen, Fan Li knew the time had come to present her to Fu Chai. Before Xi Shi left, Fan Li gave her two assignments: to ensnare Fu Chai with her beauty and to sow discord between Fu Chai and his right-hand man, Wu Zi Xu (伍子胥).

Xi Shi easily fulfilled her tasks. Fu Chai was mesmerised by her charm and lost all interest in the care of his kingdom. He also listened to Xi Shi and kept a distance from Wu Zi Xu. Wu Zi Xu was eventually driven to death. Finally, Gou Jian took the opportunity when Fu Chai left his kingdom for a meeting with his allies to attack and capture the kingdom of Wu. Xi Shi's beauty and charm is talked about today. In fact, she is commonly acknowledged as one of four great beauties in Chinese history.

STORY 2

Around 190 BC and during the reign of Emperor Xian (献帝) in China, Dong Zhuo (董卓), the premier, became very powerful. He was cunning, ruthless and intelligent. To make matters worse, he adopted Lu Bu (吕布), one of the best fighters at that time, as his son. This father-son team posed a big threat to the emperor and officials of the court. Both Dong Zhuo and Lu Bu were so arrogant that when they had an audience with the emperor, they even brought their weapons to court. These blatant acts were veiled threats to the emperor.

On one occasion and before many officials, Dong Zhuo ordered the execution of Zhang Wen (张 温) who had opposed him. At that function, Governor Si Tu Wang Yun (司 徒 王 允) was also present. He concluded that both Dong Zhuo and Lu Bu had to be eliminated before they became greater threats. However, this was not an easy task. Wang Yun knew that he was no match for Dong Zhuo both in use of strategy and physical force.

After much thinking and agonising, he decided to use the beauty scheme. Wang Yun had a maid whom he treated like his own daughter. She was not only patriotic, but was extremely beautiful and charming. Her name was Diao Chan (貂 蝉). In fact, she was another one of the four great beauties recorded in Chinese history. Like Xi Shi in Story 1, Diao Chan used her beauty to mesmerise Dong Zhuo and Lu Bu, and made every effort to sow discord between the two of them. So overwhelming was Diao Chan's charm that Dong Zhuo and Lu Bu became very jealous of each other, and failed to see through the beauty scheme. Finally, Lu Bu ended up killing Dong Zhuo. Without Dong Zhuo, Lu Bu was like a bird with clipped wings, and was no longer a threat.

COMMENTS & APPLICATIONS

One of man's greatest weaknesses is his love for beautiful women. Heroes throughout the ages have fallen for the sex trap. As one Chinese saying goes, "It is difficult for a hero to overcome a trap set by a beauty" (英 雄 难 过 美 人 关). Therefore, beautiful women were used to ensnare enemies. In fact, Sun Zi, the great Chinese military strategist also acknowledged the power of the young maiden who can entice the enemy and lower his defences (*see Strategy 27*).

Among the 36 strategies, the "Beauty scheme" is probably the most fascinating and easily adapted with the other strategies. This strategy can be applied on targets who are vulnerable to good-looks. Once their defences are down, the strategist can apply other strategies as follow-throughs to destroy the enemy. In Story 1, when Fu Chai was completely mesmerised by Xi Shi, he became vulnerable to exploitation. To a large extent, Xi Shi was applying Strategy 10, "A dagger sheathed in a smile". The smile was so lethal that she was able to use Fu Chai as the borrowed knife to eliminate Wu Zi Xi (Strategy 3 "Kill another with a borrowed knife"). When Wu Zi Xi, Fu Chai's most capable assistant, was eliminated, it was like "Pulling out the firewood from beneath the firewood" as illustrated in Strategy 19. His death was tantamount to removing Fu Chai limbs. When Fu Chai left the city, this allowed Gou Jian to use Strategy 5, "Looting a house on fire" and Strategy 20, "Catching a fish in troubled water".

The "beauty scheme" alone will not suffice to destroy the enemy. It is intended to weaken the enemy and to impair his judgement. To destroy the enemy, it must be combined with other strategies. In the case of Gou Jian, one must admire his ability in applying Strategy 27, "Pretending to be insane but remaining smart". Gou Jian did not show any mercy on Fu Chai but eliminated him completely, so that he will never be a threat to him again. As the Chinese say, "When you cut grass without removing their roots, they will sprout again when the spring winds blow" (斬草不除根，春風吹又生).

GOOD LOOKS ARE ASSETS

The beauty scheme is often used in business. Consumers are attracted to good looking sales persons. It is no surprise that hotels employ charming people to manage their front desks and as public relation officers, and marketers prefer better-looking sales people too. Interestingly, good-looking people do not only appeal to the targets of the opposite sex.

In the cosmetics business, well-known for employing pretty ladies as promoters, this goes a step further — they hire people with excellent skin, complexion and features. Their good looks, accentuated by make-up, back up their claims about what the cosmetics can do to help customers look better. In the fashion business, models such as Naomi Campbell, Claudia Schiffer, Cindy Crawford, Christy Turlington, Linda Evangelista and Kate Moss, have charmed thousands into buying products from Gianni Versace, Gucci, Christian Dior, Givenchy and others. Their astronomical salaries testify to the power of their good looks.

To be fair, the "Beauty scheme" is not confined to good looks alone. It can be extended to using well-known personalities and celebrities to market products (the more successful ones are also very well-groomed). For example, tennis player Gabriela Sabatini lends her name to a fragrance which has become a bestseller in Europe. Elizabeth Taylor, reputedly one of the most beautiful Hollywood stars in the 1960s and 1970s, is an extremely successful icon in cosmetics, with many brands under her name, including her signature fragrance White Diamonds.

Male celebrities are far left behind. Pop singer Michael Jackson, and actors Omar Sharif and Paul Newman have all lent their names to various products, especially fragrances. While products bearing their names have experienced varying degrees of success, the royalties these celebrities received were nonetheless substantial. The characteristically suave British secret agent, James Bond, played by Pierce Brosnan in "Tomorrow Never Dies," (1997) was seen using a wide range of products and services. These included a BMW car, an Omega watch, a Brioni suit, an Ericsson cellular phone, Smirnoff vodka, Heineken beer, Visa credit card, and Avis car rental. With the movie's success, Pierce Brosnan will doubtless appear in advertisements for these products/services.

The payoffs to the manufacturers who use celebrity endorsement are tremendous. To begin with, the publicity mileage generated is substantial. As celebrities have great mass appeal, the final cost of promotion may be very low on a per capita basis. In addition, the celebrity lends a lot of personality traits and possible product attributes to the brand, particularly important in marketing fragrances and other personality-based products.

Like other strategies, the "Beauty scheme" is designed to gain competitive advantages for the company. However, in the 1980s, SIA incurred the wrath of American groups who criticised its policy of hiring pretty faces as air hostesses, and condemned its advertisements as sexist.

Still, SIA's successful strategy has been copied by other Asian airlines. Besides recruiting younger and better-looking crew members, some have adopted uniforms which resemble that of the SIA girls. Having younger and better-looking crew enables these airlines to project a youthful and energetic image. A younger crew also means a lower wage bill, and therefore, lower operating costs and increased competitiveness.

REALITY IN BUSINESS

The ploy of using beauty as a bait should not be pursued all the time. A company must have a marketable product or service to attract customers, without which no amount of charm will save them. But it would be naive to assume that your competitors will not use the strategy, just because you are not using it. The reality is, beautiful people attract attention, and can hold that attention longer, fulfilling two important criteria for making a sale.

An increasing number of Asian companies, realising the power of the "Beauty scheme" are prepared to pay big bucks for the services of beautiful people in their advertisements and promotions. As an illustration, the suave Hong Kong actor, Chow Yuen Fatt, was paid S$1.28 million to appear in a three-minute television commercial for Smartone, a mobile-phone company in October 1997. In that commercial, Chow's character, a businessman, talks to someone who resembles Chinese leader Jiang Zemin in the Great Hall of the People in Beijing. The advertisement was very powerful as it capitalised on the increasing popularity of President Jiang Zemin in Hong Kong and the easily recognizable Chow.

With increasing affluence and the influence of mass media, more companies are hiring good-looking people to augment their marketing and promotional campaigns. Besides using celebrities in product endorsements, companies also invite them to grace functions such as opening ceremonies, charity events and anniversaries.

To succeed, one should face up to the realities of business. While some deny that beauty can be an effective asset in business, the truth is, beauty matters. It is better to call a spade a spade. If the "Beauty scheme" is to be used, it should be done in a tasteful and non-offensive manner.

IMPORTANCE OF TRAINING AND GROOMING

While good looks are largely determined by nature, one must not ignore nurture. With proper training and grooming, looks can be improved. Companies should give attention to projecting a strong image through well-groomed and well-trained employees. In service businesses such as banking, hotel and tourism, employees play a key role in determining customer satisfaction. So, service companies willingly spend time, effort and money to groom and train employees.

Good appearance can add power to a service presentation. Excellent manners, smart uniforms, and a good work attitude will charm the customer. Not all the SIA girls are beautiful but they are all charming. The gait, smile, make-up, uniform, hair-style and willingness to serve are all part of the trademark of the "Singapore girl".

Training in grooming, therefore, should be considered a worthwhile investment as it helps employees provide better services to customers. Companies have recourse to professional trainers who specialise in training image-building. They can also explore other ways to improve the image and self-esteem of their employees, such as smart and well-designed uniforms. This will also create a unique identity and image for the company which in turn acts as powerful marketing and promotional tools.

An intelligent company will not simply recruit good-looking people. After all, good looks only represent *external beauty* (外在美) and can be superficial and deceptive. The company should focus also on bringing out *inner beauty* (內在美), such as a good service attitude, through training and grooming. Every employee will then be able to turn on their *total charm* for the consumer. The result — a very satisfied customer and a highly motivated employee — both of which will further promote and advertise the company.

In today's highly competitive world, satisfying the customer is no longer enough. The proactive and shrewd strategist should seek to delight the customer by exceeding the his expectations. This is where training and grooming can give a decisive edge.

STRATEGY 32

空城计

EMPTY CITY SCHEME

虚者虚之, 疑中生疑;
刚柔之际, 奇而复奇。

EXPLANATION

There is no fixed method for deploying an army. It may sometimes be better to deliberately display its weakness (虚者虚之), to confuse the enemy (疑中生疑) and make the latter abandon the attack for fear of trickery. In a situation where the enemy is strong and when one is weak (刚柔之际), proper use of this strategy can appear extraordinary (奇而复奇), as in accordance with *Yi Jing's* "Jie" Theory ([易经：解] 卦).

HISTORICAL BACKGROUND

This strategy is used in a desperate situation, usually when the enemy is very strong and any direct confrontation will result in defeat. The strategy originates from the story of how Zhu Ge Liang (诸葛亮) saved the city Yang Ping with a small army, in the *Tales of the Three Kingdoms* (三国志：蜀志：诸葛亮传).

STORY 1

During the period of the Three Kingdoms, Zhu Ge Liang was in the city of Yang Ping (阳平). He sent his general Wei Yan (魏延) with the majority of the Shu (蜀) soldiers to launch an attack on the Cao Wei (曹魏) army, leaving 10,000 men behind to defend the city. The 200,000 strong Cao Wei army was led by the general Si Ma Yi (司马懿). However, due to a miscalculation, the Shu army missed the Cao Wei army.

When the Cao Wei army was about 60 miles from the city, Si Ma Yi learnt from his spy that the city held only Zhu Ge Liang and a few soldiers. Zhu Ge Liang received news that the enemy was near, but it was too late to summon Wei Yan back. The town was in panic but Zhu Ge Liang remained calm. He ordered the soldiers to keep all the army flags flying and to not leave the tents without permission. He then summoned men to open the gates and pretend to sweep the ground next to the gates.

When Si Ma Yi came with his army, he was shocked by what he saw. He knew Zhu Ge Liang to be a good strategist with many tricks up his sleeve. When he saw the city gates wide open, he suspected that Zhu Ge Liang had his men hidden within the city ready to ambush the Cao Wei army. His suspicions were further aroused by the fact that Zhu Ge Liang was sitting leisurely on top of the main gate playing his zither and sipping tea. As Si Ma Yi listened to the placid chords from Zhu Ge Liang's zither, he gathered that they did not reflect a troubled mind. He therefore concluded that the empty city was definitely a scheme to lure his troops in. Accordingly, Si Ma Yi ordered his men to retreat. Thus Zhu Ge Liang salvaged the situation.

STORY 2

In 727 AD, when Tang Xuan Zhong (唐玄宗) ruled the Tang Dynasty, the Tibetans attacked China through Gua Zhou (瓜州) of the Xi An province (西安). Emperor Tang sent General Zhang Shou Gui (张守圭) to there to defend the city. Zhang Shou Gui mobilised the residents of Gua Zhou to reconstruct the damaged city walls. However, midway through the reconstruction, the Tibetan army raided the city again.

Gua Zhou had a small population and the deaths resulting from the two attacks virtually emptied the city. Another direct confrontation would certainly them wipe out. Therefore, General Zhang advised the people against hasty retaliation. Instead, he had tables set up on top of the city walls and threw a great feast. All residents and soldiers were invited and they drank heartily.

When the Tibetans saw the scene, they wondered, "The enemies must be trying to make us believe that their defences are lax. If we enter the city, we may be walking into a trap. Their soldiers might be waiting to ambush us inside." The Tibetans decided not to risk an attack and retreated. Thus Gua Zhou was saved.

COMMENTS & APPLICATIONS

This strategy is similar to Strategy 7, "Creating something out of nothing". The difference is that Strategy 7 is an opportunistic or exploitative strategy, and capitalises on the ignorance of the other party. Strategy 7 can be used in many situations and its effects can be lasting. In contrast, the "Empty city scheme" is only used when one is in a disadvantageous and desperate position. The party using this strategy hides their real situation and creates a facade that confuses the enemy. While the enemy assesses the situation, he has a chance to escape. The "Empty city scheme" can only be used as a temporary strategy to momentarily stall the reaction of the enemy.

This "Empty city scheme" is also different from Strategy 1, "Deceiving the heavens to cross the sea" in that the latter is used in an advantageous situation. The "Empty city scheme" has to be combined with other strategies for its effectiveness to be fully appreciated. For example, Zhu Ge Liang, as illustrated in Story 1, was able to use the "Empty city scheme" to temporarily stall the enemy, giving him more time to withdraw or to wait for reinforcements to arrive. By leaving the city gates wide open, he was "Making a deceptive show of strength" as well as using Strategy 27, "Pretending to be insane but remaining smart". This would pave the way for the use of other strategies like Strategy 6, "Making a feint to the east but hitting out in the west", Strategy 8, "Secret escape through Chen Cang" and Strategy 36, "Escape — the best scheme".

A HIGH-RISK STRATEGY

This is a very high-risk strategy. The user must have an impeccable reputation, possess a lot of confidence and have a strong understanding of the enemy's psyche. This temporary measure can only stun the enemy and delay his response. It cannot be sustained over a long time. For example, Zhu Ge Liang was a well-known strategist and Si Ma Yi had always been wary of him. Zhu Ge Liang was also famous for being very thorough and detailed, and rarely made mistakes. Si Ma Yi could never envisage that Zhu Ge Liang would pull such a trick on him. Nor could he detect any strains of nervousness or stress. However, the strategy could not stall Si Ma Yi's troops for long. Si Ma Yi eventually saw through the ploy.

In the animal kingdom, this strategy is commonly illustrated. For example, the porcupine's bristles temporarily threaten the enemy, giving him a chance for a speedy escape. The octopus releases a spate of black ink to confuse its predators. Dogs bark ferociously to project bravery. However, these animals may be quite harmless and defenceless against their enemies. Their strong front deter or stun their enemies while they escape.

PUTTING UP A BRAVE FRONT

In the business world, one must also occasionally put up a "brave front" (虚张声势) to stop competitors from learning that one is under severe strain. Companies often issue press statements denying they are facing financial or business difficulties, while they secretly resolve their problems. They try to prevent competitors and the public from seeing through the facade.

An example is the South Korean Kia Group, whose flagship Kia Motors Corporation was the country's third largest car maker and eighth largest conglomerate as of July 1997. Although the company faced severed financial difficulties and was put under bank protection to save it from insolvency, its calm demeanour prevented the company from an immediate close-down. It was granted a two-month grace period by creditors to settle its debts. The Kia Group continued to conduct business as usual. Its "brave front" convinced many that the company was not beyond salvation. Its car sales in Korea had risen since 15 July and the sales figures for the period between 1 to 19 July totalled 16,079 units, up 13% compared to June. Its export sales in August increased to 31,990 vehicles, up from 22,964 for the same month in 1996. It also introduced new models of cars to boost domestic sales, and priced them attractively at 1996 prices. Kia raised 350 billion won in cash in August 1997 by selling its vehicles at a 30% discount. Sales continued to be strong. In Singapore, sales of Kia cars continued and there was no sudden avoidance of Kia cars. In fact, many in Singapore either did not believe or had not heard that the Kia Group was near insolvency.

Beneath its apparent calmness, the company was seeking desperately for a bail out from the government and creditor banks. Its 9.5 trillion won (approximately S$15.9 billion) debt to the banks was significant and it needed more than just customer support to stay afloat. As its grace period expired in September 1997, there were calls, including those from politicians such as Deputy Prime Minister Kang Kyung Shik, that Kia should not be bailed out by the government. Meanwhile, the creditors were pushing Kia Motors towards bankruptcy and receivership. Kia resisted these moves and sought court protection to freeze its debts and reschedule payments. This would allow them to continue the business. As a show of support, the workers at Kia Motors held a two-day strike at the end of September. However, this "empty city scheme" was only a temporary measure.

A second example is MBf Holdings of Malaysia. Following the currency and stock market crises in late the 1990s, there was a sudden run on MBf Finance. Rumours spread that its founder, CEO and president, Tan Sri Dato Dr Loy Hean Heong, was seriously ill. Some rumours suggested he had died of colon cancer. The run on the group's finance companies gained momentum when the public perceived there was no clear successor to Dr Loy who was regarded as a highly entrepreneurial and charismatic leader.

In an effort to calm the fears of investors and customers, MBf Holdings called an urgent press conference to deny the rumours. Dr Loy appeared in a video conference from an American Hospital in Paris where he was undergoing a check-up. He assured his viewers that he was well and "feeling on top of the world". In addition, the MBf Group took out a series of advertisements in Malaysia and Singapore to reassure the public of its sound financial position and strong backing from Bank Negara (Malaysia's Central Bank). Among the details disclosed were claims that MBf had total assets of more than M$22 billion, two million customers and 151 branches throughout Malaysia. With deposits of more than S$20 billion, it was one of the largest financial institutions in Malaysia. In addition, the group made record earnings of over S$336 million for the six months ending June 1997. With such impressive statistics and strong assurances, the brave posture put up by the top management of MBf Holdings was designed to tide the company over the temporary setback.

Unfortunately, Dr Loy died suddenly in late November 1997. The fate of MBf Holdings is difficult to establish as the full impact of the currency and stock market have not been seen. While the late Dr Loy had groomed his children to take over the business, the effectiveness of the successsion remains to be tested.

USE OF BOGUS COMPANIES AND SWINDLING SYNDICATES

In July 1997, Sim Tiang Huat was sentenced to nine years imprisonment in Singapore for engineering a scam that cheated 75 companies of S$1.5 million over a period of two years. Sim masterminded a syndicate of nine bogus companies which bought computer hardware, electrical products, furniture, household and industrial items from 75 companies over 90 occasions. These bogus companies had legitimate corporate names, accounts with reputable local and overseas banks, and registered addresses. In reality, they were all "empty shells" that obtained credit lines on goods purchased, and then refused payment. They issued cheques that subsequently bounced. Sim's "Empty city scheme" cheated unwary businessmen.

Sim Tiang Huat's tricks, however, are minuscule compared to the "get-rich-quick" scams of Nigerian swindling syndicates. The following are some examples.

The first was the fund transfer scheme. Claiming to be senior government officials, members of the Nigerian syndicates would contact businessmen in various parts of the world to say they needed foreign bank accounts to help them channel millions of US dollars out of the country. They would admit that they were money-laundering the takings from bribery, inflated project costs or aborted projects. They offered millions of dollars' commission to overseas businessmen or companies who would allow their bank accounts to be used for the transfer of funds.

Once the deal was struck, they would ask the victims for substantial sums of money in advance to cover administrative charges. To increase their credibility, they faked documents and letterheads used by the Nigerian government, Central Bank of Nigeria and other Nigerian government agencies. Once the advance fee was sent, the syndicate would vanish.

These Nigerian syndicates also conned hotels to part with large sums of money, claiming they represented large Nigerian trade or government agencies wanting to do business in the country concerned. They claimed that money was needed to facilitate foreign exchange and travel. The hotels would be assured of huge commissions upon successful conclusion of deals. But after the money was sent, no Nigerian delegation checked-in.

As corruption was rampant in Nigeria, some syndicates would entice victims to fly to Lagos to meet bogus government officials and big-time businessmen. These victims would be informed they needed to part with large sums of money and other gifts to bribe government officials who were important contacts or facilitators of the deals. Once the money was given, the poor victims would find themselves stranded in Lagos.

The scam used by Sim Tiang Huat of Singapore was an old ploy perfected by the Nigerians. These Nigerian syndicates repeatedly used the "Empty city schemes" to con greedy businessmen and companies worldwide. The problem was so serious that in 1995 and 1997 the Nigerian government had to take out advertisements in over 45 countries to warn potential victims. Despite these warnings, individuals and companies still fall victim.

The Nigerian scams preyed on the victims' greed dramatised the urgency of the transactions to impair the judgement of the potential victims and to pressure them for a decision. By the time the victims recover from the sting, it would be too late.

反 间 计

DOUBLE AGENT PLOY

疑 中 之 疑。比 之 自 内，不 自 失 也。

EXPLANATION

When the enemy lays traps, set a trap within his traps to create internal chaos (疑 中 之 疑). When one secures assistance from within the enemy's ranks (比 之 自 内), one will not lose the battle (不 失 方 也). This is in accordance with *Yi Jing's* "Bi" Theory ([易：比]：比 之 自 内，不 失 方 也).

The literal meaning of the strategy is to use the enemy's spy to counter spy on the enemy. The story from **Chang Duan Jing** describes how Chen Ping (陈 平) used this strategy to create discord between Chu's top adviser Fan Zeng (范 增) and the ruler of Chu (楚 怀 王) *(see Strategy 6, Story 2)*

[长 短 经：五 间]："陈 平 以 金 纵 反 间 于 楚 军，间 范 增，楚 王 疑 之。此 用 反 间 者 也"

HISTORICAL BACKGROUND

During the period of the Three Kingdoms (三 国 时), Cao Cao (曹 操) sent Jiang Gan (蒋 干) to spy on his enemy, Zhou Yu (周 瑜). The spy was used by Zhou Yu against Cao Cao and this led to the execution of Cao Cao's two most capable generals, Cai Mao (蔡 瑁) and Zhang Yun (张 允).

When Zhou Yu heard that Cai Mao and Zhang Yun had been recruited by Cao Cao to train the soldiers in swimming and war tactics for confrontation at sea, he knew that he had to get rid of these two generals. At that time, Cao Cao happened to send Jiang Gan to Zhou Yu's place as a guest. When Zhou Yu heard of the arrival of Jiang Gan, he knew his opportunity had come.

When he saw Jiang Gan, Zhou Yu smiled and said, "Dear friend, are you on a mission for Cao Cao?" Jiang Gan was shocked and he said, "Oh no! We have not met for quite some time and I have come just to meet you. If you suspect that I am on a mission, then it is best that I leave." Zhou Yu took him by the arm and said, "I thought that you had come to speak for Cao Cao. Since you did not, you are most welcome. Why don't you stay a few days with me?"

Zhou Yu invited Jiang Gan to a big feast attended by many of Zhou Yu's men. During the dinner, Zhou Yu announced, "Jiang Gan has been my good friend for a long time. Although he came from Cao Cao's camp, he is not here on a political mission. Therefore, no one need be wary of Mr Jiang." He then removed his sword and handed it to one of his subordinates saying, "Today we are here to enjoy ourselves and we will not talk about politics. Therefore, if anyone here mentions Cao Cao and politics, please have him beheaded."

Jiang Gan was so surprised he was speechless. Zhou Yu continued, "I have not taken wine since I started leading the army. However, it has been a long time since we met so let us drink heartily." When they were almost drunk, Zhou Yu pulled Jiang Gan out of the tent and asked, "What do you think of my men? Are they not courageous and strong?" Jiang Gan answered in the affirmative. Zhou Yu then brought him to his warehouse and asked, "What do you think of my ample supplies?" Jiang Gan was impressed with what he saw and praised Zhou Yu.

Zhou Yu then pretended to be very drunk and lifted up Jiang Gan's hand and said, "It is really good to meet a bosom friend whom one can pour one's heart out to. Nothing can change what I have been doing and nobody can make me change my mind." Jiang Gan turned pale and dared not reply.

Zhou Yu brought Jiang Gan back to the table and continued drinking until Jiang Gan could not drink anymore. Zhou Yu, pretending to be very drunk, requested Jiang Gan to sleep in his room. Jiang Gan had no choice but to agree.

However, Jiang Gan could not sleep a wink and when he thought Zhou Yu had fallen fast asleep, he snooped around in Zhou Yu's room. He saw a stack of letters on Zhou Yu's table and went through them. Among the letters was one supposedly from Cai Mao and Zhang Yun. Jiang Gan was shocked when he saw the contents of the letter which read: "We (Cai Mao and Zhang Yun) were not seeking riches but we have been pressurised by circumstances to join Cao Cao's camp. We will wait for an opportunity to kill Cao Cao and send his head to you..."

Jiang Gan quickly returned to bed when he heard Zhou Yu turn. He then heard Zhou Yu muttering in his sleep, "Jiang Gan, in a few days' time, I will bring you Cao Cao's head." Jiang Gan could hardly believe his ears.

Later that night, someone roused Zhou Yu and said, "Someone from Cao Cao's camp has come to see you." Zhou Yu quickly shushed him, looking to see if Jiang Gan had heard him. Jiang Gan pretended to be still asleep while Zhou Yu left the room to see the messenger outside. Jiang Gan overheard the messenger saying, "Cai Mao and Zhang Yun sent me to say the time has not yet come to kill Cao Cao."

Jiang Gan having heard and seen enough, sneaked back to Cao Cao's camp. When Cao Cao heard Jiang Gan's report, he ordered the immediate execution of Cai Mao and Zhang Yun without giving them a chance to defend themselves.

COMMENTS & APPLICATIONS

One good way of to defeat the enemy is to use his spies against him to create discord and confusion. Zhou Yu did just that when he fed Jiang Gan with false information to bring back to Cao Cao, causing two of Cao Cao's best generals to be destroyed. In war, espionage is a common and acceptable practice for gaining vital information of the enemy's movements.

The great Chinese military strategist, Sun Zi, clearly understood the importance of intelligence. In his well-known treatise called "The Art of War", he identified five types of spies:

> There are five types of secret agents that can be used: local agents, inside agents, double agents, doomed agents, and living agents.

故用间有五: 有因间, 有内间, 有反间, 有死间, 有生间。

The double agent is defined as follows:

> Double agents are enemy spies whom we recruit.

反间者，因其敌间而用之。

Sun Zi recommends that the enemy's spies be treated thus:

> The enemy agents who are sent to spy on us must be sought out, bribed, guided and cared for, so that they can be converted into double agents to work for us.

必索敌人之间来间我者，因而利之，导而舍之，
故反间可得而用也。

Double agents are valued highly for their services. Sun Zi gives the impression that double agents provide pivotal functions for the other four types of agents. The following quotations lend support to this:

> Through such means (double agents) the enemy's situation is known, and hence local and inside agents can be recruited and used.

因是而知之，故乡间，内间可得而使也。

> Through this medium (double agents) we learn the enemy's situation, and hence are able to use doomed agents to spread false information to the enemy.

因是而知之，故死间为诳事，可使告敌。

> Through information provided by this medium (double agents) living agents can return at an opportune time with reports on the enemy.

因是而知之，故生间可使如期。

In fact, Sun Zi went so far as to say:

> The ruler must have complete knowledge of the activities of the five types of agents. This information must come from the double agents, and thus it is essential that double agents be treated very generously.

五间之事，主必知之，知之必在于反间，
故反间不可不厚也。

Double agents are the link pin between the other agents. Among the three types of agents (local, inside and double), recruited from the enemy's territory, they are probably the most valuable and treasured. Double agents have earned the enemy's confidence, have access to enemy secrets, are able to recruit and communicate with the other types of agents and can assist in the infiltration of the enemy with other spies. What Sun Zi says about double agents still holds true today. They are still probably the most treasured but are also difficult to deal with.

INDUSTRIAL AND COMMERCIAL ESPIONAGE

In business, espionage against competitors is unethical and the use of double agents is even more unethical. However, espionage does exist in the business world. Industrial and commercial spying were very common after the cold war. It is said many Western countries recruited former Soviet Union and East European spies to work for their companies to spy on their competitors. While the use of double agents seems a remote phenomenon, they do exist.

As competition hots up, companies will inevitablely adopt more aggressive measures against their rivals, and some will compromise moral and ethical codes. Espionage is a tempting option for getting ahead. For example, British Airways was caught in 1992 trying to hack into Virgin Atlantic's computer system to steal its passenger database. The same year, a man was accused of bringing corporate documents from General Motors to Volkswagen. In Japan technological advancements have forced it to tighten security against industrial and commercial espionage.

CONSULTANTS, RESEARCH COMPANIES & AGENCIES

A company may fall victim to a double-agent ploy. The most vulnerable candidates are consultants who have access to corporate information, particularly those possessing key information that affects competitiveness such as research and development data, trademark and copyright matters, strategic plans, operational procedures and systems, and computer software. When these consultants cease working for a company, they may be tempted to sell sensitive information to the company's competitors. They may also use the information or experience gained to announce their marketability to other clients. Companies should ensure their corporate secrets are well-guarded and their corporate interests legally protected.

Market researchers and research companies are other vulnerable candidates. The privileged information they have access to might be used to benefit others, including the competitors of the clients who paid for the research. Restricting these companies is difficult as ideas and concepts cannot be patented or copyrighted. A high level of professional ethics is needed from people in these businesses.

Take the case of a research questionnaire. There is nothing to stop a research company from using the same survey instrument on different clients. Though the questionnaire may have been developed by the research company, a well-developed questionnaire is often created with clients' input. Research companies may unscrupulously use the same questionnaire, adapt it or improve it, for the client's competitors. With few regulations governing research companies, the "Double agency ploy" can easily be applied by companies operating across national boundaries. They could be serving a client in one country and its direct competitors in another.

An interesting example of the "Double agent ploy" involved the setting up of a consultancy firm in Hong Kong. After the July 1997 handover of Hong Kong to China, 75 former politicians and senior civil servants decided to set up The Hong Kong Experts Consultancy Company to provide services to organisations wanting to do business with the Hong Kong government. The company was chaired by Mr Ian Macpherson, former Secretary for Transport, together with Mr James So, former Secretary for Broadcasting, Culture and Sport. It is perfectly legal to set up such a company but there were potential ethical problems. As former politicians and top civil servants, these people hold privileged information about how the government operates. They wield considerable influence and are closely connected with government organisations. They could use their knowledge and connections to secure consultancy projects and clients. Their positions resemble that of a double agent. This company incurred fierce criticisms of a former legislator, Emily Lau who accused her former colleagues of using their connections for profit.

Advertising agencies too, may be possible double agents. To create effective campaigns for their corporate clients, these agents often require information from them on sales, marketing plans and new products or services. So, advertising companies forbid their agents from taking on clients in the same line of business. Awareness of possible abuses has caused the advertising industry to develop strict regulatory guidelines for its members.

PROTECTING THE BUSINESS

In a highly competitive environment, and in the quest for higher profits and lower costs, more companies are subcontracting work to operators. An increasing number of companies like Proctor & Gamble farm out distribution functions to logistic companies which provide a full range of services, including warehousing, packaging, repackaging, shipping, transportation and documentation. They serve multiple clients who may be competitors. This is where information might unknowingly be leaked, making the use of the "double agent ploy" possible.

Similarly, a provider of computer software may peddle the system it has developed for one company to the company's competitors, sometimes improving the product and system for the competitors. The first company which paid for the development costs loses out in the end.

Companies should protect themselves against double agent ploys, adopt strict security measures, such as protecting the copyright of their software systems and screening consultants or service providers. When the consultants have access to secret information, proper terms of reference and restrictive use of data must be clearly stated in conditions of employment. To further protect the interests of the company, it may be beneficial to draft a legal document containing confidentiality clauses.

Strategy 34

苦肉计

Self-injury Scheme

人不自害， 受害必真；
假真真假， 间以得行。
童蒙之吉， 顺以巽也。

Explanation

No one would intentionally harm himself (人不自害). Therefore, if someone is hurt, others would believe that he has been injured by another (受害必真). Pretence (假真真假) will thus gain the enemy's trust and sow discord among enemy members (间以得行). This is similar to playing with an innocent child. As long as you act according to his wishes, you will be able to trick him (童蒙之吉,), as stated in *Yi Jing's* "Meng" Theory ([易:蒙]).

Historical Background

This strategy works on the premise that the enemy will be taken in when one does something harmful to oneself. The following is one of many examples in Chinese history depicting the use of the strategy.

During the Spring and Autumn Period, Ji Guang (姬光) killed the Emperor of Wu, Wu Wang Liao (吴王僚) and declared himself Emperor. He gave himself the title Wu Wang He Lu (吴王阖闾). The deceased emperor's son, Qing Ji (庆忌), was gathering capable men to overthrow He Lu. As Qing Ji was courageous and intelligent He Lu feared for his life. He Lu's subject Wu Zi Xu (伍子胥) recommended an assassin, Yao Li (要离), to him.

Yao Li was small in size but he was intelligent and brave. He revealed to He Lu his plan for befriending Qing Ji, "Qing Ji is now looking for capable men. I will pretend to be an exile from your kingdom who wishes to join his camp. To obtain his trust, your Lordship will have to chop off my right arm and execute my entire family." Drastic action indeed! He Lu was reluctant at first, but finally agreed to the plan. Yao Li was arrested and imprisoned on the pretext of having offended the Emperor, and had his right arm chopped off as punishment. Later, the Emperor secretly released Yao Li but announced that he had escaped from prison and had his family beheaded.

Yao Li then went to Qing Ji. When Qing Ji saw Yao Li's amputated arm and learnt that his wife and children had been executed, he believed Yao Li's story and kept him as his aide. When Qing Ji planned to attack Wu, Yao Li volunteered to be the guide, convincing Qing Ji that he was the best person for the job. Troops were sent both by land and sea and Yao Li sailed on the same boat as Qing Ji. When the boat was in the middle of the sea, Yao Li took out a spear and ran it right through Qing Ji's body. Qing Ji, an experienced fighter himself, caught Yao Li and pushed his head into the water. When the men came forward to kill Yao Li, Qing Ji stopped them and said, "This man is a courageous fighter. No one should kill two courageous fighters in a day!" Qing Ji then pulled out the spear from his body and bled to death. When the boat reached the Kingdom of Wu, Qing Ji's men wanted to release Yao Li. However, Yao Li refused and committed suicide with a sword.

COMMENTS & APPLICATIONS

Sometimes, it pays to hurt oneself to gain the sympathy of the enemy, although the price may be high. In the case of Yao Li, it involved sacrificing his arm and family members, and eventually his life. The story, though rather grotesque and dramatic, reflects the tremendous loyalty of subjects to their emperor in ancient China. In warfare, it is not unusual for the general to sacrifice a section of his troops, or even a military objective (a city or town) to achieve the greatest goal. For example, in World War II, Japanese suicide bombers demonstrated the extent to which they would go for the sake of their emperor and their country.

The "Self-injury scheme" is different from finding a scapegoat. In the latter's case, it is someone else who will take the fall. Using a scapegoat to "Shift the blame to someone else" lets the real culprit escape punishment. In the "Self-injury scheme" the victim willingly takes the fall and is prepared to sacrifice himself for a higher objective. The self-inflicted injury generates tremendous credibility. In contrast, the scapegoat approach tends to create suspicion and distrust.

The "Self-injury scheme" can be used effectively with many other strategies for its credibility factor. It can be used with Strategy 1, "Deceiving the heavens to cross the sea" if the intention is to achieve a greater objective. When the enemy's defences are down, the strategist can apply Strategy 15, "Lure the tiger to leave its lair in the mountain". Having won the confidence of the target, the strategist can also apply Strategy 24, "Borrow a passage to attack Guo" by leveraging the strengths offered by the target. He could use Strategy 25, "Replace superior beams and pillars with inferior ones" to take advantage of the victim. Once the confidence of the other party is won, it opens up tremendous potential for applying other strategies. In terms of application and combination possibilities with other strategies, "Self-injury scheme" is as powerful as Strategy 31, "The beauty scheme".

PRICE DISCOUNTS AND SALES PROMOTION

In business, one can find examples of self-inflicted injury. For example, one may occasionally spot advertisements with these messages:

1   Closing down sale. All stocks to be sold at below cost!
2   Removal sale. We are moving, but not our items. All to be sold at sacrificial prices!
3   Bankruptcy sale. Our creditors are after us. We decide to benefit you, our customers, instead!
4   All items to be sold below cost. New stocks coming.
5   Warehouse sale. At least 50% cheaper than downtown stores.
6   Annual stock-taking sales. All items to go at basement prices!

Advertisements like these will always attract consumers who flock to the stores to spend their cash and use their credit cards. Such sales are especially believable when conducted by reputable stores. For instance, Diamond Industries Singapore, reputed to have the largest inventory of cut diamonds in the world, will hold "sacrificial sales" every now and then where retail prices of some pieces are slashed by as much as 80%! When the sale is on, it always attracts large crowds, including busloads of tourists.

Another example was when Genting Highland Resort Group of Malaysia wooed Singaporeans to stay at one of their four hotels for S$1 per night for a restricted period to celebrate the Group founder's birthday. In reality, there had been a noticeable drop in the number of Singaporean visitors to the resort (with the only casino in the ASEAN region). These visitors formed the largest clientele (over 30%) of the four hotels, and they needed desperately to woo them back. The Genting Group promotion used the "Self-injury scheme" by choosing to celebrate their founder's birthday for the first time in 32 years. Although the offer was restricted to weekdays, and was on a first-come-first-served basis, it was very attractive. The scheme earned high credibility and received strong media coverage in Singapore.

Dramatic and significant price discounts in the hotel industry are common ways of getting customers during off-peak periods. As it would be bad business practice to close the hotels and retrench the workers, a more viable and usual practice is to slash room rates significantly to attract visitors. This strategy can be effective when the hotels work closely with tour agencies and airlines which also participate in the scheme.

Besides resort hotels, any business subject to seasonal demands and fluctuations in sales could consider using the "Self-injury scheme" as a temporary measure. The concept of "happy hour" and "ladies' night" practised by restaurants, lounges and night-clubs operates on this principle. At certain times of the day restaurants and lounges are poorly patronised. Operators hope to attract more customers during these off-peak periods by offering price discounts. Similarly, "ladies' night" is offered to female customers, usually mid-week, when business is at its lowest.

Though "happy hour" and "ladies' night" are ventures that appear to injure the bottom-line, these are actually shrewd business schemes to keep business going during the off-peak periods. Through this they can recover part of their high operations costs. By keeping business alive during off-peak periods, a company gives the impression that it is doing well. This, in turn, will attract more customers.

Significant price cuts are not only used as a "Self-injury scheme" by companies in trouble, but also to stimulate demand and counter competition from profitable companies. A good example is Intel Corporation, the world's largest manufacturer of microprocessors. In December 1997, Intel slashed the price of its Pentium II chips by a massive 33%. The move was seen as a deliberate attempt to stave off competition from the K6 chips produced by Advanced Micro Devices Inc (AMD). AMD's K6 microprocessors were perceived a potential threat to the market share of Intel as they were sold at about 25% cheaper than Pentium II chips. Besides tackling the competition, the price reduction of Intel's Pentium II chips was aimed at helping manufacturers of personal computers (PCs) reduce prices. The chip forms a significant part of the price of a personal computer. Any price reduction is passed to the consumer, increasing the demand for PCs.

OVERCOMING SHORT-TERM DIFFICULTIES

This strategy can also be used to overcome short-term difficulties. The Great Singapore Sale was organised for this reason. For a number of years, the Singapore retail industry faced severe problems. In fact, it never quite recovered after the economic recession in 1985/86. Escalating property prices increased rents which resulted in higher operating costs.

In the early 1990s, with the support of the Singapore Tourist Promotion Board, the retail industry decided to launch the Great Singapore Sale for a month-long period from mid-July to mid-August. During this period, every retailer in the scheme would place their products on sale. The event was a great success and now attracts shoppers from many countries. The number of retailers participating has also increased significantly. What started off as a "Self-injury scheme" has now become an annual tourist attraction.

In the 1980s and early 1990s, economies in countries such as the UK, the US, Canada, Australia and New Zealand encountered severe difficulties. Property value dropped significantly. Trouble-ridden companies were forced to sell their properties, many at below acquisition and replacement costs, to raise funds. As property prices are easy to determine in terms of its acquisition value or replacement costs, these sacrificial bargains quickly attracted the attention of cash-rich companies and individuals from Asia. Asian companies such as Singapore's City Development Limited (CDL) picked up great property buys.

At the end of the 1980s, the property markets in these economies had picked up significantly. By the mid-1990s, real estate markets had risen sharply (more than 50% in markets like London). Many of the early Asian investors were still holding on to their properties hoping for further price increases. However, the Asian financial crisis in late 1990s affected investors and companies adversely. Property prices in Thailand, Hong Kong, Malaysia,

Indonesia and Singapore fell significantly. Like their Western counterparts in the 1980s, these Asian investors and companies were forced to sell their properties and assets to raise funds.

Another example which illustrates the use of the "Self-injury scheme" concerns the promotion by Cathy Pacific Airways of its two-for-one airfare to Hong Kong. The two week offer, introduced in November 1997, was intended to attract tourists back to Hong Kong. Tourist arrivals had been declining after the handover of the colony to China in July. As the offer covered flights to Hong Kong from 1 January to 15 February 1998 (the low period for tourism in Hong Kong), the response was overwhelming. Cathay Pacific had initially planned for 20,000 bookings at a promotional cost of HK$65 million. However, 80,000 bookings were received during the two-week offer period, costing Cathay Pacific HK$185 for the promotion, an increase of HK$120 million (S$25 million). As discussed earlier, the "Self-injury scheme" can be a high risk strategy, and should only be used as a plan to overcome short-term difficulties. Fortunately Hong Kong should benefit from this offer. The Hong Kong Tourist Association estimated that these tourists would spendmore than HK$500 million during their stay.

CUTTING LOSSES AND GAINING MARKET SHARE

The "Self-injury scheme" is used in business as a strategy to cut losses, or as a means to gain market share quickly. In the case of cutting losses, the principle is simple — getting even the crumbs is better than having no bread at all. Share prices inevitably plunge when the company's performance is poor. If its performance is unlikely to improve in the foreseeable future, it would be wiser to cash out and invest the money in more profitable companies as share prices may dip further, and become worthless if the company goes bankrupt.

A company may be forced to use this scheme to gain temporary market share to achieve other objectives and to remain in the market until the situation changes to its favour. The "Self-injury scheme" is necessary in businesses with high fixed investment costs and economies of scale. Unit cost decreases with increased production volume. Hence, gaining market shares becomes important. It is better to suffer losses (in operating costs) to keep an existing workforce. If production volumes are scaled down, trained workers may need to be retrenched and perhaps lost to competitors. Keeping the existing workforce will boost morale and help build commitment and loyalty within the company. This strategy of accepting losses (for a while) work well with products that can be stored and will not become obsolete. The "Self-injury scheme" used appropriately can yield surprising results.

A good example is the case of how Kia Motors of Korea managed to put up a brave front using Strategy 32, the "Empty city scheme" in conjunction with this strategy. To keep the work force and the business going, Kia Motors slashed the prices of their cars by as much as 30%. At a time when the company was faced with bankruptcy and debts of over 9.5 trillion won (approximately S$15.9 billion), this appeared an unwise move inflicting more "injury" on the ailing company. Kia's top management hoped that by keeping the business going, it might be able to get another party to bail the company out. By slashing car prices, Kia Motors managed to secure higher sales, both in the domestic and international markets. Kia Motors hoped to evoke public sympathy to the "cost" of closing down the eighth largest conglomerate in Korea. The company was still manufacturing and marketing saleable products. At the end of September 1997, the workers of Kia Motors staged a two day strike in support of the management. The "Self-injury scheme" adopted by Kia Motors therefore appeared to have some effects.

A further example to illustrate the use of the "Self-injury scheme" is the effort made by Netscape to counter Microsoft. In early 1998, Netscape announced it would distribute the standard edition of its browser, Communicator (formerly known as Navigator), free. The price of its professional edition of Communicator was reduced from US$79 to US$29 per copy. By distributing the standard edition of Communicator free and by slashing the price of its professional edition, Netscape hoped to gain market shares from Microsoft's browser, the Internet Explorer. Prior to the move by Netscape, Microsoft had been gaining significant shares in the browser's market. Some industry players accused Microsoft of trying to corner the entire market. There was an urgent need therefore to prevent Microsoft's Internet Explorer from dominating the market. Netscape had to take drastic steps to ensure its own survival. The "Self-injury scheme" was a strategic move by Netscape to gain market shares.

连环计

A SERIES OF INTERCONNECTED PLOYS

将多兵众， 不可以敌，
使其自累， 以杀其势。
在师中吉， 承天宠也。

EXPLANATION

If the enemy has a strong and powerful army (将多兵众), a head-on confrontation is not advisable (不可以敌). Instead, one should utilise a few connected strategies (使其自累) to decrease the enemy's power (以杀其势). With good leadership and careful planning (在师中吉), it will as easy to win the battle as if heaven is on one's side (承天宠也). This is in accordance with *Yi Jing's* "Shi" Theory ([易：师]).

HISTORICAL BACKGROUND

The strategy can be explained in two ways. The first is in accordance with the **Book of War Strategies**, where the strategy is derived. It considers the use of two or more strategies to overcome the enemy. It advises that a good strategist will use many strategies to achieve his aim. If one fails, another can back him up.

[兵法圆机：送]：大凡用计者， 非一计之可孤行，
必有数计以裹之也。……… 故善用兵者， 行计务
实施，…… 此策阻而彼策生， 一端致而数端起，
前未行而后复具； 百计送出， 算无遗策

    The second way to explain this strategy is taken from the words "使其自累，以杀其势", which means, use a few connected strategies to decrease the enemy's power. This explanation states that two or more connected strategies are needed. They work like interlocking rings. The first strategy weakens the enemy while the second strategy will attack and destroy him. Either one can deliver the decisive blow to the enemy. The second meaning is preferred.

The following illustrates the use of this strategy in the second meaning.

During the period of the Three Kingdoms (三国时), Zhou Yu (周瑜) and Pang Tong (庞统) set up "chain schemes" or a series of related schemes to trap Cao Cao (曹操). First, when Cao Cao sent his man, Jiang Gan (蒋干) to spy on Zhou, the latter used the "Double agent ploy" to lure Cao Cao into killing two of his best navy generals, Cai Mao (蔡瑁) and Zhang Yun (张允) (see Strategy 33). This weakened Cao Cao's navy and eventually led to Cao Cao losing the battle at the famous Chi Bi (赤壁).

Next, Zhou Yu used the "Self-injury scheme" to punish one of his best generals, Huang Gai (黄盖) to make Cao Cao believe that there was internal chaos among Zhou Yu's men. Therefore, when Cao Cao's man, Jiang Gan visited Zhou Yu the second time and "accidentally" met with Pang Tong (庞统), Jiang Gan was taken in when Pang Tong said that he had plans to defect to Cao Cao's camp.

Pang Tong's "surrender" to Cao Cao triggered the final plan. Cao Cao was pleased to see Pang Tong, and exchanged views with him on war strategies. As Cao Cao had lost his best navy generals, he was desperate to hear Pang Tong's view on naval warfare. Cao Cao's men could not swim and suffered from seasickness. Pang Tong said, "Although your soldiers are well-trained, they are not used to travelling at sea so they get seasick, especially in strong currents. You should tie your ships together, thirty or fifty in a row. This way, the ships will be stable and the soldiers can walk on the decks."

Cao Cao thanked Pang Tong for his great suggestion and ordered his blacksmiths to chain all the ships together in their next attack on Zhou Yu. However, Zhou Yu learnt of Cao Cao's plan and set fire to Cao Cao's ships. With all the ships chained together, it was almost impossible for the soldiers to escape from the burning ships. Cao Cao suffered a bitter defeat and lost many soldiers.

COMMENTS & APPLICATIONS

It may be wise to think of a series of interconnected ploys to trick the enemy when the opportunity arises. The impact of a series of strategies is often greater than that of an isolated scheme. In the episode of Zhou Yu defeating Cao Cao, Zhou Yu used a few connected schemes first to weaken Cao Cao's navy, then to gain the latter's trust and eventually to defeat him. The last scheme was a symbolic picture of this strategy. As the warships were chained together, none of them could escape when one caught fire.

As illustrated elsewhere in this book, all the strategies can be used to complement one another in an unlimited number of permutations. The "Thirty-six Strategies" are not intended to be used singly, and are most effective when used jointly. The combinations are limited only by the strategist's creativity and imagination. It pays to study each strategy to see how they can be combined effectively.

CORPORATE AND MARKETING STRATEGIES

In business, one rarely relies on a single strategy. For instance, a corporate strategy is developed using a combination of many other strategies within a company. These include the financial plan, the marketing plan, the research and development plan, the production plan, the human resource development plan, and so on. Each of these is affected by environmental constraints and opportunities. The company must also thoroughly analyse the market and consumer trends, while not ignoring competitive forces (current and future). Changes in technology, political, economic, social and cultural climate should also be factored in.

A marketing strategy typically consists strategies in product, pricing, promotion, distribution and public relations. To develop the marketing strategy, a company must first decide on its positioning, which is, in turn affected by segmentation and differentiation strategies. For segmentation of the market, a market and consumer analysis is required. Differentiating the package of benefits from those offered by competitors requires competitive analysis. Segmentation, differentiation and positioning strategies are also affected by availability of resources and by the business environment.

Using *a combination of different strategies* is more effective and allows a company greater *flexibility* because if one strategy fails, it can be replaced by another one. This also prevents competitors from preempting one's intention, and from copying a successful formula.

McDonalds' success can be attributed to its varied strategies (especially in advertising and promotion). Competitors find it hard to out manoeuvre it because of the variations. Local fast food operators too are unable to compete directly against it as local food operators compete on a very narrow strategy — the quality and taste of the food. Once these are affected, the business is as good as gone. McDonalds however, does not focus on food alone. It has a very powerful service strategy that is supported by efficient production systems, backed by highly creative advertising and marketing. On top of these, it takes pride in possessing state-of-the-art management practices and skills.

Local food court operators are catching up by learning from fast food operators like McDonalds that success is not based on serving the tastiest food alone. As local food operators learn to adopt and adapt combinations of business strategies, they will give fast food chains a run for their money.

MULTIPLE STRATEGIES IN BUSINESS

As in war, a business firm can use a series of strategies to corner its competitor(s). For example, it could pursue a combination of the following strategies designed to gain market share:
1   Aggressive sales promotion and advertising.
2   Promoting new products and brands.
3   Giving price discounts and better dealers' margins.
4   Setting up more sales outlets.
5   Offering better after-sales service and product warranties.

In addition, it can also poach key competitor's employees through head-hunting firms. If the final intention is to gain control of the competitor, it can try to acquire competitor's shares through the open market or by buying them from major shareholders. When the competitor has been ambushed by the interconnected schemes, it can then move in to acquire the company.

To compete effectively in the business world, a company cannot rely on one strategy to win. Instead it must create competitive advantages on several fronts. A good example is the fast food industry in many Asian economies today. Most local food operators typically focus on food as the basic strategy. They make little attempt to improve their services and other aspects of the eating environment. Once another operator comes in with better food, they would easily lose out. This is because other than the food itself, there are no other competitive advantages. Theirs is essentially a single-strategy approach.

In contrast, Western fast food chains like McDonalds, Burger King and Kentucky Fried Chicken rely on "A series of interconnected ploys" to win customers. They provide a comfortable (air-conditioned), hygienic eating environment, good service and food of consistent and acceptable quality. These are backed by efficient purchasing and operation systems, well-trained managers and crew, and creative advertising and promotions. More importantly, they often vary their advertising and promotional strategies to create excitement and sustain consumer interest. Small wonder then, that fast food chains are giving local operators a run for their money. Through these competitive edges (and series of schemes), they have captured a significant market shares in the prepared food business in many Asian cities. Their success nudged Asian operators to modernise and to extend their competitive edge beyond food alone.

The use of multiple strategies also implies the need to go after different markets. Take the example of the property markets in Singapore and Malaysia. Developers in Malaysia began to market their properties to Singapore, Hong Kong, Taiwan and Indonesia due to a property glut in 1997. In fact, in the 1997 currency turmoil in Malaysia in which the ringgit lost more than 30% against regional currencies such as the Hong Kong and Singapore dollars, its properties had become relatively cheap and attractive. Singaporean developers also marketed their properties to Hong Kong, and Taiwan, with the more innovative developers coming up with attractive financing schemes to promote sales.

The case of Kia Motors of Korea provides another good example of how, in the face of bankruptcy, the company had to resort to "A series of interconnected ploys". As mentioned in Strategy 32, the "Empty city scheme", Kia Motors put up a very brave front to project that it was not in serious financial trouble and went about business as usual. It even used Strategy 34, the "Self-injury scheme" to boost sales. With prices of several car models slashed, export and domestic sales rose. Kia Motors also used Strategy 13, "Hitting the grass to startle the snake" when the management allowed its workers to go on strike, demonstrating the "danger" of closing down the country's third largest car manufacturer. By arousing public attention, Kia Motors hoped to win support and sympathy, putting pressure on the Korean government and Kia's creditors to come up with a rescue package to bail out the company.

INNOVATE AND CREATE ADVANTAGES

In seeking growth, a company should not rest on its laurels. Instead, it should constantly seek to use more than one strategy to win. Singapore Airlines (SIA) is an excellent example. Despite being one of the most profitable airlines, and being voted the best airline in the world year after year, it does not rest on its laurels. Continuing to innovate and improve its services, SIA strives consistently to maintain one of the youngest fleet of aircrafts in the world. To expand its market share and profitability, it entered into a strategic alliance with SwissAir and Delta Airlines in the 1980s to ensure that it could benefit more on the Atlantic and Pacific routes. When the alliance did not work out to its advantage, SIA terminated it and forged a new alliance with Germany's Lufthansa. This new alliance is likely to pave the way for SIA to join the more powerful Star Alliance in which Lufthansa and five other major airlines are members (*see Strategy 23*).

In June 1997, SIA entered into another strategic alliance with Ansett Airways (of Australia) and Air New Zealand to benefit from the lucrative "kangaroo" route between Asia and Australia. SIA continues to pursue other avenues for growth. These include a possible joint venture with the Tata Group for a domestic airline in India, and the exploration of more access routes to various cities by advocating an open sky policy. Most significantly, at a time when British Airways (one of SIA's biggest competitors) was besieged with a strike by members of its own cabin crew, SIA announced on 12 July 1997 the appointment of Mr Lim Boon Heng, a Singapore cabinet minister, to its board of directors. This move was widely seen as a strategy to further strengthen and improve the already close union-management relations in SIA. This is because Mr Lim is currently the Secretary-General of the National Trade Union Congress of Singapore. Thus, it can be seen that SIA is definitely pursuing a multiple of related strategies to ensure that it remains as the best and one of the most profitable airlines in the world.

As another illustration, SIA spent millions of dollars to develop the world's first inflight system that offers both audio and video shows on demand. Called the "Wisemen", it was launched in October 1997 for its First and Raffles class passengers. What is unique about the "Wisemen" system is that it allows the passenger to choose from a vast array of the latest digital movies, sports, news and other entertainment programs. Features like *fast forward, rewind, pause or switch features* are also included. These would then allow the passenger to enjoy his choice of programs at his own pace and pleasure — something not available in other airlines. The "Wisemen" system definitely projects SIA as an innovative and caring airline that is prepared to tailor-make its already well-known inflight service.

In a further attempt to cater to the increasing number of international passengers, SIA embarked on a concerted effort to train its cabin crew to speak passengers' languages. Thus far, it has refrained from recruiting non-Asian crew in order not to affect the "Singapore Girl" image. Whether it would depart from such a policy remains to be seen. To minimise operation costs and maximize utilization of aircrafts, it shifted its less critical corporate functions to lower cost countries such as India, and bases as many employees as possible in their home countries. Its fleet of aircrafts has been regularly upgraded/replaced with planes that are more fuel efficient. Idle-time of aircraft has been looked at to see how the aircraft can be better utilized.

The end result of these efforts in using "A series of interconnected ploys" is that SIA has, thus far, minimized heavy price discounting to gain market share. Indeed, even heavyweights like British Airways and other American airlines have resorted to price discounts to lure passengers. The irony is that their load factors have not increased significantly. In contrast, despite the intense price competition, SIA (which is known to charge higher ticket prices) has continued to excel in the industry. Credit must go to its ability to use multiple strategies.

The largest conglomerates in Japan, known as the *zaibatsus*, are experts of this strategy. Today, they are highly diversified not only in terms of products and industries, but in markets that range from the least to the most developed economies. In addition, many *zaibatsus* have begun to invest in high growth regions like Asia and have entered into strategic alliances with Western companies (for example Fuji-Xerox) to protect market share and to access foreign technology. Thus, despite the economic problems in Japan in the 1990s, many Japanese companies are poised to roar again by the turn of the century. Their formula — never to rely on a single strategy to succeed.

One of the darlings of the computer industry, Apple Computer has learned that it was not sufficient to rely on a single strategy to succeed. Its products took a hard knock when the rest of the industry moved towards the DOS operating system with Microsoft Windows. Apple rigidly stuck to its own system and suffered severely. However, as of mid-1997, Apple has made a come back. It developed a wide range of connected products to ensure competitiveness. For example, in mid-1997, it developed the fastest notebook computer (Macintosh Power Book 3400c), the fastest home computer, an impressive palm top (Newton Message Pad 2000), a new digital camera for both Macs and PCs (QuickTake 200) and PC compatibility cards. Besides hardware, Apple also worked on the software. For example, its QuickTime has been accepted as the industry standard for desktop publishing. Its Mac OS is also moving closer to the DOS system, and soon users should have little difficulty working between the two systems. Thus, Apple Computer, still a giant company by any standard (it is bigger than McDonalds with sales of US$10 billion annually), is now taking on its competitors by using a multi-pronged approach.

STRATEGY 36

走为上

ESCAPE – THE BEST SCHEME

全师避敌，左次无咎，未失常也。

EXPLANATION

In a situation where the enemy is obviously stronger, total retreat may be the best option (全师避敌). As stated in *Yi Jing's* "Shi" Theory, there is nothing wrong with a retreating to avoid confrontation with a stronger enemy ([易经：师] 卦：左次无咎，未失常也).

This strategy advocates retreating as a means to plan for the next attack (以退为进). As stated in the Introduction, this strategy is taken from *Book of Nan Qi* (南齐书：王敬则传). "Escape — the best scheme" does not mean this is the best of all the strategies. However, in a desperate situation, it is the best or prime option (上策). As the Chinese saying goes, "As long as trees on the mountains are preserved, we need not fear a shortage of firewood" (留得青山在，不愁无柴烧). This strategy recommends that one preserves one's energy instead of making pointless sacrifices, as it is better to suffer some humiliation and temporary setback than to lose everything. In fact, there is a Chinese saying, "For a man to take revenge, it is not too late to wait ten years," (君子报仇，十年未晚).

HISTORICAL BACKGROUND

During the Spring and Autumn Period (春秋时期), the state of Chu (楚国) was surrounded by many smaller states who paid homage to the ruler of Chu. However, during the reign of Chu Zhuang Wang (楚庄王), when the state of Chu suffered serious famine, the surrounding states attacked it. The Chu ruler did not want to summon the main army guarding the northern border for fear that stronger states like Qi (齐国) and Jin (晋国) might ambush Chu. Therefore, only a small troop was sent to defend the country against the attacks by the smaller states.

The Chu troop, led by general Ji Li (戢黎), attacked the state of Yong (庸国). Ji Li was familar with the terrain of Yong and the Chu army quickly invaded the Square City (方城). But the people of Yong defended their state bravely and the Chu army could not take it down. Ji Li ordered general Zi Yang Chuang (子扬窗) to guard the Square City. Zi Yang Chuang was captured by the Yong army, but escaped after three days. He reported to Ji Li that the Yong army was strong and well-equipped and that it would be difficult to conquer Yong with only a small troop. He therefore suggested that they ask the ruler of Chu to summon the main force to Yong so that they could take down the entire state.

Ji Li disagreed and said, "It may not be to our advantage if we were to attack Yong hastily. We should win the Yong army with tact and not with brute force. We should retreat now in view of the strong Yong army and even pretend to be defeated by them. The prouder they are, the stronger the morale of our soldiers will be, and we can then strike at the best opportunity."

He therefore ordered a retreat and the Chu army pretended to lose the subsequent seven battles with the Yong. The Yong army became very proud and thought that they would be able to defeat the Chu army anytime. The ruler of Chu later led reinforcements to meet up with Ji Li and his men and launched a massive attack on the Yong army. The Yong army did not expect the Chu army to be so powerful and the state of Yong was eventually conquered.

COMMENTS & APPLICATIONS

Of all the strategies, "Escape — the best scheme," to the Chinese, is perhaps the most commonly known but misunderstood strategy. Many fail to realise that it is a strategy for a desperate situation. For example, when faced with a definite defeat, one can act in three ways: surrender, negotiate for peace, or escape. Surrendering is admitting total defeat. To negotiate for peace is to acknowledge that one is already half-defeated. However, running away does not mean defeat. By running away, one can still stage a comeback and may eventually defeat the enemy to win the battle. This is particularly important as it gives one time to understand the enemy, and to build one's strengths before launching another attack.

KENTUCKY FRIED CHICKEN

Kentucky Fried Chicken (KFC) is a good example of the use of this strategy. As part of its globalization efforts, KFC entered the Asian market in the late 1960s through Hong Kong. Unfortunately, the Hong Kong market was not ready for western fast food. It was also difficult for KFC to compete head-on against the much cheaper local food and "dim sum". Instead of persisting, KFC withdrew from Hong Kong. It took time to study the Asian market, reevaluated their strategy and launched a second attack on the Asian food market, this time in Singapore.

The Asian market then (Singapore, in particular) was ready for Western fast food because of affluence and a pro-Western attitude. With their years of experience in Hong Kong, KFC marketed the whole concept of Western fast food as a life-style phenomenon, instead of just as fast food. Through advertisements, KFC projected the impression that eating at KFC was modern and stylish, befitting the affluent person and family.

Its success in Singapore allowed KFC to re-enter the Hong Kong market. Over the years, KFC (and other fast food chains) expanded aggressively into Asian cities. Today, KFC outlets can even be found in China and other newly-opened economies in Asia.

DOING BUSINESS IN A CORRUPT ENVIRONMENT

Doing business in some economies is not easy because of corruption. Corruption exists everywhere, only differing in degree from place to place. Severe corruption can pose great difficulties to a company and can destroy a company if incorrectly handled.

How should a company deal with corruption? Since bribery is definitely out of the question, and ought not be condoned or encouraged, to "survive", one must definitely have a strong understanding of the situation. We would like to propose the following guidelines for dealing with "greasy situations" when operating in a corrupted environment.

Firstly, *know the rules* of the game. Know the extent of corruption. Is it a common practice to "pay" for services rendered? Is gift-giving a norm, like in Japan? Where is the dividing line between gift-giving and corruption? What practices are considered as gifts or bribery? Is the legal framework governing illegal payments well-established? These questions must be answered before entering any country.

Secondly, when you are asked to pay, it is important to *investigate and verify*. When in doubt, always stall for time to find out more about the background of the person who is demanding payment. Uncover his background, connections, and whether he is backed by others. He may turn out to be a fake or a con.

Thirdly, *cover your back*. Ensure that you are acting within your limits or authority. Anything beyond your jurisdiction should be brought to the attention of the next higher level of authority in the company. In particular, when it involves granting favours, it is crucial that your immediate bosses are kept informed. Otherwise, you may end up being made a scapegoat!

Fourthly, no matter what kinds of payments you have to make, ensure you are *above board*. In other words, be legal and ethical. Do not do things that might jeopardise your position, especially when they are against the laws of the host country. One can easily end up in jail, or even be blackmailed into making more payments.

Fifthly, *know the purpose* of the demands being made on you. Do not be easily threatened just because someone approaches you for contributions. Knowing the purpose will also provide you with the leads to investigate and verify the background of the person making the demands and the people or organisation he represents. It will also provide you with strong indications and directions as to whether you should accede to the request.

Sixthly, always *explore alternatives* to the demands. It is absolutely untrue that one has to bribe to win! By exploring alternatives, one may be able to come out with a response that is creative, and legally and ethically acceptable. For example, while attracting talent, it may be possible to provide scholarships and training rather than to make outright payments. It is better to leave product samples behind than to provide gifts! Similarly, it is more appropriate to organise training programs for overseas trips than to offer packaged tours that resemble junkets. Of course, when the *purpose of the demand* can be clearly established, it would be much easier to explore *alternative ways* to solve the problem in a way that is *above board*.

Seventhly, be fully aware of the *"dracula" effects* when one becomes too willing to respond to such demands. When it comes to bribery and corruption, the receiving party is likely to grow quickly into a "dracula" with a thirst for more. He may suck you dry. Therefore, if possible, never breed nor groom a dracula in your own backyard! In fact, an external dracula may breed internal draculas — internal corruption could set in.

Eighthly, any contributions made to obtain a business deal should be factored into the *costs of doing business.* These will include scholarship grants, training costs, product samples, overseas trips, and donations made to charitable organisations. In business, there is no such thing as a free meal. Every expense should be accounted for.

Finally, the company must be prepared to *walk away* if necessary. This is what Strategy 36 is all about. At the end of the day, it is important to know that if one cannot win, it is better to run away rather than to hang onto a dying situation. The business world is very large, and there are plenty of opportunities awaiting any shrewd entrepreneurial company. The key is to find one's niche and exploit it fully. If the situation is difficult, avoid the market for a while, and wait for the right moment to strike again. It is bad enough to rush in blindly. It would be worse to stay on to face certain defeat.

OPERATING IN UNFAMILIAR MARKETS

Escape as a strategy is not confined to operating in difficult environments. It can be applied to any market. Take Singapore, for instance. In the late 1980s and early 1990s, when the government advocated that companies expand overseas, a number of manufacturing companies decided to enter the US market. But it proved a difficult market with its different time zones, cultures and business practices, and very tough competition. Recognising their weaknesses, these companies did not stay on. Many quickly bailed out and redirected investments to Asia.

IPC, a computer manufacturer from Singapore, had a similar experience in Australia. Sensing that the market for personal computer was growing in Australia, IPC decided to set up their own distribution channels there thinking that direct and exclusive distribution would allow it better control. Unfortunately, Australian consumers preferred to buy from outlets that carried several brands and models so that they could compare them. The Australian dealer's performance was also far from satisfactory. IPC finally decided painfully (they already lost millions of dollars in the project) but necessarily (they could continue to lose more) to shut down the Australian operation in 1996. It was better to "escape" from Australia, recuperate and then launch another "attack" later. The departure from Australia was a wise decision for IPC. Like many other Singapore companies, IPC is now focusing its attention on Asia, China in particular.

To escape from a desperate situation is indeed a worthwhile option. Far from being an act of cowardice, it takes courage and decisiveness to do so. When on a losing streak, the smartest thing is to know when to stop, and recoup one's capital some other day. In war, it means no unnecessary sacrifice of lives and resources. In business, it means there will be no unnecessary loss of employment or bankruptcy.

KNOWING WHEN TO QUIT

In international business, Japanese companies are very willing to forgo businesses in which they are no longer competitive. The Japanese started producing cheap and labour-intensive products after World War II, but they have cleverly given these up in favour of high technology projects. Even in car manufacturing, Japanese companies realise that they can no longer compete against Malaysia and Korea at the lower-end of the market. Thus, they have moved to the higher-value end of the products, and into the luxury car market. By applying the "Escape — the best scheme", they free up resources to focus on areas in which they can excel. Of late, many Japanese companies have also moved the production of their lower-end products to developing countries such as Malaysia, Thailand and Indonesia where costs are lower.

The Japanese experience provides useful lessons for other companies. Often a company may face declining market shares as products are overtaken by competitors with better technology. Or, a product may outlive its usefulness due to changing tastes and preferences. When faced with these challenges, a company should confront the problem. If there is no way to beat the stronger competitors or if the product has become obsolete, it is better to adopt the "Escape — the best scheme" strategy. Rather than hang onto a losing business, it is better to walk away and find new markets or create new products.

Unfortunately, some companies linger too long in the market or are unwilling to get rid of weak products and declining businesses, arguing that these products complement the overall business of the company and that a change of strategy should improve the situation. Others claim that declining sales are temporary hiccups caused by economic downturn. Amazingly, some stubbornly cling on to dying products for nostalgic reasons. Their rationale — these products were the ones that started the company and brought in the profits in the good old days! Thus, emotional feelings run deep, and resistance runs high against dropping these products.

A company does well to remember that they are in business to create profits, not to lose it. Failure to eliminate dying products and businesses will prove costly, preventing valuable resources from being used in more productive areas. Weak products may also bleed the company to death. Therefore, it is better to take a pragmatic "escape route". It is better to live and fight another day than to die unceremoniously and be forgotten!

Similarly, a shrewd investor must know when he should quit. The smart investor liquidates his shares and other investments the moment the situation sours. By cashing out, he has the cash to move in once the market bottoms out. With the market in the doldrums, holding hard cash becomes even more important, especially when interest rates begin to climb. The stubborn investor who persists to hold on may be badly "burnt".

It is wiser to withdraw now and return to fight another battle. Afterall, in war, just like in business, victory or defeat is seldom determined in a single battle.

INDEX